Utopia Undone

Utopia Undone

The Fall of Uruguay
in the Novels
of Carlos Martínez Moreno

Kenton V. Stone

Lewisburg
Bucknell University Press
London and Toronto: Associated University Presses

© 1994 by Associated University Presses, Inc.

All rights reserved. Authorization to photocopy items for internal or personal use, or the internal or personal use of specific clients, is granted by the copyright owner, provided that a base fee of $10.00, plus eight cents per page, per copy is paid directly to the Copyright Clearance Center, 27 Congress Street, Salem, Massachusetts 01970. [0-8387-5193-8/94 $10.00 + 8¢ pp, pc.]

Associated University Presses
440 Forsgate Drive
Cranbury, NJ 08512

Associated University Presses
25 Sicilian Avenue
London WC1A 2QH, England

Associated University Presses
P.O. Box 338, Port Credit
Mississauga, Ontario
Canada L5G 4L8

The paper used in this publication meets the requirements of the American National Standard for Permanence of Paper for Printed Library Materials Z39.48-1984.

Library of Congress Cataloging-in-Publication Data

Stone, Kenton V., 1958–
    Utopia undone : the fall of Uruguay in the novels of Carlos Martínez Moreno / Kenton V. Stone.
       p. cm.
    Includes bibliographical references and index.
    ISBN 0-8387-5193-8 (alk. paper)
    1. Martínez Moreno, Carlos, 1917– —Criticism and interpretation. 2. Uruguay in literature. I. Title.
PQ8519.M367Z87 1994
863—dc20   93-36324
                                                            CIP

PRINTED IN THE UNITED STATES OF AMERICA

To Lisa

¿Nos contarás tu historia?
¿Nos hablarás al oído alguna vez?
. . .
Ciudad enmascarada que nos escondés el rostro
a nosotros tus hijos:
¿Bailan juntos en tus noches
los vivos y los muertos?
. . .
Ciudad mía, ciudad nunca:
¿Seré digno de hundir la cabeza entre tus pechos?
¿Mereceré beber tus jugos
amargos, poderosos?
¿Podré cantar tu canción boca arriba sobre la hierba?
¿Cantar con voz de ciego tu canción?
                              —Eduardo Galeano
                              La canción de nosotros

[Will you tell us your story?
Will you speak into our ear sometime?
. . .
Masked city that hides its face from us
us your children:
Do the dead and the living
dance together in your nights?
. . .
City of mine, never city:
Will I be worthy to burrow my head between your breasts?
Will I deserve to drink your juices
bitter, powerful?
Will I be able to sing your song lying on my back in the grass?
Sing with a blind man's voice your song?
                              —*Song of Ourselves*]

Contents

Preface	9
1. The Life and Times of Carlos Martínez Moreno	15
2. *Los aborígenes:* The Drama of Latin America's Elite	35
3. *Cordelia:* Mental Architecture	50
4. *El paredón:* The Ethics of Revolutionary Justice	62
5. *La otra mitad:* Know Thyself	88
6. *Con las primeras luces:* The Darkness before the Dawn	109
7. *Coca:* Cupid, Cocaine, and Military Corruption	127
8. *Tierra en la boca:* Decadence, Death, and a Decent Burial	145
9. *El color que el infierno me escondiera:* After the Fall	166
Chronology	195
Notes	199
Bibliography	205
Index	209

Preface

This study of the novels of the Uruguayan Carlos Martínez Moreno has an obvious purpose: to show that he is a writer of the "boom" in the Latin-American novel of the 1960s who deserves much more critical attention than he has received to date. Thus far, only three comprehensive studies of the author's work have been done.

Nora Orthmann's *Life and Works of Martínez Moreno* (1976) was the first. In it she collected important biographical and bibliographical information that has become indispensible to any further scholarship on the author's canon, as well as the first outline of its general characteristics. Six years later, two follow-up studies appeared almost simultaneously: Ana-María Ravazzani's *La narrativa de Carlos Martínez Moreno* (1982), and Liz Salisbury-Ginsburg's *Downfall of a Democracy: Carlos Martínez Moreno and the Uruguayan Experience* (1983). Both studies have proved to be most useful to this analysis. Ravazzani's analysis could perhaps be best described as a New Critical close reading that results in a sociopolitical emphasis in its interpretation of the author's works. Salisbury-Ginsburg, as the title of her study indicates, begins with that sociopolitical emphasis in mind. Her procedure, then, is to interpret the author's canon in a largely allegorical fashion against the background of an historical context which she builds around his body of work.

Through the author's novels themselves, the fall of one of Latin America's most well-established democracies can be traced as it pushes an experimental writer beyond the limits of the literary avant-garde boom in the Latin-American novel of the 1960s. In tracing the development of Martínez Moreno as a novelist, one must account for the causes and effects of a significant shift in the relationship between literature and society, which is reflected in the works of a serious artist.

That shift, which has characterized the recent watershed between the boom and postboom in Latin-American fiction, has been more evident in some authors' work than in others. In Martínez Moreno's case, it is central to understanding his life's work.

Martínez Moreno's novels, whether "intimist" or social commentary or both, consistently deal with the two-decade decline of Uruguayan democracy *(la deca)* to dictatorship in 1973 and its aftermath. The trajectory of Martínez Moreno's novelistic career, the rise and fall of the boom in the Latin-American novel, and the national crisis that made him a member of Uruguay's *Generación crítica*, all coincide. Thus, his works provide an extraordinary opportunity to trace the relationships between the artist, his social milieu, and the artistic influences that mold his modes of expression.

Throughout the study, I emphasize relationships observed between Martínez Moreno's own treatment of the sociohistorical phenomenon he calls *la deca* and his stylistic experiments as a novelist of the boom. As his perspective of *la deca* evolves in his novels, that evolution produces an ever-widening ripple effect upon his treatment of it until it is no longer possible to speak of him as a boom novelist. This moment is what I call the *postdeca* watershed in Martínez Moreno's own canon, and its implications for contributing to a definition of the Latin-American postboom are significant.

In proposing such a rereading of Martínez Moreno's works, I have tried to let the novels themselves dictate the critical methodology most appropriate to each case. Thus, following my historical-biographical introduction, my first two chapters establish Martínez Moreno's thematic and stylistic concerns by a close reading of his two early novellas, *Cordelia* and *Los aborígenes* (the aborigines). Proceeding chronologically, I attempt to shed some new light on his most controversial novel, *El paredón* (The executioner's wall) by drawing on the work of the intellectual historian Hayden White regarding native language and ideological implication, since that novel raises certain questions about the Cuban revolution. I found Roland Barthes's cultural codes to be useful in the case of *La otra mitad* (the other half), a novel that explores questions of personal identity revealed through intimate relationships in a way that challenges social convention. For what is perhaps Martínez Moreno's most structurally experimental novel, *Con las primeras luces* (By dawn's early light), and for the subsequent *Coca* (Cocaine), I inform my reading with the deconstructive writings of Jacques Derrida. In the instance of Martínez Moreno's last fictional novel, *Tierra en la boca* (A mouthful of dirt), the insights of Michael Holquist on the postmodern detective story seemed to be the most helpful. As for the novelist's last work, the nonfiction novel *El color que el infierno me escondiera* (The color hell would hide, translated into English as *El Infierno*), Lennard Davis's thoughts on the social history of fact and fiction in Edward Said's *Literature and Society* served as a worthwhile resource.

In no way, however, are these readings meant to be definitive. Rather, I hope they open up Martínez Moreno's work to a new generation of critics who will bring a variety of approaches to bear on the interpretation of his novels. It is my experience that, perhaps as a cultural side-effect of the Uruguayan cultural diaspora of 1973 to 1985, many are only familiar with contemporary Uruguayan fiction by way of writers whose critical reputations were well-established by the 1960s, such as Juan Carlos Onetti or, at best, Mario Benedetti. Obviously, much has changed since then; today these authors and their contemporaries represent only a handful of the country's many excellent writers. Hence, this study is not offered merely as an opportunity to put forth some new readings of Martínez Moreno's works, based on a variety of methodologies that were developing in a manner roughly contemporary to the novelist's literary production. It is also one man's contribution to an endeavor that lies before this entire generation, writers and critics alike: to account for and redress the disruption of Uruguay's cultural continuity in the last generation.

I would like to thank many people for their help in my endeavor. First and foremost, I am grateful to Professor John Brushwood, whose encouragement and guidance as a mentor and friend were invaluable. I would like to express my gratitude also to the members of the Department of Spanish and Portuguese of the University of Kansas who sponsored me for a Fulbright-Hays Research Grant, the fellow members of the Faculty of Foreign Languages and Comparative Literature of the Kendall College of Arts and Sciences at the University of Tulsa who sponsored me for a Summer Research Grant from the Ford Foundation, both of which aided me in completing the research for this study, and the Center for the Humanities of Drake University, which provided support for the final editing of this book's manuscript. Thanks are also in order to my lifelong friend Julio Silva for his valuable research assistance from Uruguay and for his hospitality during my stay there. I am especially indebted to Juan Carlos Legido, a fine novelist in his own right, for his valuable reminiscences about his old friend Carlos and years of encouragement, friendship, and hospitality in Uruguay. Last, but never least, I would like to thank my wife Lisa Langan, without whose encouragement and support this might never have been written.

It is inevitable, of course, that I have overlooked several others who in some way contributed to this study, and for that I beg pardon in advance. This project has allowed me the opportunity to incorporate a wide variety of influences that I have accumulated over many years. Having spent my childhood and adolescence as a United States citizen in Uruguay during most of the years covered by Martínez Moreno's writing, I have had the challenge and personal satisfaction of incorporating into this critical endeavor many insights gained by firsthand experience. That experience was capped by the privilege of meeting the author himself in his exile in Mexico City, only months before his untimely death in 1986. I shall ever be grateful for the friendship and hospitality extended to me by Don Carlos and his wife, Carmen. He is sorely missed.

While all of these experiences may have to some extent threatened my critical objectivity in this analysis of the author's works, I believe I have managed to achieve an equilibrium by virtue of remaining essentially a North American reader as well as one with a firsthand knowledge of Uruguayan culture. The challenge of that balancing act has been, I believe, a fitting response to the works of such a master of juxtaposition as Martínez Moreno. I hope the reader finds it challenging as well.

Utopia Undone

1
The Life and Times of Carlos Martínez Moreno

Martínez Moreno's double last name bespeaks the legacy he inherited from both of Uruguay's traditional political parties—the rejection of which is the subject of much of his writing. On his mother's side, his heritage is that of the landowning rural gentry of the National or Blanco party. On his father's side, he is heir to the traditions of the urban, Eurocentric, liberal bourgeois idealists of the Colorado party. Throughout most of the latter half of the nineteenth century, these two parties were at war. Their civil war over the shape of Uruguayan society after Independence is known to history simply as the *Guerra Grande,* or Great War. It roughly followed the lines of the epic nineteenth century conflict of "civilización/barbarie" ("civilization/barbarism") between the neighboring Argentine Federalistas and Unitarios. However, Uruguay's Blancos produced no Dictator Rosas, and, though they laid siege to it for years on end, they never conquered their nation's capital. Martínez Moreno outlined his family's relationship to the *Guerra Grande*—used in his 1966 novel *Con las primeras luces* (By dawn's early light)—and Uruguay's two major factions in a conversation with critic Nora Orthman:

> Mi bisabuelo paterno era de orígen portugués y aquí se castillanizó (cambiando el Martins por Martínez). Hizo su fortuna introduciendo ganado a la plaza sitiada de Montevideo, durante la Guerra Grande (1842–1851). Entre los sitiadores estaba, como uno de los Comandantes de Oribe (es decir, blancos, es decir, aliados de Juan Manuel Rosas) mi virtual bisabuelo materno: el entonces Comandante y luego General Lucas Moreno. Y digo virtual bisabuelo porque era el tío carnal de mi abuelo materno pero, huérfano mi abuelo desde muy joven (su padre era Gregorio Moreno, también—en sus días—diputado blanco), protegió a mi abuelo y es fama que llegó a preferirlo a sus propios hijos. O sea, que mis orígenes reconcilian a dos facciones tradicio-

nales, que han hecho el país comportándos las más de las veces como enemigas, y ocasionalmente, en momentos entendidos como muy difíciles para el país, como patrióticamente conciliadas. (Orthmann 1976, 21)

My paternal great-grandfather was of Portuguese origin and Castilianized his name once here (changing Martins for Martínez). He made his fortune by supplying cattle to the town square of Montevideo under siege during the Great War (1842–1851). Among those laying siege was, as one of Oribe's Commanders (that is to say, one of the Blancos, or rather, allies of Juan Manual Rosas), my virtual maternal great-grandfather: the then Commander and later General Lucas Moreno. And I say virtual great-grandfather because from a very early age he (his father was Gregorio Moreno who was also—in his day—a Blanco congressman) protected my grandfather and it is said that he eventually came to prefer him over his own children. In any case, my origins reconcile two traditional factions who built the country behaving most of the time as enemies and, occasionally in moments understood to be very difficult for the country, as patriotically reconciled.

With time, the war degenerated, for all practical purposes, into a family feud of *caudillos,* spilling over into the twentieth century until its end was mediated by Uruguay's great statesman, José Batlle y Ordóñez, in 1903.[1] Batlle, as he is referred to today, brought the country's warring factions into an agreement to disagree for the sake of mutual benefit during his two presidencies. Batlle's legacy is remarkable. In his first presidential term his role was similar to that of Abraham Lincoln in his resolution of the country's long-standing civil strife. In his second term, he could be compared to Franklin Roosevelt in that he completely modernized Uruguay's social and political institutions with one of the most sweeping reform programs any Western democracy has ever seen. Creating the political philosophy of *batllismo,* still current in Uruguay today, he preserved the union and, with great vision, took advantage of the opportunity to legislate a Uruguayan New Deal. Batlle's leadership took the country, in one seemingly impossible leap, from a nineteenth-century feudal society to a twentieth-century welfare state with reformist liberal policies. Those policies, adopted from the small, neutral European buffer state that Batlle's model, earned Uruguay the nickname of the "Switzerland of the Americas."

By the 1950s, however, Uruguay bore more resemblance to the Weimar Republic than to Switzerland. By 1959, even Uruguay's government had to acknowledge that its welfare state was in serious trouble. Economic factors brought back to the surface nineteenth-century structural problems of Uruguayan society that Batlle's peace-making and reforms had failed to address. As long as Uruguay enjoyed prosperity from its export of wool and beef, Batlle's reforms were sufficient to mitigate issues such as the fact that Uruguay, like all other Latin-American countries, still suffered from an unbalanced distribution in the ownership of land. Rather than radically alter land ownership through agrarian reform—which, after all, would have impinged on the Blancos—Batlle's reforms had managed to create a middle class by following a welfare state model without touching the country's capital base, its land.

Batlle's reforms had a tendency to defuse revolt by creating public dependence on a system of governmental benefits and industries. By the 1950s this system fostered such a massive bureaucracy that, as Mario Benedetti put it, many Uruguayans began to boast darkly that they had created the world's first country of office workers. Obviously, such dependence on the government was contingent on the government's economic ability to deliver on its promises; in a 1955 white paper on the economy, the government admitted that it would soon not be able to do so. Furthermore, it forecast that, with the invention and mass manufacture of synthetic fibers, its ability to do so in the long term could only diminish. The market for one of its two basic exports, wool, was shrinking in direct proportion to the spread of synthetic fibers in worldwide textile production.[2]

The effect of this announcement was no less severe than the devastating effect that the replacement of natural rubber with synthetic substitutes once had on Brazil's rich Amazonian region. Uruguay's response was general shock and outrage. In 1958, feeling betrayed by a government that had allowed this state of affairs to build to such a level without taking preventive measures, Uruguayans voted the Colorados out of office for the first time in ninety-four years. However, in so doing, they voted in the Blancos who, as the rural, landowners' party hardest hit by the state of the economy, were perhaps even less prepared for dealing with the crisis than the Colorados had been. For the first time in Uruguay's modern history, inflation began to eat away at real earnings at an alarming rate. In addition, the currency was devalued for the first time this century. Public unrest began to fester, unions became restive, hundreds of strikes and student protests began to break out. Panicking, the new government imposed martial law for the first time since the Terra government of the early

1930s, a measure that became more and more routine until it became the regime in 1973. In retrospect, the similarity between Germany in the 1930s and Uruguay in the late 1950s and 1960s is ironically clear. It is not too forced an analogy to say that the late fifties and sixties were the years of Uruguay's Weimar Republic, years characterized by economic chaos and public loss of faith in institutions, and the seventies the years of its Reich—its collapse into dictatorship.

The crisis of faith that led Martínez Moreno—along with the Tupamaros and other writers, activists, and intellectuals of his Generation of 1945 (or, as Angel Rama called it, "la Generación crítica")—to break with *batllismo* and its sociopolitical duality is clearly portrayed in the first pages of his novel *El paredón*. That generation, anchored by the journal *Marcha*, founded by its lifelong editor and Martínez Moreno associate Carlos Quijano, had been traumatized once before by the brief Terra regime of the early 1930s. The Terra regime, though little discussed in Uruguayan history, was an aborted attempt to establish a dictatorship in 1933. It came about as a result of a dispute within the Colorado party itself, interestingly enough for those in the late 1960s who rightly suspected Colorado President Jorge Pacheco Areco of coup tendencies. To Martínez Moreno and his contemporaries, then young men, the Terra regime, short-lived as it was, indicated that *batllismo* was not as solid after Batlle's death as the country would like to believe. In what then was a radical move, he, Carlos Quijano, and other young colleagues broke with *batllista* duality with the establishment of *Marcha* in 1939. *Marcha* was to play a central role in Uruguay's social, political, and cultural crisis leading up to the events of *El color*, a period Martínez Moreno called "la deca."

The members of the Generation of 1945 and the intellectuals of *Marcha* broke with *batllista* duality in search of what Martínez Moreno called *tercerismo*. The Cuban revolution was, nonetheless, a challenge for which Uruguay's *terceristas* were ideologically unprepared. The Generation of 1945 was divided as to how to respond to the sudden success of these young Cubans in ridding themselves of the old colonial structures that had hobbled Cuban society. Though Uruguay had a bloody history throughout the nineteenth century, the country's more recent past led most citizens, rightly or wrongly, to consider themselves a nation of neutrals and near pacifists akin to the Swiss. To embrace the violence of the Cuban revolution was to fly in the face of this mythological national character. Many, like Mario Benedetti—author of, among other things, the bitingly satirical essay *El país de la cola de paja* (The cowardly country)—were glad to do so. They announced the formation of what some see as a precursor to the Tupamaro movement, the Movimiento Nacional de Solidaridad con Cuba (MNSC) on 12 January 1961, the day the Uruguayan government expelled the Cuban ambassador and broke relations with Cuba under pressure from the U.S. A minority, while emphasizing the obsolescence of Uruguay's traditional parties and institutions, rejected the relevance of the Cuban experience to their own nation's problems. From the publication of *El paredón* in 1963, Martínez Moreno was the leading voice of this leftist minority.

The divisions in the Left worsened as the crisis deepened in the 1960s. Warnings of *golpismo* ("coup tendencies") were almost routine in *Marcha*'s editorials from the early 1960s on. They rose to a crescendo as Uruguay reformed its constitution along North American lines in 1966, strengthening the powers of the presidency to a degree that presaged the coup of 1973. The issue was not a matter of differences over recognition of the problem, but of finding a solution. On that point Uruguay's Left became sharply divided into two camps that could roughly be characterized as "soft" and "hard" responses to the government's failure and its growing repression.

By the mid-1960s, while *Marcha*'s independents and the Communist Party fought against the government's slide toward dictatorship in their journals and in the streets, others in the Left decided that more direct action was necessary. This group, which formed the basis for the creation of the Tupamaros, concluded that, given the country's basic socioeconomic structure, Uruguay's elite would prefer to sacrifice the country's political institutions to fascism rather than sacrifice their economic advantages to any comprehensive reform. That assent, they said, would be more than passive: key elements of the elite would, they said, collaborate in the creation of a violent apparatus for the suppression of dissent and the protection of privilege, all in the name of anticommunism. What they called Uruguay's "bourgeois" democracy, in their view, would prove to be more bourgeois than democratic. Reliance on its institutions, allowing it to define the limits of resistance and thus manipulate the rules of conflict by manipulating legality itself, was self-defeating.

The struggle was, ultimately, they said, over land ownership. They pointed to Uruguayan liberator José Artigas's betrayal by the nineteenth-century elite of both capitals of the River Plate in his endeavor to redistribute land after Independence as evidence of the priorities of Uruguay's elite. Thus, these pre-Tupamaros, though they had participated in the university demonstrations,unions, intellectual dissent groups, and party programs that attempted to bring the government to account through constitutional, nonviolent resistance, rejected the methods of those groups as inadequate to the task and embraced the Cuban model. The struggle over ideas in the capital was so much hot air, they said. The struggle must be made to focus on a more concrete element: the land.

It is interesting to the student of Martínez Moreno's canon that his publication record of novels dealing with *la deca* (1963–1974) coincides with the rise and fall of the urban guerrilla movement that sought to respond to it with armed revolt. Pablo Cejudo Velázquez has chronicled the history of the Movimiento de Liberación Nacional–Tuparmaros (MLN–T) in four stages:

> Pueden distinguirse cuatro etapas en el movimiento tupamaro. Los años que van de 1962 a 1968 son un período de formición y organización. Los tupamaros se comportan a modo del famoso bandido Diego Corrientes, que quitaba a los ricos para dar a los pobres. En escritos de lengua inglesa, se los han comparado a Robin Hood. Sus acciones iban especialmente dirigidas a bancos o casinos. Parecían buscar una adhesión popular a su causa, que nunca llegó de verdad.
>
> De 1968 a 1971, a lucha armada tupamara se hizo encarnizada y sin tregua. El Movimiento de Libercion Nacional–Tupamaro (MLN–T) creó el cuadro más caótico que se haya experimentado en país alguno, perpetró numerosos asaltos y mantuvo en jaque el ejército y la policía.
>
> Las instituciones del estado y toda la vida uruguaya se tambaleaban cuando entraron en acción masiva las Fuerzas Armadas, el 9 de setiembre de 1971. Le tercera etapa se concentra, precisamente, en esta lucha frontal entre MLN–T y ejército y policía combinados. La declinación de la guerrilla tupamara (cuarta etapa) no se advierte sino hasta mayo de 1972. La curva clínica baja casi del todo a fines de 1973. (Velázquez 1985, 14–15)

> Four stages can be distinguished in the development of the Tupamaro movement. The years from 1962 to 1968 are a period of formation and organization. The Tupamaros behave in the manner of the famous bandit Diego Corrientes, who took from the rich to give to the poor. In English language writings, they have been compared to Robin Hood. Their actions were especially directed at banks and casinos. They seemed to be looking for a popular rallying to their cause, something that never truly came to be.
>
> From 1968 to 1971, the Tupamaro armed struggle became bloody and gave no quarter. The Movement of National Liberation–

Tupamaros (MLN–T) created the most chaotic scene any country has experienced, perpetrated numerous assaults, and kept the army and the police in check.

The state institutions and all of Uruguayan life were teetering when the Armed Forces entered into action en masse on 9 September 1971. The third stage is concentrated, precisely, on this frontal struggle between the MLN–T and the combined army and police. The decline of the Tupamaro guerrillas (fourth stage) cannot be detected until May 1972. The clinical curve almost drops completely by the end of 1973.

Thus, it must be kept in mind that Martínez Moreno's literary and legal response to the deteriorating state of his country belonged to that of the nonviolent left in Uruguay. It paralleled a brutal fight by the violent left, led by the Tupamaros, to forestall a military dictatorship. Martínez Moreno had some legal dealings with Tupamaros representing them as a defense attorney. However, he refrained from making literary comment on their movement until his last novel, the documentary novel written in exile, *El color que el infierno me escondiera* (*El Infierno*) (1981). The controversy that ensued can be traced back to Martínez Moreno's position vis-à-vis the group from which the Tupamaros evolved. The Movimiento de Solidaridad con Cuba or National Movement of Solidarity with Cuba (MNSC), was founded on 12 January 1961, the day the government expelled the Cuban ambassador to Uruguay at the U.S.'s bidding. Martínez Moreno was in no way a defender of U.S. policy or an apologist for bowing to its pressure. However, after his visit to Cuba as an observer of the trial of Batista government official Sosa Blanco, he was no great admirer of the Castro regime either, as his novel *El paredón* (The executioner's wall) bears out. Yet, as Cejudo Valázquez points out, others who made the trip took the opposite path:

> A la sombra del MNSC, muchos uruguayos, incluidos futuros dirigentes tupamaros, visitaron Cuba y se hicieron verdaderos importadores de ideología y los métodos de la revolución cubana.
>
> El Movimiento de Liberacion Nacional . . . surgió . . . a base de la primera célula militante, formada en 1962 por Raúl Sendic Antonaccio, con un grupo de trabajadores de la Caña de Azucar.
>
> En abril y mayo de 1962, cientos de militantes de UTAA (Unión de Trabajadores Azucareros de Artigas) recorrieron a pie la ruta Artigas–Montevideo (todo el país, de norte a sur), a fin de atraer la atención sobre las precarias condiciones de vida existentes en las plantaciones. . . .
>
> Sendic, en esta primera época, semeja una especie de figura mítica,

> que desaparece aquí y aparece allá, que es detenido y se evade en varias oportunidades. . . .
> Al MLN–T, gestado en ambiente cañero, se adhirieron después profesionales, médicos, ingenieros, y abogados. . . .
> Sendic escogió el camino de la guerrilla urbana, por cuanto la rural no tenía perspectivas de éxito en la geografía uruguaya, carente de altas montañas. (Velázquez 1985 18–19)

> In the shadow of the MNSC, many Uruguayans, including future Tupamaros leaders, visited Cuba and became true importers of the methods and ideology of the Cuban Revolution.
> The Movement of National Liberation . . . arose . . . from the first militant cells formed in 1962 by Raúl Sendic Antonaccio, with a group of sugar cane workers.
> In April and May 1962, hundreds of UTAA (Union of Sugar Workers of Artigas) militants walked from Artigas to Montevideo (the entire country, north to south), with the goal of attracting attention to the precarious conditions of life on the plantations. . . .
> Sendic, in this first period, seems to be a sort of mythical figure, who disappears here and reappears there, who is detained and escapes on various occasions. . . .
> The MLN–T, born among the canefields, later is joined by professionals, doctors, engineers, and lawyers. . . .
> Sendic chose the path of urban guerrilla warfare since rural warfare had no chance of success in Uruguayan geography, so lacking in high mountains.

This discrepancy was to put Martínez Moreno and like-minded leftists at odds with the more militant leftists for the next decade. The Tupamaros did support the leftist electoral coalition of which Martínez Moreno was a charter member, the Broad Front. In addition, the MLN–T observed a truce during the 1971 electoral campaign. Nonetheless, hindsight reveals that the differences between the two factions resulted in a lack of coordination of political and military strategies that effectively weakened the opposition as a whole at critical junctures as the government drifted to dictatorship.

Still, the Tupamaros nearly succeeded in bringing down the repressive government of Jorge Pacheco Areco, Uruguay's president from late 1967 to 1971. Pacheco Areco had been the little-known vice presidential running mate of Oscar Gestido, the moderate Colorado general some compared to Eisenhower in the country's first election under its U.S.-style 1966 constitution. Pacheco Areco, a former boxer and sportscaster who was known for his demagoguery on behalf of the right wing of the party, had been made a candidate to mollify the Right. When President Gestido died of a heart attack on 6 December 1967, most Uruguayans considered it the gravest national tragedy in recent history and sincerely feared for the future of democracy. They had good reason to fear: one week after taking power, Pacheco Areco shut down two newspapers for printing material he found offensive, and banned six leftist groups, including the Socialist Party.

The effect of Pacheco Areco's actions was to polarize the already volatile situation in Uruguay's leftist opposition. Pacheco Areco's unpopular image unwittingly provided the Tupamaros with the best recruiting tool they could have wished for. As he gratuitously applied and lifted his famous "Medidas Prontas de Seguridad" ("Emergency Security Measures"), the MLN–T, known to its members as "la Orga" ("the Organization") broadened and deepened its effectiveness. In 1970, it struck in force with a wave of kidnappings. The most notorious of these was the kidnapping of a foreign official in a spectacular operation that attracted worldwide attention and inspired a major motion picture. The official was alleged to be a secret organizer of schools for the teaching of professional torture techniques to Uruguay's security forces, a task he had allegedly accomplished previously at the service of another South American dictatorship.[3] Whatever his actual position, the effect of such activities was tens of thousands of unfortunate broken bodies and minds for the next decade across the entire Southern Cone region of South America.

The Tupamaros' main demand in the kidnapping of the U.S. official, the resignation of the unpopular Pacheco Areco government, came within hours of being met. Had it actually taken place, the MLN–T might have garnered massive support from the citizenry; it might even have been able to emerge from clandestinity, gaining political respectability and legitimacy. It certainly stood a good chance of producing an outpouring of approval among the undecided in Uruguay's conflict. Then Pacheco benefited from a huge stroke of luck in the fortuitous capture of Raúl Sendic in a fateful MLN–T mix-up. With Sendic in hand, the Pacheco government no longer felt it needed to deal with the MLN–T and decided to call the Tupamaros' bluff. The Tupamaros, feeling their credibility was at stake, executed the kidnapped foreign official in what their current leader, Eleuterio Fernández Huidobro, now acknowledges was their greatest and most dramatic mistake. Public support for the MLN–T fell as they were perceived to have killed a man in cold blood as the government had done to dissidents for years. An all-out war between the security forces and the Tupamaros ensued over the heads, as it were, of the vast majority of Uruguayans caught in the middle until the Tupamaros were defeated in 1972.

Though the Tupamaros' armed resistance had been the pretext for granting the Uruguayan military vast powers until 1972, that year it became clear that it was just that—a pretext. The army's hard-liners purged the soft-liners by setting up false peace-talks with the MLN-T and then arresting those army officers who came forward to participate.[4] On 8 February 1973, the army and air force mutinied, seizing key positions in the capital. The navy and President Bordaberry, the obscure conservative who had just been elected amidst allegations of fraud, had not been consulted as to the coup; together they denounced the coup in public, while negotiating their own interests in private. The other two branches of the armed forces backed down. Then the armed forces and the president combined to launch an intense propaganda campaign against the nation's congress. Serious charges of corruption against parliamentarians were made almost daily for the next three months. Meanwhile, the president and the joint chiefs hammered out a power-sharing deal. Bordaberry was to be allowed to remain in office as titular head of state with a cabinet approved by the joint chiefs and watched over by a colonel in each ministry. On 1 June 1973, President Bordaberry granted himself an extension of special powers without congressional approval. On 26 June 1973, following rumors that the president was about to dissolve congress, the Uruguayan senate occupied its chambers for over twenty-four hours in an attempt to head off any such action. The senators finally left at 1:40 A.M. on 27 June. Within a couple of hours the army moved on congress. President Bordaberry went on the air to announce that the measure had been taken because of congress's "grave violation of the fundamental principles of the Constitution." At the same time, in what would have been an Orwellian doublespeak farce had it not caused such hardship, he announced strict censorship against attempts "to attribute to the executive power any dictatorial purposes."[5]

The general in charge of the operation against the congress, General Gregorio Alvarez ("Goyo"), was the brother of a colonel assassinated by the Tupamaros. Colonel Artigas Alvarez had been in charge of an elite torture team after the introduction of systematic torture to Uruguay's security forces. Hence, Goyo's eagerness to take a firm hand against "subversives" such as the members of the nation's congress. In the 1980s Goyo would go on to be the last—and only military—president under Uruguay's infamous

1: The Life and Times of Carlos Martínez Moreno

dictatorship. Following the return to democracy, he would be court-martialed on charges of petty corruption. As for Bordaberry, he wouldn't last as long as the term to which he had been fraudulently elected. In 1976 he was replaced by Aparicio Méndez, a senile lawyer from the Interior, after a squabble with the joint chiefs over their power-sharing agreement. In his first televised speech to the nation as successor to Bordaberry, a victim of stage-fright and the involuntary muscle spasms of old age, the poor man allegedly urinated on himself before the cameras. Uruguay was about to set a new low for travesties of justice. For the remainder of the decade, it would be denounced internationally as one of the most repressive police states the continent has ever seen—and Latin America has seen its share.

Few countries in the Western world have ever suffered such a complete purge of dissidents as that which occurred after the military takeover of 1973. In 1977 Amnesty International denounced Uruguay as the country with the most political prisoners per capita in Latin America. Conditions became so repressive that they drew the concern of Andrei Sakharov and forty of his fellow dissidents in the Soviet Union, who sent a letter of protest to the Uruguyan regime that year. Once the proudest of Latin America's liberal democracies, Uruguay became, in the words of a U.S. Congressman, "the torture chamber of Latin America."[6] The government instituted a comprehensive computer system used to classify all citizens into three categories of political desirability—a desirability that controlled all areas of life. In addition, one of every four hundred Uruguayans was sent to a concentration camp, as opposed to a rate of 1/55,000 in Brazil, 1/12,500 in Bolivia, 1/1200 in Argentina, and 1/600 in Paraguay.

Yet few countries have witnessed such a turn of events as Uruguay's return to democracy. Uruguay is the first country in Latin American to overthrow a dictatorship through peaceful demonstrations and the ballot box. Today, as we become accustomed to the dramatic events of Eastern Europe, this may not seem so dramatic. In 1980, however, when the dictatorship sought to legitimize its rule with a "yes" or "no" vote, no one expected the landslide rejection that followed. No advertising or campaigning against the military's proposal had been allowed, while over one million dollars had been spent on a public relations campaign for the "yes" vote. Rumors had circulated that the secrecy of the balloting would be breached in order to punish any "no" voters and that the whole plebiscite was a ruse to stage another purge.

When voters went to the polls, no one knew the true measure of public opinion regarding the military's bid for indefinite rule.

The overwhelming results proved that, although Uruguay's armed resistance had been defeated, its citizens' nonviolence in no way had constituted consent for military rule. Conceding to the exposure of the reality that they ruled only by force, the next year the military removed their last civilian puppet president and openly installed a general as chief of the executive branch. Yet the momentum was irreversible: as many Uruguayans put it, they had lost their fear in the 1980 plebiscite. On 27 November 1983, emboldened by the fall of Argentina's dictatorship in its defeat in the Falklands war, nearly half a million Uruguayans demonstrated for an end to dictatorial rule. Almost two years later to the day, on 25 November 1985, they got their wish: the first elections for public office since 1973 were held. They were elections somewhat strained by the military's attempts to bargain for certain guarantees to insulate them from the consequences of their harsh rule. General Seregni, the nominee once again for the Broad Front after his release to a hero's welcome from nine years as a political prisoner, was "proscribed" from running for president. The opposition's other seasoned presidential candidate, the moderate Blanco party Senator Wilson Ferreira Aldunate—who had, in fact, actually gained the plurality in the 1971 elections—was robbed of a last run at the office as he was imprisoned upon his return from exile. Thus, the field was left to the remaining party's candidate, Julio Sanguinetti. Though widely respected, many were uncomfortable with the fact that Sanguinetti belonged to the same party as the collaborating Bordaberry. Their fears were realized when, within months of winning such a questionably influenced election, Sanguinetti announced an amnesty for all military accused of human rights crimes. The remainder of his presidential term was spent defending his administration from a grass roots call for a referendum to nullify the amnesty. It finally reached a vote in early 1989 and was defeated. However, its effects carried over into the next election. The Colorados were thrown out of office for the second time this century as the Uruguyans elected a Blanco to the president's office. The Broad Front won the highest office it had ever attained—the mayorship of Montevideo.

Meanwhile, perhaps most astounding of all, the MLN–T, released from horrible years of secret torture houses, secret political prisons, and outright concentration camps, regrouped as a political party. In four years, the Tupamaros went from defeated guerrilla movement to newspaper and book publisher and radio station owner. In a move few thought they would ever live to see, the Tupamaros applied for and were granted admission as a party into the Broad Front coalition as official members. The application of their legendary grass roots organizing skills to the 1989 electoral campaign is partially credited with gaining the Broad Front the mayorship of Montevideo, the second most powerful elected post in the country. Problems persist: the amnestying of the military has emboldened them to the point that they are quite belligerent in their demands. In addition to freedom from prosecution for their crimes, they have let it be known that they expect that their disproportionately large portion of the budget be left intact. This is a constant drain on an economy whose failure was, after all, the beginning of Uruguay's troubles. Yet much remains to give one hope that in reestablishing democracy, Uruguay can claim once more: "Como el Uruguay no hay" ("There's no place like Uruguay").

Life

Carlos Martínez Moreno was born in the Western city of Colonia, Uruguay in 1917. His father, a Montevidean, had settled there with his bride, a native of Colonia, upon inheriting a small piece of land. The farming endeavor went sour three years later, however, and the elder Martínez Moreno had to move his family twice more before settling down permanently in Montevideo.

Carlos was a precocious child whose literary inclinations were evident from the time he learned to read and write. He wrote poetry, made up his own newspaper, and read extensively in his grandfather's excellent library. His grandfather, Eduardo Moreno, had been an historian and novelist himself, while his godfather, uncle Afredo Martínez, was a poet. Hence, young Carlos's literary ambitions were welcomed and encouraged in the family when it became obvious that the boy, in the author's own words, had "una necesidad irreprimible de expresarme por escrito" ("an irrepressible need to express myself in writing") (Orthmann 1976, 25).

For all his advantages, however, by Martínez Moreno's account, his was not a happy childhood. Reports of his preferences as a young boy lead one to surmise that the nearly misanthropic, Flaubertian tone of his novels was a personal trait developed very early in life. A timid introvert, his propensity for reflection drew him more to realism than to the usual escapist fantasy even in his childhood stories, traits he imparted to his character Susana in his early novella *Cordelia*. According to Martínez Moreno,

> Yo, por mi idiosincracia, no pude tener una niñez feliz, tuve una niñez confortablemente asistida y hoy me parece que en esa época me incorporé conocimientos capitales y, en germen desarrollé principios fundamentales de mi persona. Pero no fui feliz, porque me acecharon innumerables fantsmas y porque yo era un niño tímido, sin ningún coraje, con bastante lucidez para saber que no lo tenía, con cantidad de represiones e inhibiciones que la educación no me fomentaba demaisiado pero que estaban dentro de mí. (Orthman 25)

> I, by virtue of my idiosyncrasies, couldn't enjoy a happy childhood. I had a comfortable childhood and today, it seems to me, I incorporated capital knowledge and developed the seeds of the fundamental principles of my personality. But I was not happy because innumerable phantoms haunted me and because I was a timid child, totally lacking in courage, with enough intelligence to know it, with a host of repressive characteristics and inhibitions that education didn't promote too much but that were within me nonetheless.

Timid and introverted, Martínez Moreno was closer to his mother than to his father as a child, although he did admire his father for his candor and steadfastness and used him as the basis for the protagonist's father in his first acclaimed novel, *El paredón* (The executioner's wall).

The Spanish Civil War and the brief quasi-dictatorship of Uruguayan Colorado party leader Gabriel Terra in the 1930s shaped Martínez Moreno's university years. As a result, he developed a deep-seated antiauthoritarian, civil-libertarian streak in his character. Martínez Moreno's tenacious loyalty to these ideals is evident in both his literature and his life up to the day in 1986 when he died in exile in Mexico.

The author's first published narrative, a short story entitled "El niño que prepara su muerte" (The boy who prepared his death), appeared in the weekly *AIAPE* (Asociación de Intelectuales, Artistas, Periodistas, y Escritores), when he was only twenty-one. The same year, he landed a job as drama critic for one of Montevideo's two leading dailies, *El país* with which, along with stories and articles written for *Mundo Uruguayo*, he supported himself and his young family. In 1943 he joined the staff of *Marcha*, the magazine that would play an enormous role in his life as well as in the life of the country during the tumultuous 1960s and early 1970s. From the outset, Martínez Moreno was its drama critic—

a feared and revered one, it is said—as well as its political commentator under founder, editor, and friend Carlos Quijano. The two would die as exiled next-door neighbors in Mexico City over four decades later.

In 1944 Martínez Moreno's literary work gained its first recognition when he was unanimously awarded first prize by *AIAPE* and *Mundo Uruguayo* in a contest for the short story "La otra mitad" (The other half). "La otra mitad" was later to be the title of his second full-length novel in 1966. This novel became notorious for falling into disfavor with the censors in Franco's Spain. While working for *Marcha* and, at the same time, taking on the editorial page for the daily *El Diario*, Martínez Moreno graduated as valedictorian of his law school class in 1948. He quickly established himself as one of the most competent criminal public defenders before the courts of Montevideo. His legal career extended for over twenty-five years until his defense against the imprisonment of writers, and his subsequent legal showdown with the military dictatorship before the supreme court in 1974.

In the 1950s, he began traveling as an international correspondent. In 1952 he covered the Bolivian revolution and befriended its leaders, Paz Estenssoro and Siles Suazo. The experience is reflected in his first novella, written in 1956, *Los aborígenes* (The aborigienes), as well as in his later novel *Coca* (1970). In 1959 he traveled to Cuba at the invitation of the Castro government as an observer at the trials of the members of deposed dictator Fulgenico Batista's regime. The trial turned out to be, in Martínez Moreno's own words, one of the most upsetting experiences of his life, and its effects were well documented in 1963 in his first full-length, and most controversial, novel, *El paredón* (The executioner's wall).

After his first award-winning short story in 1938, Martínez Moreno did not publish any creative writing until 1960. In 1960, his first collection of short stories appeared, *Los días por vivir* (The days we're about to live). The novellas *Los aborígenes* and *Cordelia* were to follow shortly, then a steady stream of novels from 1963 until the hiatus in dictatorship and his exile in 1974. According to Juan Carlos Onetti, Martínez Moreno demanded too much of himself as a writer during this period, aspiring to perfection before allowing his work to be published (Orthmann 1976, 33). Martínez Moreno admits to a certain amount of pessimism and doubt as to his writing abilities, but in an interview with Jorge Ruffinelli also points to his involvement with *Marcha* as another reason for "blooming late" as a fiction writer:

Marcha lleva el mérito—no voy a decir la culpa—de que no haya publicado en este tiempo. Porque el compromiso intelectual. . . , el compromiso de calibrarse frente a un público exigente todas las semanas, que para mí representaba la crítica de teatro y después la factura de algunos editoriales, ya significaba una forma de cotejarse o de probarse ante la gente; also así como un sucedáneo de la posibilidad de escribir. Todos nos postergamos. Para consolarnos Quijano a veces nos decía que ésta era la época del magazine y no la del libro, y que hay obras que pueden dejarse dentro de un semanario, pues son más importantes allí que en un libro. Fíjese: es un hecho que yo estoy en *Marcha* desde fines del 43 hasta comienzos del 61 y que publico recién a fines de 1960. Es cuando me rito de *Marcha* que me encuentro confrontado a la experiencia de la soledad, que es la creación. (Orthmann 1976, 34)

Marcha bears the merit—I'm not going to say the blame—for the fact that I didn't publish during all this time. Because the intellectual commitment . . , the commitment of gauging oneself before a demanding readership every week, which for me was theater criticism and later the authorship of some editorials, was already a form of proving myself before an audience—something like a substitute for the possibility of writing. We all put things off. As a consolation, Quijano sometimes used to tell us that this was the age of the magazine and not of the book, and that there are works that must be left within the pages of a weekly since they are more important than in a book. Look: it's a fact that I was at *Marcha* from the end of 1943 to the beginning of 1961 and that I begin publishing toward the end of 1960. It is when I retire from *Marcha* that I find myself confronted with the experience of solitude, which is creativity.

Martínez Moreno lost no time in taking advantage of his retirement from *Marcha*, as his publication record in the 1960s proves. In 1960, he published his first volume of short stories, aptly named *Los días por vivir* (The days we're about to live). In 1961, his two novellas *Los aborígenes* (The aborigines), based on his experiences in Bolivia, and *Cordelia,* appeared. The year 1963 saw the success of his first full-length novel, *El paredón* (The executioner's wall), the controversial work based on his observations of the Cuban revolution in 1959. In 1964 Martínez Moreno was brought up short by a problem that increasingly was to become an issue for him, both as a writer and a lawyer: censorship. This time it was Spanish censors who refused to allow his novel *La otra mitad* (The other half) to be published by Seix Barral. What was curious about Franco's censors' decision was that they chose to censor Martínez Moreno's least political novel. It was objectionable, they said, because it explored adultery and thus undermined the institution of marriage. In a measure soon to become a routine hindrance to the development of his career, Martínez Moreno was forced to have the novel's publication postponed until it could go to press in Mexico three years later, in 1966. Unfortunately, this meant that it competed with his next novel, which came out the same year, *Con las primeras luces* (By dawn's early light).

The next year saw past collections of Martínez Moreno's short stories reach second editions. However, the sharpening of the conflicts in Uruguay with the emergence of the MLN–T as an effective fighting force and the death of Che Guevara in Bolivia drew Martínez Moreno back into the political arena as a writer. A trip to Mexico City and another to New York, both times as a delegate to conferences on writers and their social responsibility, provided Martínez Moreno with a jarring contrast in experiences. The year 1968 saw the resulting publication of *Los prados de la conciencia* (Conscience meadows), another book of short stories delving into the ethical dimensions of the growing crisis in his country. Though Uruguay was at war in 1969, Martínez Moreno's short story publication continued unabated with three books: *La sirena y otros cuentos* (The siren and other stories), *Las bebidas azules* (The blue drinks), and *Cuentos de la ciudad* (City stories). In 1970, his response to Che Guevara's failed revolution in his old familiar reporter's beat of Bolivia yields his first novel in four years, *Coca* (Cocaine).

However, the next year brought Martínez Moreno back into the public arena, this time as a charter member of the leftist coalition, the Broad Front. His involvement and prestige were such that he was considered seriously for the vice presidential spot on the ticket with Líber Seregni. He published yet another book of short stories, this one reflecting the times in its title, *De vida o muerte* (Of life or death). In addition, he argued a milestone case before the supreme court challenging the constitutionality of the ever-increasing practice of extending military jurisdiction to civilians. The experience resulted in the publication of a book on the law, *Jurisdicción civil y jurisdicción militar* (Civilian jurisdiction and military jurisdiction).

To the extent that he resisted the growing threat of military rule in the courts, in his writings, and at the ballot box, however, Martínez Moreno also rejected the path of violent resistance chosen by the MLN–T. As the situation worsened, the consequences of this divergence in strategies of resistance became more acute. Martínez Moreno the lawyer took great exception to revolutionary justice as he had seen it practiced in Cuba in the trials and executions of members of the Batista regime after the revolution.

Meanwhile the government entrenched itself more and more in the politics of repression and became ever more closely allied to the U.S.'s policies of anticommunist containment. The government effectively offered the entire country to the U.S. as a "domino" in North American foreign policy in exchange for some form of aid. The short-term result, according to former C.I.A. agent Philip Agee in his book about the time he spent stationed in Montevideo, *C.I.A. Diary*, was that Montevideo was made into the main C.I.A. station for South America.[7] A bunker-style U.S. embassy was built that allegedly bristled with intelligence devices and employed over five hundred people. Foreign embassies were allegedly electronically "bugged" with the Uruguayan government's tacit approval and cooperation, and attempts were allegedly made to make Montevideo a station for Eastern bloc defectors. The long-term result of the distorting influence of U.S. aid on the course of Uruguayan politics was the interference of antidemocratic elements within the U.S. intelligence community in local Uruguayan politics. These elements consisted of disgruntled right-wingers in the National Security Council and other agencies allegedly answering to groups such as the "Forty Committee," the task force Henry Kissinger ostensibly organized at President Richard Nixon's bidding, allegedly in order to bring down the government of Chilean president Salvador Allende with a military coup in 1973.[8] These elements, who were failing miserably in their "counterinsurgency" efforts in Asia, were determined not to suffer defeat in the Southern Cone. They embarked on a concerted program to expand and improve the "counterinsurgency" effectiveness of long-neutral Uruguay's military, which, in 1967, had fewer soldiers than Montevideo had firemen. As they increased its effectiveness, "soft-liners"—i.e., officers who had qualms about the proper relationship between the military and constitutional democratic leadership—were purged. These men included officers such as General Líber Seregni, who resigned his command rather than mobilize his unit against civilians in a labor dispute in 1968. In an editorial that caused its closing by the government, the newspaper *Extra* commented in September 1968:

> Seregni en franca discrepancia con sus pares, no se limitó a desobedecer las órdenes de su jefe constitucional, el presidente de la República, sino que protestando formalmente por la conducción represiva intentó con éxito apartar a los autores del clima de violencia del escen-

ario de los hechos, y se convirtió en el seno del Ejército en el líder de la línea democrática, del diálogo y del sentido común. Cuando vio que el régimen se encaminaba aceleradamente hacia la dictadura y que nada podía hacer para evitarlo, se negó a desenvainar la espada contra su propio pueblo y en un gesto que lo honra les arrojó la renuncia y cruzó al otro lado de la trinchera. (Fasano 1980, 91)

In frank discrepancy with his peers, Seregni did not limit himself to disobeying the orders of his constitutional commander-in-chief, the president of the republic. Rather, formally protesting against repressive conduct, he successfully attempted to divert the creators of the climate of violence from the scene of the events. He became the leader of the democratic line at the heart of the inner circles of the army, the proponent of dialogue and common sense. When he saw that the regime was hurling along the path toward dictatorship and that there was nothing he could do to stop it, he refused to unsheath his sword against his own people and, in a gesture that brings him honor, he threw them his resignation and crossed to the other side of the trenches.

Seregni went on to be the leftist coalition's presidential candidate in 1971, only to serve nine years in prison as a political prisoner after the 1973 military coup he had tried so earnestly to prevent.

The year of the coup, Martínez Moreno responded with the publication of a bold book exposing in detail the illegal steps the government had adopted to defeat the Tupamaros. Harking back to the prophetic tone of the title of his 1960 short story collection, *Los días por vivir,* he called his 1973 book *Los días que vivimos* (The days we're living through). In 1974 Martínez Moreno was drawn directly into the battle over civil liberties when he was called upon to defend Juan Carlos Onetti and several others against government persecution. In the end, all but one of his clients, Nelson Marra, was released into exile. However, Marra was forced to serve five years in prison for penning a short story offensive to the military, and *Marcha* was closed down for publishing it. The result is perhaps Martínez Moreno's darkest, most pessimistic novel, *Tierra en la boca* (A mouthful of dirt), originally written under the title *Alguien tiene que enterrarnos* (Someone will have to bury us).

After 1974, Martínez Moreno was never to publish in Uruguay again. Dismissed from his twenty-five-year post as criminal public defender, his private legal practice consisted mostly of consoling and aiding the families of the growing ranks of the "disappeared." Such activities, once again, did not serve to endear him to the military, and in 1978 his home was the target of a right-wing death squad bombing. Though he obstinately refused to allow that to force him into exile immediately, a phone tip from a former adversary in court convinced him that the military intended to "disappear" him as well. He quickly arranged a two-week vacation in Spain for himself, his wife, and his youngest daughter, leaving everything they owned behind in Montevideo except for what could fit in two suitcases. On arriving in Spain, he finally told his wife what he had resisted saying for five years: they could not go home again. Opportunities to start over took them on to Mexico City, where Martínez Moreno was offered a position as a professor at the national university and as a columnist for the daily *La Jornada*. He and his family settled into a Mexico City apartment complex next-door to that of his old friend, *Marcha*'s Carlos Quijano, also—like most of Uruguay's intellectuals—in exile.

In 1981 Martínez Moreno's was vindicated with the publication and critical success of *El color que el infierno me escondiera (Él Infierno)*. *El color* is his only narrative ever to completely combine the two careers he had been forced to pursue under such desperate circumstnaces for over a decade. It is also his only work ever to achieve critical success in English translation, being published in North America and the United Kingdom in 1988. By then, however, it was too late. Martínez Moreno never was to see his homeland again: he succumbed to a heart attack in Mexico City on 6 February 1986 at the age of sixty-eight. It had been a decade since his novels had been allowed to circulate in his home country. However, his death two months after Uruguay's first democratic elections since 1973 meant that his hometown press at least had the freedom to eulogize him. Though he did not live long enough to return to his country's reborn democracy, Martínez Moreno had lived long enough to be remembered by it for his tireless efforts in its behalf, as a writer, a lawyer, and principled human being.

2
Los aborígenes: The Drama of Latin America's Elite

Though his career as a fiction writer began in the 1940s, Carlos Martínez Moreno's first full-length novel was not published until 1963, when *El paredón* (The executioner's wall) appeared. In the interim, his dedication to his legal practice and his extensive writing for the prestigious magazine *Marcha*, both as essayist and theater critic, made it impossible for him to devote himself to the extensive undertaking of producing a full-length narrative.[1]

This delay is completely understandable in retrospect, given the tremendous care with which he did construct his novels when he set out to write them in the 1960s and 1970s. Yet *El paredón* did not come out of nowhere. Between 1956 and 1960, he wrote two novellas, *Los aborígenes* (The aborigines) and *Cordelia*, which show the development that would later become Martínez Moreno's hallmark as a novelist, both in style and in thematic concern. Before analyzing the novellas themselves, it is important to consider these two early works as blueprints for Martínez Moreno's life's work.

Each of these novellas is worthy of close analysis for the different ways in which they treat *la deca* through their respective characters. Both stories contain the germinal stage of a theme that developed to become suitable for treatment later as a full-length novel and ultimately characterizes the writer's canon. *La deca*, or decadence and decay, is the term used by Martínez Moreno to decribe the theme that unifies all of his works. All of his characters experience a sense of decay and are confronted with a critical moment of self-recognition that causes them to analyze the relationship of past and present. These two novellas depict that theme and Martínez Moreno's treatment of it in its genesis.

Los aborígenes was written in 1960 and published in 1961. It, in turn, can be seen as a predecessor to *El paredón* in that it depicts the plight of an intellectual alienated from his Latin-American reality. In the later novel, *El paredón* (1963), we are to see the full-scale development of the protagonist to whom we are introduced in *Los aborígenes*. This protagonist is a character who feels powerless and is unable to mature and assume responsibility in his society. In Primitivo of *Los aborígenes* we also see the introduction of the theme that is to be Carlos Martínez Moreno's overriding concern in his novels, *la deca*. *La deca* is, in Martínez Moreno's canon, both a sense of decaying values in society that is felt by his characters, as well as their often decadent response to that sense of decay.

Los aborígenes is a precurson to *El paredón* (1963), Martínez Moreno's first full-length novel. It represents a tendency in his works to treat *la deca* on a large scale: it focuses on an alienated protagonist who not only reflects upon his personal history in relationships, but also looks at his entire country from without, as an exiled Latin American. In *El paredón*, Julio Calodoro reflects on the state of Uruguay from the vantage point of the Cuban revolution, which symbolizes of the future. In *Los aborígenes*, Primitivo reflects on the condition of Bolivia from the vantage point of Rome, which symbolizes of the past. In both cases, the theme is that of an individual alienated from his society. Furthermore, both reflect a particularly Uruguayan cultural phenomenon: dealing with the implications of the country's famous slogan, "como el Uruguay no hay" ("There's no place like Uruguay"). Although *Los aborígenes* is set in Bolivia, its suggestion of a cultural conflict between Europe and Latin America brings to mind the issue of Uruguay's "Europeanness" and its lack of cultural solidarity with the rest of Latin America.

The reasons for this have to do, once again, with the heart of the poetics of *la Generación crítica*, the generation to which Martínez Moreno belonged. As Uruguayan society reached a crisis during its decline in the 1960s and revolutionary movements pushed the idea of Latin-American solidarity to the point of armed conflict, "como el Uruguay no hay" was transformed from a boast to a lament. As it had been the Latin-American exception to the rule of underdevelopment in its golden years, the "Switzerland of South America" now found itself isolated in its crisis. Attempts were made to find points of contact with other Latin-American countries; the later novel on the Cuban revolution, *El paredón*, is an example of that search.

Los aborígenes looks to an Andean nation. In a different way,

2: *Los aborígenes:* The Drama Of Latin America's Elite

the decade's most important Uruguayan guerrilla movement, the Movimiento de Liberación Nacional–Tupamaros (National Liberation Movement–Tupamaros), did also, taking its name from the leader of a indigenous uprising against colonial rule in Peru.[2] Both phenomena, though very different in nature, are symptomatic of an unprecedented Uruguayan tendency to reject its identity as the Athens of the River Plate, always looking out to Europe, to look inward to the continent for a new identity that would serve to cope with its crisis.

In its sociopolitical aspects, it is both the strength and tragedy of Martínez Moreno's writing that it was prophetic in addressing the issues that eventually destroyed the cherished stability of Uruguay's social and political institutions. This fact makes him perhaps the most prominent, earliest, and most profound member, in terms of his social criticism, of *la Generación crítica*. While not its most strident member, his analysis is earlier, more dispassionate, more intellectualy profound, and, above all (for this is his hallmark) has the balance of intimism that bridged the gap between personal and social reality in a way no other writer has attempted.

The circumstances that led to Martínez Moreno's choice of Bolivia as the referent for *Los aborígenes* are the same as those that led to his choice of Cuba for *El paredón*: his role as a journalist and political editorialist. As far as his political views were concerned, he was a committed democratic socialist to his death.[3] At the time of the Bolivian revolution of 1952, he became close friends with President Paz Estenssoro, the revolution's leader. This relationship was to endure for decades beyond that revolution's failure, which ended in Paz Estenssoro's exile in Uruguay. Martínez Moreno chose to identity himself with the Bolivian revolution in a much closer way than he did with the Cuban revolution. It became again part of the referent of his fiction in the later novel *Coca* (Cocaine) (1970), in which its events are narrated in even greater detail than that found in *Los aborígenes*.

The Bolivian revolution is the central mechanism of *Los aborígenes*'s scant plot. Primitivo (literally, "Primitive"), the diplomat who has been long estranged from his native country, loses his job because of a political upheaval back home with which he finds himself totally out of touch. But the issue this mechanism represents goes far beyond mere political considerations. It is the same one that motivated the radicalism of the Cuban revolution and the later movements of the 1960s: the rejection of "genteel barbarism," to borrow a term from John Brushwood.[4] This rejection came from a sense that the bourgeois, European, nineteenth-century liberalism that had achieved Latin-American independence—and, in Uruguay's case, a golden age of affluence and peace—had become irrelevant to its development in the second half of the twentieth century. It is fitting that a Uruguayan should most directly address this concern, since perhaps no Latin-American country so totally embraced that liberalism as did Uruguay. It follows, then, that no country's writers would become as sensitive to the question of its irrelevance as they did. *Los aborígenes* deals directly with this issue, which Martínez Moreno describes as one of *sobrevivientes* (survivors) and *sobremurientes* (his neologism, literally "the sur-dead-ors," or survivors who are as good as dead).

Once again, it must be pointed out that in doing so Martínez Moreno bridges a gap in the novelistic literature of his generation. Juan Carlos Onetti's work is filled with *sobremurientes*. The term brings to mind Onetti's title *Juntacadáveres* (The gatherer of cadavers). Onetti's landmark novel, *El astillero* (The shipyard), is in itself an allegorical tale of irrelevance denied. Yet Onetti's focus remains on the individualist, philosophical level, whereas in Martínez Moreno we see this level joined inextricably with the broader sociopolitical referent that is almost the exclusive focus of the other pole of his generation, writers such as Benedetti. By maintaining the contact between the intimist and the social, the philosophical and the political, all by means of a deep psychological analysis, Martínez Moreno attempts a totality that the others of his generation do not.

Whereas Onetti's *El astillero* uses a shipyard as its referent, Martínez Moreno's story juxtaposes the ruins of a great ancient civilization, that of Rome, with the modern ruinous state of his native culture. Simultaneously, Rome's ruins serve to identify Primitivo with an attachment to an eclipsed culture of the Old World, as opposed to the demands of the New. Thus, the European ruins of the novella's opening scene become symbolic of the condition of Latin America's "genteel barbarism." The story's title and the protagonist's name evoke images of New World noble savagery, and yet the Primitivo's opening scene shows him to be an empty parenthesis between the ancient and the modern, just as his nineteenth-century liberal values are: "Sentado sobre una de aquellas piedras ilustres, veía correr los autos que flanqueaban el Coliseo" ("Seated upon one of those illustrious stones, he watched the rush-hour traffic flow past the Coliseum" (Martínez Moreno 1967, 7). Primitivo is the very picture of irrelevant genteel barbarism, a misfit in a picture of ancient Roman ruins and twentieth-century

2: *Los aborígenes:* The Drama Of Latin America's Elite

rush hour traffic. Unlike the "Primitivo" of Carlos Reyles, he is an absurd form of syncretism incarnate:

> . . . ese Primitivo Cortés había quedado como la cifra de sus contradicciones: su achaparrada figura de indio, su alquitarada deferencia doctral. (11)
>
> . . . that Primitivo Cortés had become the sum of his contradictions: his stunted Indian features, his misery doctoral deference.

In his case, this syncretism proves to be less than the sum of its parts. While attempting to maintain an identity both as "indio" and Old World cosmopolitan, he knows he has succeeded only in becoming one of those "caricaturas políticas" ("political cartoons") he dislikes, an anachronism, an absurdity.

Events in his home country serve to underscore his sense of alienation and threaten the passive exile he has imposed upon himself as a truce between his contradictions. Even the manner in which he learns of these events is significant. Rather than through any Latin-American source, even though he is a diplomat representing a Latin-American country, his source is a corner of an Italian newspaper: "todo eso se filtraba hacia el mundo por el estrecho cuello de aquel cuentagotas" ("all of his information was filtered into the world through the narrow neck of an eyedropper") (13).

The fact that Primitivo refers to Rome in his thoughts as "el mundo" ("the world") emphasizes how, absurdly enough for this little Indian doctor, he has become a victim of Eurocentrism to the extent that his native culture has become otherworldly to him. His alienation is so complete that Bolivia has become little more than an obituary to him: "diez líneas de texto con sus muertes elípticas: eso era la patria lejana" ("ten lines of text with its elliptical deaths: to him, that was the old country") (13). He imagines himself before a psychoanalyst, exploring his alienation, but even in reflection he finds himself isolated:

"[s]i el psicoanalista imaginario no conocía el alma de América, acaso tampoco pudiera llegar a conocer la suya." ("If the imaginary psychoanalyst did not know the soul of America, then there was no way he could fathom his") (14).

As events across the sea disrupt the truce he has maintained with his own soul for these many years, the stage is set for Primitivo's self-analysis of the forces that have brought him to become a victim of circumstances: "Pero creía saber lo suficiente de Psicoanálisis como para estudiarse a sí mismo" ("But he believed he knew enough about psychoanalysis to study himself") (14). Such reflections blur the distinction between the personal and the social, the sociological and the psychological. Primitivo had attempted a form of narrative self-analysis before in an "autobiografía étnica" ("ethnic autobiography") that he, too, had titled *Los aborígenes*. This metalepsis blurs the line between the level of the character's reality within the novel itself and the reality of the text-act reader of Martínez Moreno's novella. Thus, it ironically distinguishes between the purpose of Martínez Moreno's text and the text his character attempted to write, suggesting, by contrast, that the purpose of the novella is not to provide ethnic rationalizations for his character's situation. It only seeks an understanding of what seems a fatalistically predetermined situation before which, by choice or not, Primitivo finds himself helpless.

His point of departure will be his marriage, an intimate contract entered into for social gain in the genteel tradition. He remembers the day in which he announced his marital plans to his father, an old professor with a "bigotito afrancesado" ("pretentiously Parisian moustache"). His father's reaction had been to become "abismado en quién sabe cuál momento de su íntimo pasado, ése que nunca llegan e conocer los hijos" ("absorbed in who knows what moment of his own private past, that past that sons never get to know") (16). The implication is that Primitivo's own father had grappled unsuccessfully with the same sense of absurdity himself, and had no wisdom to give, or at least none that was capable of being communicated. Each generation, then, repeats the pattern of the past, pushed by unseen, mysterious forces. His father is able only to warn his son that marriage, like life, is "el azar, el temor, y el misterio" ("chance, fear, and mystery") and even this he says without "rastro de pasión" ("a trace of passion") (17).

Primitivo, in attempting to write his "autobiografía étnica" had attempted at least to escape some of that indeterminacy by "una forma de disolución de propio ser en el ser de la raza" ("a form of dissolution of his own sense of self in his sense of race") (17). But death is the only ultimate resolution possible for the problem of the self, and his satisfaction with his failure was now itself dissolved. The problem had come back yet again to haunt him; the scant difference between *sobrevivientes* and *sobremurientes* (survivors and "sur-dead-ors") was yet again the issue.

The problem is established in the narrative present by the first chapter: the second and third are an analepsis that depicts Primi-

2: *Los aborígenes:* The Drama Of Latin America's Elite

tivo's attempts to come to terms with his identity—both personally and sociopolitically—as a youth in his homeland. He had been a "snob" at the university, and had submitted himself to a company wedding, one with promise for his vague ambitions. Yet, at the very beginning, external factors had intervened in his attempt to yoke together the personal and the social; it had literally blown up, not in his, but in his wife's face. A strike gainst the oligarchy of which he formed a part erupted in violence, and a bomb was thrown that disfigured his wife's features. Sociopolitical events symbolically marred her identity at the same time their marriage was on the verge of collapse; Primitivo sends her to the U.S. to have her face reconstructed.

She becomes the first to assimilate a false cosmopolitan sensibility that leads her to deny her culture. At the same time, Primitivo begins to justify his passivity as a form of revenge, giving way to corruption so as to pay for his wife's plastic surgery: "'Ellos me lo hicieron y tienen que pagármelo—solía pensar con artificioso conformismo" ("They did it to me and they're going to have to pay for it," he used to think to himself with contrived conformity") (37). His wife begins to write home, speaking of Bolivia as "ese ombliguito de terracota en que hemos vivido por tanto tiempo como si fuera El Mundo" ("that little belly-button of a place in which we lived for so long as if it were the whole World") (37).

As occurs so often in Martínez Moreno's works, however, the couple's bitter alienation from their homeland is complicated by personal alienation, one that is very contradictory. During his wife's absence while convalescing, he has an affair with a Bolivian woman who, in spite of his resentment toward his homeland, comes to represent to him "el amor, la lumbre, y el abrazo del país" ("love, light, and the embrace of the motherland") (39).

His having an affair is the only way in which he comes to feel any sense of hope or connectedness with his country; his "tertulias literarias" ("literary soirées") with the young, up-and-coming oligarchs-to-be are unproductive events in which

> se discutía, hasta la saciedad del ripio mental y del aguardiente, la tesis del "pueblo enfermo" de Arguedas o cualquier otra doctrina a la moda, de ésas que parecen más visibles que la propia faz de América (25).

> they discussed, to the point of exhausting both their minds and their liquor supply, Arguedas's theory of a "diseased people" or any other

of the many fashionable doctrines that are always more visible than the true face of America.

His best friend from these *tertulias* one day proclaims, under the heavy influence of alcohol: "Este país no tiene salida, estamos todos perdidos. Yo lo resuelvo aquí mismito y me mato" ("This country has no way out; we all are doomed. I resolve to kill myself right here and now") (27). He doesn't kill himself, of course. Instead, Cándido Lafuentes' desperation carries him to become leader of his country, a position that secures Primitivo his means of escape into Roman self-exile. That dependency proves to be ill-advised, however, because the ousting of Cándido forces Primitivo from the sanctuary that shields him from life's realities in the story's narrative present.

but Cándido's presidency is yet to come at the time of Primitivo's wife's separation from him. He does not have the courage to pursue the feelings—patriotic or otherwise—that his affair stirs in him. Upon her return, it loses its lustre, just as her life in the U.S. gradually does for her. The truce into which they fall is punctuated by the mention, five times on one page of the words that sum up their lives: "Orgullo, miseria, y pena" ("Pride, misery, and pain") (40).

The fourth and final chapter presents the reader with Primitivo's ultimate failure: to escape his dissatisfaction through resignation to decadence. *La deca,* as Martínez Moreno presents it, is decadence, but not the bacchanal of the Roman empire that serves as the story's backdrop. Nor is Latin-American decadence, in Martínez Moreno's fictive universe, the imperial decadence of the European Neros, Borgias, and Bonapartes. *La deca* is never so conveniently divorced from a simultaneous and nagging sense of the difference between the twilight of a great culture and the agonizing stillbirth of another. It is decadence without the comfort of sentimental, nostalgic yearning for past grandeur. Thus, the relationship between decadent behavior and its cause and effect does not go unperceived by his characters. Its cause is a fear rooted in an awareness of the slow destruction of the values of the past. Its effect, decadent behavior, is recognized as an irrational reaction to the fear produced by witnessing the withering away of the past so evident around them. *La deca* represents the dynamic of the two as a vicious circle, each perpetuating the other. Thus, *la deca* is a process that Martínez Moreno's characters are painfully aware of and yet feel unable to do anything about—not even merely accept it. As the rumors of troubles back home

2: *Los aborígenes:* The Drama Of Latin America's Elite

threaten to destabilize the complacent status of Bolivia's Roman mission, Ventura, Primitivo's junior colleague, an inadequate painter who has gained a coveted European post as "asesor artístico" ("cultural attaché") through high society connections, delights in the opportunities for decadent celebration his position entitles him. "¡Qu'hemos d'hacerle!" ("Whatcha gonna do!") he declares to Primitivo (43). "'Para eso se hacen las revoluciones en América'" ("'That's what revolutions in America are for'"), he boasts cynically to his Italian friends at cocktail parties, using as an example how a colleague of his abused the diplomatic travel budget to transport a pet first-class: "Para que un par de maniáticos financie el viaje de un perro idiota en un camarote de lujo" ("So a pair of maniacs could finance an idiotic dog's trip in a first-class cabin") (58).

Such talk sends Primitivo into his last set of reminiscences, this time to remember his brief participation in Bolivia's upper-class, bohemian, escapist decadence in his relationship with a cocaine-using daughter of the upper class, Ilse. In the account of Primitivo's brief experience with Bolivia's local chapter of international Bohemia, Martínez Moreno makes clear the dangers of ignoring the distinction between literature and reality: "Aquello suponía un mundo de refinamientos desconocidos para un joven paisano que sólo conocía los de la literature" ("All of which had presupposed a world of refinements unknown for a young peasant who only knew the refinements of literature") (49).

Primitivo's naive relationship with Ilse was a series of drug-fueled soirées hosted at Ilse's parents' stately home. It ended when one of the young bohemians overdosed and the little circle's activities were exposed. Primitivo was confronted with actual, and not just chemical, escape: Ilse offered to finance their escape to Paris, leaving Bolivia and all its troubles behind. As Primitivo remembers wistfully, he declined out of a feeling of obligation, a feeling he has never been able to escape.

Thus, in reviewing his life, Primitivo begins to see it as a series of judicious and sensible compromises that have, nonetheless, left him lonely and on the verge of being exiled from exile itself. His reflections lead him to remember another book he once tried to write, this one a novel that had the purpose of justifying his lifelong compromises by means of genealogical analysis:

En algún cajón yacían los rollos de los tres primeros capítulos y el tíulo definitivo de aquella larga historia, que bajaba de epopeya a letanía: *Y luego descansaron* (54, emphasis in original).

In some desk drawer somewhere lay the rough draft of the first three chapters and the definitive title of that long story that descended from epic to litany: *And Then They Rested.*

He realizes now that, never having confronted his contradictions in the past, none of them are at rest. Rest implies the need for a break from some sort of activity; such is not his case. His passivity is a symptom of a futile irrelevance. When Primitivo's "end" comes in the form of his dismissal as diplomat in Rome, the end of his good fortune fulfills a sense of meaningless inevitability that has been with him all his life: "Y 'eso' tenía que acabarse un día; acabarse o desfondarse una mañana como cualquier otra, a la hora del desayuno y los periódicos" ("And that 'something' had to run out someday; run out or have its bottom fall out some morning just like any other over breakfast and the morning paper") (59). The end does come just as he predicted. As Primitivo contemplates its inevitability, his secretary informs him that his protector, President Cándido Lafuentes, has been assassinated. Primitivo seems almost to envy Cándido's fate. "Esa diferencia de suertes se medía por la distancia. . . . Se medía por la diferencia entre una vida y una muerte igualmente inútiles" ("The difference in their fates could be measured by the distance between them. . . . It was the measure of the difference between a life and a death equally useless") (60). The fact that Primitivo practically begrudges Cándido his assassin is a testament to the scant difference between the *sobrevivientes* ("survivors") and the good-as-dead *sobremurientes* ("sur-dead-ors") among the characters in Martínez Moreno's works. Their comparison serves as a metaphor for all of Martínez Moreno's work: a comparison of life to death when intellectual reflection (or the lack thereof) only leads to inactivity, a paralysis of active affirmation. In *Los aborígenes,* the comparison is made clear. Primitivo privately concludes that "Otros mueren a menudo por nosotros. Pero ése es también, a veces la forma más engañosa de nuestra propia muerte" ("Others die for us all the time. But that, too, is sometimes the most deceitful form of our own death") (64). Primitivo has, at times, been almost moved to voice his own feelings, or at least to give them form and not depend on the sacrifices of others.

> Había estado muchas veces tentado de escribir, en sus ensayos, frases como 'el drama de las clases cultas, el aislamiento y la incomunicación de las élites en esta nuestra América Española;' pero le había parecido antipatriótico afirmarlo sólo porque se lo dijeran sus sentimientos. (58)

2: *Los aborígenes:* The Drama Of Latin America's Elite

> He had been tempted many times to write in his essays phrases like "the drama of the cultured classes, the isolation and confinement of the elites in this, our Spanish America." But it had seemed antipatriotic to write it just because he felt it in his gut.

This drama of the elites in Latin America, their isolation and uncommunication—in addition to the intelligentsia's inability to stop rationalizing it—is the reason for the theme of *la deca* in Martínez Moreno's work. It is Martínez Moreno's answer to the call of *la Generación crítica* to declare, unpatriotic as it may seem, that in the case of the Latin-American elite, that the "emperor has no clothes." Primitivo's decision to repress and deny this is the same tendency against which Julio Calodoro attempts to act in *El Paredón*, when he searches for an alternative to the view of the past he inherits from his father, a man at the same juncture of life as Primitivo (his father's political party has been ousted from power in his old age). In *El paredón*, this tendency toward *la deca* is viewed from without and treated with rejection by the protagonist. He gives it a name, "quietismo" ("quietism"), and a derogatory metaphor, that of the ostrich with its head in the sand. In *Los aborígenes* we find the definition of *la deca*, and a description of how it is experienced from the inside by a member of the generation that engendered it.

It is important to note that while Martínez Moreno most persistently writes of *la deca* and most clearly defines this personal and sociopolitical *quietismo* of the elite that he depicts as the malaise of his reality, he never prescribes the intellectual's role in the Latin-American crisis of conscience and intellect he so accurately and incisively portrays. This contrasts him sharply with his colleague Mario Benedetti, whose later books of the 1970s, *El escritor latinoamericano y la revolución posible* (The Latin-American writer and the possible revolution) and *El ejercicio del criterio* (The use of judgment), do. Martínez Moreno's treatment of *la deca* never attempts to override individualistic considerations of the type attended to by Onetti in his more narrowly focused works. Rather, he attempts to bring to bear the personal repercussions of social or political events, be they random accidents or revolutions, never sacrificing one level of reality for the other, but showing them always in juxtaposition.

Thus, *Cordelia* and *Los aborígenes* serve, each in its way, as models for Martínez Moreno's canon. While accepting its reasons for being and its causes, each points out the need for ending the denial that forms the basis of *la deca* both on the micro- and the macrocosmic levels. In *El paredón*, that need is seen through the eyes of a member of a generation that assumes responsibility in a society in which its elderly members, genteelly barbaric, have never taught them how to face change. In *La otra mitad*, the consequences of the avoidance of responsible personal commitment is seen as the reader is led to experience the grief of Mario Possenti, a character who, like Robledo, is left behind by a loved one with a debt of conscience unpaid.

While much has been said here of Martínez Moreno's first two full-length novels because of the unique relationship each of these novellas has with them, the treatment of *la deca* seen in *Cordelia* and *Los aborígenes* develops into a pattern that persists throughout the rest of his canon as well. In *Con las primeas luces* (1966), the price of irresponsibility is portrayed by yet another character, quite similar to Robledo, who impales himself in the groin while drunkenly trying to jump the iron fence around his family's dilapidated mansion; his death by castration symbolically ends a decadent dynasty. *Coca*'s (1970) protagonist could be said to be a younger Primitivo: having passively risen to the middle ranks as an officer on the coattails of others in the Bolivian revolution of 1952, he allows himself to be manipulated into a decadence for which he pays with a cocaine-smuggling conviction at his diplomatic post in Montevideo.

Martínez Mareno's last fictional novel, *Tierra en la boca* (1974), is quite unlike the rest in that it does not concern itself with *la deca* of the elite, as the othes do. Nonetheless, it does portray its trickle-down effect on the lower-class, the lumpen proletariat, and shares much with *Cordelia* in the fortuitous nature of its central event, even though it is a murder. Its title comes from a phrase used twice in *Los aborígenes* in connection with Primitivo's *sobremuriente* sensibility. The concept of being buried alive, dead in life, decaying, is extended to include, then, not only those alienated as the elite, but also those alienated as the underclass. In both cases the characters leave the consequences of (in)action to fate, to similar effect. In *Tierra en la boca*, we see a last and fitting turn in Martínez Moreno's choice of character (from elite intellectuals to lumpen proletarians) that generalizes the theme of *la deca* beyond being a condition of class.

Perhaps even more significantly, at the same time we see a stylistic turn in which the author's fragmented, avant-garde, Faulknerian style (avant-garde in that it is initially beyond the conventional canon) meets that which is beneath the canon in

2: *Los aborígenes:* The Drama Of Latin America's Elite

the kitsch genre of the crime novel. While *La otra mitad* calls itself a "policial metafísica" ("metaphysical detective story") and *Coca* also deals with a crime as its central event, none carries the influence of the genre so far as does the author's last novel. It was a sign of things to come, if not in Martínez Moreno's own works (since the turmoil of war and exile ended his novelistic career), then in the Latin-American novel and, arguably, in the novel as a whole. A sense of moral decay and decadence, *la deca*, led quite logically to a questioning of moral causality in the genre of crime and punishment. Michael Holquist has called this the most marked literary symptom of the postmodern condition (Holquist 1971, 135).

While the exact definition of this condition is a topic of much theoretical debate in the United States, a sense of it as it is currently being understood in the River Plate may be represented by reference to a recent interview with the Italian philosopher Gianni Vattimo (author of *El fin de la modernidad* [The end of modernity], published in 1985) in the cultural supplement of *Clarín* in the fall of 1987.

> La modernidad es no solo una época sino también una forma de pensar, de mirar la existencia. La forma moderna de vivir la historia era progresista y progresiva. Imaginaba un desarrollo indefinido del tiempo. Este progreso era un valor, como si la historia mejorara. El concepto moderno se acaba cuando ya no sentimos que es necesario ese avance. No hace falta más ser vanguardista. . . . Asistimos al final de la creencia generalizada en el progreso. Ha caído la fe en la modernidad porque ha desparecido también la expectativa por la novedad. . . . [La situación] posmoderna es una actitud que concilia estos cambios. Es algo que está occurriendo y en consecuencia no vemos aún con demasiada claridad. Advertimos una nueva experiencia del tiempo, ya que todo tiende a ser simultáneo. . . . Los medios de comunicación tienen una necesidad cuantitativa de usar y recuperar el pasado . . . y de transformarlo en presente. Pero no hay en ello nostalgia ni ingenuidad sino una simultaniedad de presencias. . . . La información nos brinda todo y la historia procede también por ironizaciones. De tal modo, la historia nos ofrece una multiplicación de modelos que pasan a ser compartidos parcial y simultáneamente en el presente. Por eso este peso del pasado tiene en la situación posmoderna una respuesta irónica. La ironía relativiza el pasado y lo incorpora sin drama al presente. . . . El mismo psicoanálisis sufre esta ironización. El psicoanálisis produce mentalidades posmodernas. Un hombre menos pasional, menos intenso. Podría decirse que hay una reducción de las intensidades y una diseminación de los sentimientos. (Vattimo 1987, 8)

> Modernity is not only a period but also a way of thinking, of looking at existence. The modern way of living history was progressivist and progressive. It imagined an indefinite development of time. This progress stemmed from a value that held that history bettered itself. The concept of modernity comes to an end when we no longer feel the need for such advancement. We no longer need to be avant-garde. . . . We are witnessing the end of the generalized belief in progress. Faith in modernity has fallen because the expectation of innovation has disappeared. . . . Postmodernisty is an attitude that reconciles those changes. It is something that is occurring and, in consequence, cannot be seen yet with much clarity. We are aware of a new experience of time since everything tends to be simultaneous. . . . The communications media have a quantitative need to use and recover the past . . . and transform it into the present. But there is no nostalgia or ingenuity in it, but, rather, a simultaneity of presences. . . . Information offers us everything and history proceeds by way of ironies. Therefore, history offers us a multiplicity of models that are shared partially and simultaneously in the present. That is why the weight of the past is met with an ironic response in the postmodern situation. Irony relativizes the past and incorporates it into the present without dramatics. . . . Psychoanalysis itself is suffering from this irony. Psychoanalysis produces postmodern mentalities. A less passionate, less intense man. It could be said that its result is a reduction in the intensities and a dissemination of feelings.

This relativized sense of the relationship of past and present without drama is central to Martínez Moreno's narrative. As Orthmann puts it, in Martínez Moreno's works

> The typical personage tends to overanalyze his problems, often very shrewdly, but fails to do anything practical or concrete about them. Reflections are more important than actions; reason lies above passion. . . . Consequently, characters are devoid of sentiment. This analytical attitude is supported by a variety of cultural references that emphasize the preference to meditate rather than to act. (Orthmann 1976, 109)

It is my suggestion that perhaps what Orthmann sees vaguely as "a variety of cultural references that emphasize the preference to meditate rather than to act" is slowly evolving today into a more defined "analytical attitude" that is shared by more than Martínez Moreno's characters. Perhaps it is what Vattimo describes as the postmodern attitude. Martínez Moreno's characters, as seen in *Los aborígenes* as well as the later *Cordelia*, suffer the psychological effects described by Vattimo as a result of being forced, through one means or another, to confront the conse-

2: *Los aborígenes:* The Drama Of Latin America's Elite

quences of a general loss of faith in progress, *la deca*. Though Martínez Moreno never displays an overt sense of reconciling those changes in society that affect his characters (quite the contrary), his presentation of them without drama, as it were, clearly indicates what one could describe as a sense of the postmodern condition.

If so, this raises the possibility of viewing Martínez Moreno as a precursor of a philosophical movement, a "deca," that goes far beyond his native Uruguay. He becomes not only a figure who bridges the intimist and social tendencies of the novel cultivated by Onetti and Benedetti in a vertical, metaphorical sense within his own generation; he also becomes a figure who bridges a transitional moment between generations in the novel, in a metonymical, chronological sense. His works become a much-needed, concrete manifestation of a movement away from Faulknerian modernism toward a postmodern novel, with a sense of this movement (from *deca* to *postdeca*) throughout his works. If so, Martínez Moreno's works can be seen as being at the center of an important intra- and intergenerational axis; worthy signposts not only in marking the past, but perhaps in understanding the present and, at least, the immediate future of the novel in Latin America—and even the future of Latin America itself. *Cordelia* and *Los aborígenes* are clear points of departure for analyzing that transitional view of reality that is the essence of Martínez Moreno's works.

3
Cordelia: Mental Architecture

Cordelia is a forty-eight page novella that won a contest run by Uruguay's *Número* magazine in 1956. However, the magazine ceased publication before *Cordelia* could be published. Hence, *Cordelia* was published five years later, in an anthology published in 1961. There has been ever further confusion regarding *Cordelia* because when it was published the publisher decided, for reasons unknown, to print the word *novela* (novel) under the title of the anthology in which it was included. This confusion regarding its publication date and its genre label has caused certain otherwise very accurate literary historians to list *Cordelia* in literary history books as Martínez Moreno's first novel.[1] *Cordelia* is important in that it clearly heralds the style of shifting focalization and temporal analepsis that was to become standard throughout Martínez Moreno's work. More specifically, in *Cordelia*'s protagonist, Robledo, we see the prototype of the main character of *La otra mitad* (The other half), his own favorite novel and the one most carefully constructed in his personal style.

Cordelia is most clearly a precursor to *La otra mitad* (1966) in its characterization and in its structure. It represents the more intimist pole of Martínez Moreno's writing (Brushwood 1984, 289). In *Cordelia, la deca* affects its protagonist on an intimdate, individual level, within the margins of interpersonal relationships—in this case, the family unit. In *La otra mitad*, a similar character's decadence comes back to haunt him in the same way that one of life's realities—death—intrudes upon him in his relationship with his lover. *La otra mitad*'s Mario Possenti grapples with a grief exacerbated by the guilt of adultery. Possenti's precursor, *Cordelia*'s Robledo, grapples with the same grief under the guilty burden of irresponsible parenthood.

In *Cordelia*'s style one can clearly see, along with the casting of a mold for later characterization, the development of the narrative

3: *Cordelia:* Mental Architecture

structuring preferred by Martínez Moreno. This consists of, to use Susana's words to describe her father in *Cordelia,* a lack of sentimentality in favor of "mucha arquitectura mental" ("much mental architecture") (Martínez Moreno 1961, 46). To borrow from Gerard Genette, it involves the use of careful shifts in focalization (or *aspect,* as the literary theorist would call it), a shifting of "tense" (i.e., the use of analepses or flashbacks so as to arrange chronological order of the *récit* for narrative effect), and a diegetic "mood" of discourse (i.e., one of "pure narrative" rather than "mimetic representation").[2]

These choices of narrative strategy are what have earned Martínez Moreno, for good or ill, the reputation of being an "existentialist" or "intellectual" writer, just as his characterization has often brought up the question—ill-conceived, in my opinion—of whether he "hated" his characters.[3] Both issues stem, I believe, from the unsettling effect on some readers of his detached treatment of often unsympathetic characters as they struggle with their lives' painful consequences. Angel Rama says of the author that

> Martínez Moreno es más intelectual, más sistemático y lógico (que otros de su generación), mientras que Benedetti es más sensible y más lírico, lo que no hace sino definir una mentalidad que, como la de Flaubert, ha frecuentado los códigos y la jurisprudencia. . . . A partir de . . . materias reales . . . traza una contrucción narrativa a la que mueve una constante apetencia interpretativa, razonando motivaciones, descubriendo el modelo verdadero que los sentimientos o las ideologías escamotean. (Rama 1972, 94–96)

> Martínez Moreno is more intellectual, systematic, and logical (than others of his generation), while Benedetti is more sensitive and lyrical. This only describes a mentality which, like that of Flaubert, has frequented legal codes and jurisprudence. . . . Beginning with . . . real raw material . . . he traces a narrative construction consistently driven by a constant interpretive craving, weighing motives against logic to uncover the truth behind the sleight of hand of sentiments or ideologies.

According to Rama, Martínez Moreno uses sociological methods in his stories not by way of apology for his characters, but in a "función desenmascaradora" ("unmasking function"). The consequent lack of melodrama with which he presents characters in painful situations is thus explained by the fact that in Martínez Moreno's narrative,

> la operación artística es entonces una operación cogniscitiva y aquí, principalmente, crítica. Por eso todo el arte de Martínez Moreno corresponde al hemisferio iluminado de la razón . . . lo que implica el incesante análisis de los comportamientos, retrotrayendo las acciones y voliciones a sus causas, y una claridad intensa sobre las conciencias que diluye a las sombras románticas. (Rama 1972, 4)

> the artistic operation is, then, a cognitive one and, here, mainly a critical one. For this reason all of Martínez Moreno's art corresponds to the illuminated hemisphere of reason . . . which implies the unceasing analysis of human behavior, tracing action and volition back to its source and casting an intense light upon consciences that dilutes romantic shadows.

This being the case, Rama maintains that stylistically

> el elemento conductor más adecuado a tal enfoque es una lengua discursiva, rica, estructurada sobre una sintaxis precisa y lógica, abundosa de palabras y giros casi barrocos, done se percibe la distancia que el autor fija entre la realidad y su concepción objectivante de ella. (Rama 1972, 94–95)

> the element most conducive to such a focus is a rich, discursive language, structured by precise, logical syntax and abounding with almost baroque turns of words in which the distance that the author maintains between reality and his objectivizing concept of it is clearly perceived.

Martínez Moreno's deliberate pursuit of a dispassionate way of depicting *la deca* and its effect on his characters, in addition to his lack of dramatics, result in stories of much thought and little action. In *Cordelia*—as in all of his works, except for his last one—the decisive action, or at least the chain of events leading to the inevitable moment of the story, have already occurred when the story opens. Thus, what the story largely consists of is not the telling of what happened so much as of how it came to happen—the process and not the product. As Nora Orthmann puts it in her study of the author's works,

> in most of Martínez Moreno's narrative the protagonist's life is already determined, and very few events occur during the story's development. The main character has been defeated before the novel or *cuento* begins, and he becomes an impotent spectator of a world already in ruins. He reflects on the causes that produced the disaster without suggesting a solution (Orthmann 1976, 109)

3: *Cordelia:* Mental Architecture

The protagonist's reflections upon his or her past and how it has brought him or her to the present set of circumstances results in an analeptical mode of narration and in diegetic discourse— the telling of his or her story, rather than the showing of it. What matters is not so much the action itself, but the narrator-protagonist's interpretation of it in the light of present circumstances. This interpretation, in turn, is contrasted with the interpretations of other characters who reflect upon their part in the present circumstance, and in great detail as well. The reader's interest, then, depends less upon discovering what has happened, than on discovering which interpretation of events presented by the characters has been, in the end, privileged by the implied author.

To some readers, such an enigma may not be enough to capture their interest, and they may find such detailed analysis of motives boring. Such readers, I would argue, would find *Madame Bovary* boring as well. That novel's central action, Emma's adultery, is a commonly known fact to almost any reader before she or he opens the novel. What is unique about Flaubert's novel is not so much what happens (middle-class marital problems are not new), but the fact that he tells his story of adultery from the point of view of the adulteress herself. The reader is invited to see the action from the inside, where it is somewhat more difficult to judge.

That Martínez Moreno has often been referred to as a twentieth-century Flaubert stems from this tendency in his own work as well. In novel after novel, as in *Cordelia*, he chooses to invite the reader to experience a freakish or commonplace event from the point of view of the least likely sympathetic participant in it. In *La otra mitad*, the reader is invited to experience the consequences of a murder-suicide of a husband and wife from the point of view of the adulterer, Mario Possenti, who must try to live with the question of whether his affair with a married woman provoked her husband into killing her and himself. In *Cordelia*, the reader is invited to experience the consequences of a young woman's death, from the point of view of her estranged father who has just returned, after years of absence, to involve himself in his daughter's life.

Through such a strategy of treating events in a manner devoid of any obvious empathic significance, examining them on a multiplicity of levels and from such unusual angles, Martínez Moreno achieves that which is his main purpose: to show that even the simplest or most random of events has complex causes and repercussions. To use a theoretical term much in postmodern vogue,

Martínez Moreno *problematizes* these events to show life's complexity and the difficulties of ordinary people in facing it. He is, in effect, a narrative "problematizer" par excellence.

In *Cordelia*, structure and focalization are of paramount importance to the story's effectiveness. The *histoire* is not unusual. A daughter loses her mother. Her father, unable to cope, turns her over to the mother's family for rearing, and dedicates himself to a life of escapist debauchery, earning the scorn of the family. Upon coming of age, the girl, having always been taught what a scoundrel her irresponsible father was, decides to find out about him for herself and arranges a meeting. The father-daughter reunion goes well, but days later the girl dies in a plane crash in a distant tropical country. The airline, in order to protect itself from lawsuits from the victims' relatives, offers to fly the relatives to their loved ones' graves, once a year. The girl's father, reaching the height of insensitivity, uses the occasion to manipulate the company into promsing him tickets for himself and his philandering friends, so they can use the yearly excursion as a party junket—instead of offering to share the tickets with those who raised her. The man who the reader may have hoped would deal with this second loss with more dignity than upon the loss of his wife does not use the occasion as a turning point in his life; he turns out to be a weakling and a scoundrel after all.

Telling the story carefully from his point of view instead of that of the relatives, and contrasting Robledo's interpretation of events with his daughter's thoughts on their brief reunion, Martínez Moreno asks a disturbing question of the reader, who may have reacted to the story judgmentally and according to convention. How does a "scoundrel" become one? How does a "scoundrel" feel? What is it like to be one of these censured members of society, especially in that fundamental unit of social order, the family? The investigation into those questions is what makes up the *récit* of *Cordelia*, and is what makes it an incursion into the human soul rather than a diatribe against parental irresponsibility. The implied author in no way defends the scoundrel Robledo's actions, opinions, or feelings. Rather, he merely confronts us with them in a most believable fashion, showing us the humanity in even the pettiest of characters, with implications that reach far beyond the issue of familial concerns to that of challenging the reader to consider how marginalized people are judged and dealt with in society in general.

As with most of Martínez Moreno's works, the best place to begin interpreting *Cordelia* is with the title itself. *Cordelia* is only

3: *Cordelia:* Mental Architecture

the story's title, not the name of Robledo's daughter. Since Robeldo's daughter, Susana, is not the story's protagonist, the intention is clearly not only to associate Susana with the only faithful daughter of Shakespeare's *King Lear,* but to stamp the whole story with the imprint of Shakespearean intertextuality. In *King Lear,* Cordelia is the somewhat alienated daughter (she is married to the King of France) who comes to the aid of her father when he is literally cast out in the cold by her greedy sisters. In *Cordelia,* Susana feels unjustly alienated from her father upon reaching womanhood, and risks estrangement from the relatives who raised her in his stead in order to seek some sense of solidarity with him, the black sheep of the family. The question she seeks to resolve is whether her estrangement from him was imposed only by her guardians' prejudices, or whether it was his own wish to abandon her as a child.

From Robledo's point of view, we see that his estrangement from his daughter has more complex motives than merely being at odds with his relatives. The estrangement is symptomatic of a deeper denial that has produced an unwillingness to mourn the death of Susana's mother years before. In Susana's death, Robledo is confronted with this unfinished business of loving and losing yet again. The reader expects that his defenses will finally be overcome. Hence, there is every expectation that the point of the story will be Robledo's coming to terms with the grief of loss, his acceptance of it, and his conversion into a potentially responsible member of his family. Yet, as in many of Martínez Moreno's works, such expectations are created in the character but not fulfilled by him. Precisely because it runs against all sense of conventional duty, Martínez Moreno drily presents the reader with the opportunity of experiencing a grief unresolved. Robledo refuses to accept the potential loss inherent in any emotional involvement, just as he refuses to accept his own mortality. This refusal poisons all of his attempts at sincere intimacy, even though he blames others for doing the poisoning. His refusal to accept the consequences of the passage of time is central to their reunion scene.

—Tenemos que vernos a menudo, cuando vuelvas de tu viaje—le habia pedido, fingiendo a su vez que aquélla era una proposición de igualdad. "Tenemos que vernos para que yo no envejezca, para que sienta que te he hecho y que me llenas la vida," era la oculta y verdadera propuesta.
—Claro que sí—se había apurado a asentir Susana, con una extraña

rotundidad, de fondo abstracto y pensativo. Papá—había añadido al cabo de una pausa—¿por qué me viste tan poco de chica?
—No fue por culpa mía ni de Mamá—respondía él, con un acento insólito de ternura en la última palabra. Fue por culpa de esa gente que te ha criado, tu abuela y esos tíos que envenenaron todo le que había entre Elvira y yo, y a veces creo que hasta a ella misma contra mí. (32)

"We'll have to get together on a regular basis when you get back from your trip," he had ventured, pretending that it was a suggestion of equality. "We'll have to see each other so I can keep from aging, so I can feel that I have made you and that you fill my life," was the hidden, true response.

"Of course we will," Susana hurried to agree, in a strangely categorical manner that was, at bottom, abstract and pensive.

"Papa," she had added after a pause, "why did you see me so little when I was a girl?"

"It wasn't my fault or your mom's," he answered, with an oddly tender accent on the last word. "It was because of those people who brought you up, your grandmother and those aunts and uncles who poisoned everything there was between Elvira and me and sometimes, I think, even pitted her against me.

That Robledo seeks some sense of immortality through his daughter is by no means a character defect; it is perhaps what most ensures the survival of the human species. That it becomes a hidden motive in his relationship with her and that his bitterness prevents him from exposing his true self to her are defects of character. And, as in many of Martínez Moreno's characters, though Robledo is clearly capable of self-analysis and aware of his motives, he is unwilling to do anything to change the pattern of his life, making him a prototypical Martínez Moreno *deca* character.

Contrast this situation with that of *King Lear*, and the intended ironic *deca* difference of the story's title becomes clear. In *King Lear*, Cordelia comes from France to rescue her father. He, having suffered so much at the hands of his own kin, is reluctant to allow himself to be rescued, to trust his daughter.

> *Cordelia.* O my dear father! Restoration hang
> thy medicine on my lips, and
> let this kiss repair those
> violent harms. . . .
> *Lear.* You do my wrong to take me out o' the
> grave; thou art a soul in bliss;

3: *Cordelia*: Mental Architecture

> but I am bound upon a wheel of fire, that
> mine own tears
> do scald like molten lead . . .
> Do not mock me;
> I am a very foolish fond old man.
>
> (*King Lear* act 4, scene 1)

Though reluctant to be reconciled with his family, Lear does speak his pain truthfully; it is recognized in the last line quoted above. By contrast, though Robledo is not a victim of his family so much as of his own attitudes, it is he and not Lear who speaks most of how others have ruined his life. Lear's reluctance is finally overcome by love, and justice is served. Robledo clings to what injustice death (a fact of existence) has dealt him, blaming others for his pain, and only passes it on by disservice to Susana's memory and her attempt at healing old wounds. Lear comes around, as it were, recognizing the risk in his daughter's overtures toward him:

> *Cordelia.* We are not the first who, with best
> meaning, have incurr'd the worst.
> For thee, oppressed king, am I cast
> down. . . .
> *Lear.* Upon such sacrifices, my Cordelia,
> the gods themselves throw incense.
>
> (*King Lear* act 5, scene 3)

Instead of "throwing incense" upon it, Robledo uses Susana's sacrifice as an extortion tool to maintain his lifestyle of denial and irresponsibility. Thus, the ironic twist of Martínez Moreno's intertextuality is that the "worst" is yet to come. *King Lear* ends didactically, with the words of the Duke of Albany:

> The weight of this sad time we must obey;
> Speak what we feel, not what we ought to say.
> The oldest hath borne most: we that are young
> Shall never see so much, nor live so long.
>
> (*King Lear* act 5, scene 3)

Martínez Moreno's *Cordelia* grants the reader no such didactic resolution, at least not on a literal level. Robledo refuses to "obey" his "weight" in Susana's death, just as he did in Elvira's. He does not "speak what he feels" and therefore never shows vulnerability or even respect for intimacy. In Martínez Moreno's *Cordelia*, consequently, it is the youngest (Susana), not the oldest, who hath borne most." Characters do not gain wisdom with age or through suffering.

Yet we are shown what Robledo does bear, and hence, are less able to condemn him outright. Furthermore, in Robledo we find one whose denial goes beyond replacing his feelings with words born of a sense of what he "ought to say." He rejects both the formulae of conformity and the risk of spontaneity as options for responding to tragedy. The result is his inexcusable extortion.

For the reader the inexcusable is made understandable in a Flaubertian sense, from the inside out. This is what John Brushwood has called the "intimist" aspect of Martínez Moreno's works. Larger events are seen in their personal dimensions. Yet, at the same time, Martínez Moreno extends his "intimism" in an attempt to suggest its social implications. By his unusual choice of subject matter (accidents, revolutions, drug crimes, etc.) and his original treatment of them, focusing on them from the most unlikely vantage point, he manages to bridge a gap in his own generation's novelistic tradition. That gap, the one between the intimate and the social, can be seen in the Generation of 1945 (*la Generación crítica*, as Angel Rama named it), between the poles of the social realist narrative of Mario Benedetti and the introspectively philosophical narrative of Juan Carlos Onetti. Only a writer such as Martínez Moreno would have attempted to bridge that gap between the personal and the social, and he does it with great care in juxtaposing the past and the present, and in painstaking use of internal focalization.

In *Cordelia*, the use of narrative structure is essential to this strategy of juxtaposition. The structuring of the story, in a series of chapters that shift temporally and in focalization, maintains the thread of irony. The reader is drawn into the story's question regarding ways of confronting mortality, found at the story's key moment—"quiénes son los más felices" ("who are the happy ones")—by way of the process of experiencing dispassionately the protagonist's way of confronting (or not confronting) life (29). Robledo's answer to his own question, "nunca sabremos" ("we shall never know"), responds to his own defeatist sense of impenetrability of the other, just as Possenti's does in *La otra mitad*. As in the later novel, however, the protagonist's conclusion is confirmed by his actions, which respond to the process he represents. It is simultaneously contradicted by the fact that it **has** been penetrated by both the implied author and the reader in the narrative act. We share an understanding of the "other," albeit a detached one, while the characters, persistent in their impotent view of *la deca*, never reveal it anywhere but in their most secret thoughts and doom themselves to alienation and misunderstanding, to "arquitectura mental" ("mental architecture").

The implied author's attitude toward this "arquitectura mental" is never seen by way of direct commentary, but is abundantly evident in his ironic ordering of the *récit* and in his shifts in narrative voice and focalization. The first chapter begins as extradiegetic narration, as the reader is introduced to Robledo and the accident from an objective point of view. The point of view of this first chapter is contrasted with the internal focalization of Robledo in the third chapter. In this third chapter, he phrases his thoughts to himself in the form of an imaginary telegram. Thus, his feelings are revealed to the reader, through his own thoughts, in an ironic parody of the sort of objectivity displayed at the novella's beginning. Such a contrast highlights the real importance of an internal focus on the interpretation of each of the characters surrounding the novella's main events. The second chapter shifts to internal focalization on the part of Susana, shifting the narrative present to the eve of the father/daughter reunion only days before the accident that is announced on the novella's first page. That narrative present, in turn, is interrupted by a flashback as Susana looks at herself in the mirror while dressing for dinner with her long-lost father. She presents the reader with her version of the family's history, which has brought her to this point: "La famosa educación recibida . . . había consistido en privarla por igual del dolor y de la alegría" ("The famous education she had received . . . had consisted of depriving her of suffering and joy in equal measure" (17). The fourth and final chapter of the novella shifts back to the extradiegetic narration of the first chapter, in which we again focus externally on Robledo's actions, which contrast with the feelings we know he harbors (though he denies them) from chapter three.

Thus, the stage is set for a final, potentially redemptive act that might transcend and resolve the story's ironic conflict. By this point, this conflict is as much one that takes place within the characters themselves—most notably Robledo—as it is a misunderstanding between the characters. Yet the final chapter, rather than resolving these conflicts, projects them onto the ultimate plane. The reader finds her or his expectations unfulfilled as well. The final act presented is a symptomatic one that perpetuates the insoluble nature of the conflicts, maintaining the distances between reader and character and between the characters themselves, rather than transcending them. The setting is the airline company's funeral for Susana, and its attempt to dispense with its responsibility in her death, which the company has reduced to a business matter. Robledo's playboy partner, Aldo, represents the cynical attitude that pervades the approach to death presented in the story:

> Esto es también la compañía—Pensó Aldo. Es la compañía de un modo ligeramente más tenebroso, porque cuando estas organizaciones son así de fuertes, hasta una tragedia sirve en la línea del tiempo a los fines de su propaganda. (46)
>
> "This, too, is the company," thought Aldo to himself." "It's still the company, just in a slightly shadier way. Because when organizations are this powerful, even a tragedy must take its place in the timely order of things to serve the company's public relations image."

From a structural point of view, this statement is most revealing because it shows how skillfully Martínez Moreno manages to bridge political commentary and make it reverberate in reverse on the intimist level, bridging the gap between them. "Fuertes organizaciones" ("powerful organizations") depend on a "línea del tiempo" ("time line" or "the timely order of things") in the service of "propaganda" on a personal level as well. Characters such as Robledo cling to their view of the past, their line, as it were, selling themselves their own "propaganda" in stiff resistance to the challenge of present tragedy. Even as they are able to point it out in others, as in "la compañía" ("the company"), they refuse to do so in themselves. Blind allegiance to their defensive worldviews dooms them. They are just as powerless against "la deca" in themselves as they are against "la deca" in others. Robledo does not learn, even as he receives a posthumous letter from Susana with her observation, here remembered, that her father had "mucha arquitectura mental" ("much mental architecture") just like the story itself. In Robledo, that "arquitectura" consists of maintaining a system of defenses against the effects of miscommunication rather than making any radical attempts to resolve it. In the story, that "arquitectura" consists of maintaining tensions juxtaposed and unresolved between issues of the past and present, and among points of view of different characters reacting to the same phenomenon, each isolated by allegiance to his or her own "línea del tiempo" (timely order of things).

As Martínez Moreno makes clear in *Cordelia*, in a character who has surrendered to *la deca*, innovation is impossible. There is no

3: *Cordelia:* Mental Architecture

faith in transcendence, no faith in change, and therefore no future. There is only "arquitectura mental" regarding the past and the present. To misunderstand the close relationship between the "arquitectura mental" of Martínez Moreno's characters and that of his implied author's narrative structure, represented here by the example of *Cordelia*, is to miss the point in all of his narratives. His message, his call to allow for the reworking of one's understanding of the past as prologue to the future, is implicit, not explicit, in the ironic complexity possible even in such a random event as an act of God, as it were, an accidental death. Without such a reworking of the past, the consequences of the sins of the father are sure to be visited upon the child, even if only in ways known only to him.

4
El paredón: The Ethics of Revolutionary Justice

El paredón (The executioner's wall) (1963) is Carlos Martínez Moreno's first full-length novel, and without a doubt his best known. Acclaimed for its literary qualities as runner-up for the Premio Seix Barral, it nonetheless became a literary pariah due to the controversy that surrounded it in the critical community. That controversy, as Emir Rodríguez Monegal has so succinctly indicated, did not center on any literary qualities of the novel itself, but rather on the entirely extratextual and political matter of whether the novel "was in favor of Cuba or not" (Rodríguez Monegal 1967, 79–85).

Obviously, centering the novel's interpretation upon such ideological considerations led to a hermeneutical discussion of it that was almost entirely centered outside the text. In fact, as Ana María Ravazzani has noted, the controversy was already raging full force even before the novel's publication:

> Como es fácil suponer, cuando en 1963 se tuvo noticia de la inminente publicacíon que trataría de un tema extremadamente controversial . . . el revuelo fue enorme. Unicamente se sabía el título de la obra, el cual fue tomado por la mayoría como símbolo del contenido. . . . Una polémica a tapas cerradas, ya que la novela todavía no estaba en circulación fue el resultado. (Ravazzani 1981, 81)

> As it is easy to suppose, when the news of the imminent publication of a novel that would deal with this extremely controversial theme broke in 1963 . . . the commotion was enormous. Only the title of the work was known, which was taken by the majority to be a symbol of its contents. . . . A closed-book polemic, given that the novel was not yet in circulation, was what ensued.

By taking "the executioners' wall" as its title, the novel created

4: *El paredón:* The Ethics of Revolutionary Justice

expectations of a clear position in favor of the judicial practices of the Cuban revolution. All the while, it was merely meant to confront the reader with its reality and leave him or her to decide as to its ethical, not political, place in modern society. Thus, the novel was a disappointment for readers of both the left and the right. Ravazzani continues:

> Quienes le leyeron porque creían que su contenido era pro-Castro, se sintieron defraudados por la forma en que la Revolución había sido tratado. . . . Los que estaban en contra de ella, criticaban su título y la portado con el retrato de Che Guevara, ya que consideraban esto detalles como una propaganda abierta a favor del comunismo.
>
> Those who read it because they believed its contents were pro-Castro felt betrayed by the manner in which the Revolution was treated. . . . Those who were against the book criticized its title and the cover with the portrait of Che Guevara, since they considered these details to be open propaganda in favor of Communism.

The result was that there was a sharp critical backlash. Both camps had been armed, critical guns loaded to do ideological battle upon the battlefield of the text. When the text did not actually afford them that space, they created their own by attacking the text that was presented to them; they did so, as the quotation of Ravazzani implies, by creating a controversy where none had existed. The left's attack was based not on an interpretation of what the text was, but what it was not. The right's attack was a little less sophisticated—they objected to the novel's cover because they could not find objectionable material in its contents.

The position taken by the left, then, is more interesting, since its arguments surrounding the novel are more strategically sophisticated. Upon finding a valued colleague and well-known leftist writer under ideological attack, several of Martinez Moreno's peers came forward with critical studies whose aim was to establish a defensive reading of the novel. Because the problem with it was, however, an extratextual one, such a reading was bound to distort the text even as it defended it by attempting to accommodate the ideological concerns of the moment (i.e., what the novel "should" have been about regarding the Cuban revolution) rather than interpreting it on its own terms.

A quarter-century's distance allows a perspective considerably freer of such considerations. It is easy to see now that *El paredón* is a novel only incidentally set in Cuba, and that its political commentary on that historical moment is secondary. Its primary theme is not political, but ethical. *El pardeón* explores the problem of intellectual ethics in the gap that exists between theory and practice. It does this by raising the question of means and ends in a process of social change that is provoked by a general perception of *la deca*. By taking the macrocosmic level of revolutionary executions and juxtaposing that with microcosmic ethical decisions, its author asks whether equality and justice have more than rhetorical value in the new social order being proposed and modeled by Cuba. He presents the possibility that it might not be more than a mere inversion of the old hierarchy in which there is a double standard with regard to the morality of murder both at the macrocosmic level and at the microcosmic level. In daring to raise such questions, Carlos Martínez Moreno goes to the heart of a matter that still has the inteligentsia perplexed: At what price change? Today such a consideration is expected of any intellectual who discusses issues of social order or change. In 1963, it was the question that could end the intellectuals' honeymoon with revolution, and no one was quite ready for it when Martínez Moreno brought it up. He was, literally and figuratively, spoiling the party to which he had been invited. As a rude guest he first had to be scolded, then his actions explained away.

Because this critical reaction set the tone for the novel's misreading for the next two and a half decades, the accepted approach to the novel now must be reexamined. Before the morally powerful issues raised by the novel can be discussed, a brief discussion of its canonical readings must be presented.

As Ravazzani's quotation implies, the main critical strategy for defending the novel, in spite of its being ideologically "incorrect," centers on the reader's response to the title itself. A *paredón* is an executioner's wall. In the novel it refers to the walls against which the Castro government executed hundreds of former cronies of deposed dictator Batista, because of the public outcry over television images of firing squads at work, these executions eventually took place at night out, of the public eye, following a series of very public and judicially-suspect trials by the "people." These trials and executions chagrined the leftist community worldwide, and especially that of Latin America, as they made supporting similar social revolution ethically difficult in other countries and spread fear among the intelligentsia. In order to mend fences, Castro staged a public relations offensive called "Operación Verdad" ("Operation Truth"), the purpose of which was to dispel rumors that, according to Castro, were disinformation spread by agents of capitalist propaganda. Martínez Moreno himself was

4: *El paredón:* The Ethics of Revolutionary Justice

one of the Latin American journalists invited to participate in Operación Verdad, and this experience became the basis of his novel. Its failure as a public relations success as far as the novelist was concerned is made clear by the fact that, in spite of Castro's counterpropaganda campaign, Martinez Moreno chose the embarrassing *paredón* for the title of his novel.

Thus it became the central strategy of all Martínez Moreno's leftist defenders to become apologists in the ensuing scandal created by this title, and the details surrounding it included in the novel. That meant accounting for more than one third of the novel's content without appearing, ultimately, to be critical of the Cuban regime. It took some strategic extratextual leaps to get that job done.

The most significant of these readings is that of Martínez Moreno's colleague and compatriot, novelist Mario Benedetti, who set the pattern followed by others. This pattern consisted of cancelling out the literal meaning of the title and substituting a figurative, allegorical meaning more suited to ideological necessities. Benedetti sees the theme of the whole novel as that of its first part alone, a denunciation of the Uruguayan reaction to *la deca* as *quietismo* ("quietism") or "el extremo quietista de una publicitada alternativa electorera: 'que todo siga como está'" ("the quietist extreme of an alternative electoral publicity campaign: 'so everything will go on the way it is'" (Benedetti 1969, 188). This reading requires an almost exclusive emphasis on the novel's Uruguayan first and last parts. At the same time, it demands an almost complete suppression of its second part, which takes place in Cuba. In other words, in order to save the revolution's image, it becomes necessary to do away with it as it is presented in the novel: i.e., the protagonist's observations regarding Cuba's journalistic offense, Operación Verdad. Indeed, Benedetti avoids discussion of the novel's Cuban section so thoroughly that he nearly excludes it from his analysis in favor of the first section, one which is much more in keeping with his own ideological agenda. He seeks an authority outside the text itself to justify this, claiming that his emphasis has foundation in a remark made by the author to the effect that "aunque más de la mitad del relato transcurriera en La Habana, en realidad el tema de la novela era siempre el Uruguay" ("although more than half of the plot takes place in Havana, in reality the theme of the novel is always Uruguay") (Benedetti 1969, 1987). While the remark is undoubtedly true, Benedetti's use of it does not answer the inescapable question of the meaning the Cuban portion of the novel does have. It dedicates 180 pages to yellow journalism, radical chic parties, kangaroo court trials, and nighttime executions. What stance does the novel mean to take for or against these activities, either individually or collectively, and what significance would such a stance have with regard to the novel's first Uruguayan portion? Benedetti—and others—are silent on the matter. From this point on, Benedetti proceeds to define the novel's thematic scope by reducing it even further. To him, not only is *El paredón* a political novel as opposed to anything else—say, for example, a moralist novel—is really a mere denunciation of Uruguayan "coloradismo," the loose ideology of Uruguay's predominant liberal political party. Thus, in defending his friend and colleague's novel against its initial misreading, Benedetti divests it of any universal or even continental significance. With regard to the narrow purvue of politics, he also divests it of any national significance within the tiny home country of its author by confining it to the narrow, parochial concerns of only a few politicians and columnists in Uruguay itself. It is hardy conceivable that such narrow concerns attracted attention from the jury of Spain's Premio Seiz Barral to the extent that it cast four tied ballots before awarding the price to a safer choice.

To be fair to Benedetti, he does recognize the novel's merits, though he actually says nothing about them. He does declare that it is not "un libro panfletario" ("a pamphletering book"). Yet he treats it as just that. By the end of his analysis, having reduced the novel's relevance to that of mere parochial political concerns, he reaches once again to the *paredón*. He sees it again not as a symbol of oxymoronic revolutionary justice from its literal use, an "obvio sentido" ("obvious meaning") to which he makes oblique reference, but which he avoids addressing; rather, this time it is

> un símbolo de la incomunicación entre dos realidades latinoamericanas . . . un tremendo esfuerzo de comprensión, de inminente liquidació de prejuicios. . . . En otras palabras: un sincero esfuerzo por que la comunicación sea reestablecida. (Benedetti 1969, 192)
>
> a symbol of the lack of communication between the two realities of Latin America . . . a tremendous effort to comprehend and liquidate prejudice. . . . In other words, a sincere effort to reestablish communication.

This is perhaps the oddest statement of all. While recognizing the novel's sincere attempt to bridge two realities (that of morality in theory and in political practice), Benedetti implies something quite different that is more molded to his own agenda. *El paredón*

4: *El paredón:* The Ethics of Revolutionary Justice

is indeed a sincere effort, not for communication between political bodies, but for an intellectual relationship between fundamental terms in the Latin American referent: revolution and justice. Benedetti may be the first man ever to propose that execution is a form of communication between adversaries, a call for tolerance, openness, and dialogue, a "liquidation of prejudices." It seems somehow more to the point to discuss the reverse when speaking of liquidation, which from the novel's plot suggests that the purpose of Operación Verdad was to be a smokescreen behind which to hide mass liquidation of untried political prisoners, and not a program aimed at liquidating prejudices through open discussion. Several hundred men, not their ideas, were liquidated at the *paredón*. This method of disposing of perceived prejudices, the novel seems to say (contrary to Benedetti's reading), is not new at all, but one of the oldest despotic practices known to man, and not a method for resolving differences worthy of any revolution claiming to have a corner on the market of new ideas.

Nonetheless, Benedetti's "antiquietista" reading became the standard one for the analyses generated by the literary left in the years that followed. All as well-meaning as the first, they tend to echo its glosses of the *paredón* issue whole-heartedly. Among these is the study by Ana María Ravazzani. In her study, she improves on Benedetti at least insofar as she stays within the text for her gloss of the *paredón*. She does so by quoting a reference to a speech given by Fidel Castro in the novel, in which he excuses his atrocities by employing an argument of proportions. In this argument he claims that his mass executions are justified because Batista was a fascist like the imperial Japanese and that, after all, he had only eliminated a few hundred of his fascist opponents in the process of doing away with their regime, while the North Americans had murdered hundreds of thousands in Hiroshima and Nagasaki.

This is a clever way to sidestep the issue, a good offense as defense of the indefensible. It is unusual, however, that Ravazzani would take it seriously. In this argument, Fidel seeks to sidetrack his critics into a discussion of the ethics of warfare and the atomic bomb. The problem is that his defense does not work if one brings to mind that what is at issue in Fidel's Cuba is not the ethics of different methods of waging war, but that of postwar justice in trying war criminals after the war is over. Thus, if he wants to draw legitimate analogies between is war and World War II, it is more appropriate to discuss the Nuremburg Trials than Hiroshima and Nagasaki. If one amends the analogy in this manner, it becomes quickly apparent that it would not have been to Fidel's advantage to bring up any World War II analogy at all.

Martínez Moreno gives Fidel's speech ample contextual treatment; he does not merely include it as a viable defense for his actions. Ravazzani seems to miss this point, or at least prefer to pretend she does, by taking it out of context and using it as an actual defense. Julio Calodoro and his colleagues to not see Castro's statement as a defense at all, but as an argument that opposes imperialism not by proposing a new form of justice, but by imitating it, only on an appropriately "underdeveloped" scale.

Liz Salisbury-Ginzburg, in her study, *Downfall of a Democracy*, takes her turn at the issue. She not only imitates Benedetti more closely by going outside the text in her role as an apologist, she goes outside the novel's—and the author's— language as well. Her reading consists of coining a pun with the novel's title, playing the title's *"Paredón"* against the English expression "back up against the *wall.*" It is clever, but, being based on an English idiom that does not hold in Spanish translation (since the Spanish *paredón* is specific to executions and no other form of wall) it could not possibly have been an intended interpretation by the author.

> *El paredón* is, of course, a synonym of the [sic] revolutionary justice, i.e., the wall of the firing squad, used to annihilate the previous regime in Cuba. More meaningfully, though, it was the wall against which Uruguayan society was inexorably backing itself (Salisbury-Ginsburg 1982, 65).

No one would disagree that Uruguayan society was backing itself up against a wall in 1959, nor that the novel treats the issue of Uruguayan political stagnation in its first part. One must take issue with the figurative wall being the *paredón* of the novel. The *paredón* is a Cuban phenomenon that creates a moral dilemma regarding justice and social change. The moral dilemma is brought back to the Uruguayan referent with its protagonist in the novel's third part. It is a moral dilemma as to the ethics of capital punishment and social change. In no way does it stem only from Uruguay's internal stagnation, but rather from the desire to follow foreign models as a way out of it. Could it not be that, just as Martínez Moreno was willing to depict a Uruguay being slowly backed up against a wall by its *quietista* response to the glacial sociopolitical erosion of *la deca* he was also showing that Cuba was not the model for a way out, since the wall against which it was killing its own ideals of justice was more concrete and imme-

4: *El paredón:* The Ethics of Revolutionary Justice

diate than that of Uruguay? Salisbury-Ginzburg—like the other critics who, along with this author, are sympathetic to the left—is strangely silent on this question.

On the critical Right, Emir Rodríguez Monegal was no more willing to deal with the issue of the *paredón* and its relationship to *quietismo* and *la deca* than were the leftists. Nonetheless, he is at least in the advantageous position of having less need to suppress discussion of the Cuban portion of the novel because of some politically delicate issues it might raise. Therefore, though he allegorizes the entire novel, he includes the Cuban portion in his reading. For Rodríguez Monegal, the struggle of the novel's protagonist, Julio Calodoro, is not a political nor an ethical struggle regarding the implications of social change, but an individualistic Oedipal struggle that depicts "la muerte del mundo paterno" ("the death of the paternal world") to be followed by the death of the "mundo materno" ("maternal world") in Martínez Moreno's next novel, *la otra mitad* (The other half). It is obvious that such a limit of emphasis to the novel's microcosmic level distorts its meaning as well, and Josefina Delgado has been quick to make that point in her chapter in *Nueva Novela Latinoamericana* (The new Latin American novel).[1] Yet she does not offer any alternative, either to Rodríguez Monegal or to the leftist readings, and seems to favor the latter as they are, which leaves one on the ideological treadmill upon which criticism regarding El paredón has been trapped. It seems that the best way to avoid getting caught on that treadmill would be simply to get off. That does not mean abandoning the idea that the novel has any political implications, but achieving some distance from them in order to appreciate whatever broader implications the novel might contain. As our outline of both "leftist" and "rightist" readings has shown, ideological readings tend to pick and choose between parts or levels of the novel in a most inflexible manner in order to avoid acknowledging portions of it that may be in disharmony with ideological presuppositions. A reading that sought to step out of such a restrictive frame, on the other hand, would be able to appreciate the patterns in the novel to which both kinds of readings point. It would be able to do so without needing to suppress any ideologically contradictory elements. Such a reading would then be able to draw conclusions from the contradictions themselves, rather than attempt to artificially harmonize or eliminate them. The divergent readings I have described are all, in one way or another, made possible by something in the text itself. I propose here to attempt to stay within the text as much as possible in order to discover what it is that has provoked such divergent interpretations.

First, it is worth pointing out that the difficulty of even sympathetic criticism in defending *El paredón* is in part a generic problem. According to Jacques Leenhardt, in his article entitled "La estructura ensayística de la novela latinoamericana" (The essayistic structure of the Latin-American novel), works like *el paredón*—such as *Sobre héroes y tumbas* (Of heroes and tombs) by Ernesto Sábato, for example—represent a recent Latin-American phenomenon that requires a peculiar understanding, since they attempt to discuss a problem usually left to the essay form; i.e., questions of national identity:

> El problema de la identidad nacional aparece frecuentemente en el ensayo. Raramente, el mismo se constituye en el meollo de una novela. . . . El problema se hace singularmente más difícil desde que se trata menos de acciones que de estados, menos de hechos que de situaciones, es decir, de una compleja articulacíon de hechos, de sentimientos, y de representaciones. . . . A pesar—o a causa—de la ambigüedad . . Fuentes, Cortázar, Roa Bastos—por no citar más que e ellos—han intentado un nuevo enfoque de la narración a partir de este tipo de técnica. (Leenhardt 1981, 138–39)

> The problem of national identity appears often in the essay. Rarely does the same problem constitute the marrow of a novel. . . . The problem is then made singularly more difficult since it consists less of actions than states, less of deeds than situations; that is, it becomes a complex articulation of deeds, emotions, and representations. . . . In spite of—or, perhaps, because of—this ambiguity . . . Fuentes, Cortázar, and Roa Bastos, just to mention a few, have attempted to bring this new focus to narrative on the basis of this kind of technique.

Hence, part of the problem is a critical misunderstanding of a peculiar adaptation of a genre to a subject matter. This, says Leenhardt, is a problem of technique, not content. His observations apply especially well to *El paredón:* Julio Calodoro is mostly an observer both in Uruguay and in Cuba, one who mainly gives us "estados" ("states") and "situaciones" (situations"), instead of the action expected of a protagonist in a traditional realist novel. That Julio Calodoro is a truthful observer is never in doubt. Thus, the conclusions that reveal Julio Calodoro's inability to act in the face of death, on the microcosmic level (his father's death from

4: El paredón: The Ethics of Revolutionary Justice

cancer) and the macrocosmic level (Cuba's executions) imply an interesting attitude toward accurate observation: It is to be condemned when it conflicts with "correct" action. But how is one to decide what constitutes correct action without truthfully observing circumstances? This is the dilemma posed by the novel itself.

Posing that question is precisely what Leenhardt says is the purpose of this new type of Latin-American "novela ensayística" ("essayistic novel"). Rather than merely echo popular attitudes to denounce political events and attitudes in the style of the tabloid, they seek to reveal the ethical problems beneath the surface of a popular political discourse that seeks to oversimplify reality in Manichean terms of "good" or "bad." Since the novel provides a medium for such an "ethical aesthetic," novels have arisen that tend to test the conventional wisdom of political-historical stereotypes. The more recent novels—novels such as *Yo, El Supremo*, (I, the supreme), for example, in addition to *El paredón*—challenge those stereotypes in a more comprehensive manner than that with which the conventional reader might be comfortable. These novels do not seek to invert the hierarchies of "good" and "evil" established by popular cultural discourse, but rather to step out of the way and let the polarities artificially maintained by ideological prejudice meet head on, hoping for at least a rearrangement of priorities in discussing sociohistorical problems such as national identity. Such a rearrangement of priorities, though not proposed as a solution, is seen as positive and worth the confusion it might create in conventional wisdom. It is precisely because these authors are concerned with the unresolved issue of national identity that they refuse merely to reinforce it and attempt to return to its origins to reexamine the issue of how that "wisdom" was produced in the first place. As Leenhardt concludes:

> A mi manera de ver, la importancia de *Yo, El Supremo* (como ejemplo de este tipo de novela), reside en el hecho de que constituye una puesta en obra de una forma estética adecuada al problema ético que se les plantea a todos los escritores latinoamericanos. (Leenhardt 1981, 138–230)
>
> To my way of seeing it, the importance of *I, The Supreme* (as an example of this kind of novel), lies in the fact that it constitutes the casting as work of art of an aesthetic form adequate to the ethical problem that confronts every Latin-American writer.

That critics are confused by *El paredón, Yo, El Supremo,* and other novels like these may owe itself in large part, then, to reader expectations. In *El paredón* this is particularly easy to see. Most novels in three parts that show the first two to be contradictory in relation to each other are expected to resolve themselves dialectically, in a neat thesis-antithesis-synthesis process. Tzvetan Todorov's "grammar of narrative" describes this conventional process as one of "equilibrium-disequilibrium-equilibrium." In his view, this process can be traced by reducing the novel down to elements equivalent to parts of speech: "we shall understand narrative better if we know that the character is a noun, the action a verb (Todorov 1977, 118–19).

But what happens when a novelist deliberately throws the expected final "equilibrium" off balance, short-circuiting the equation by not having the protagonist act on any level at all? Unfortunately in this novel's case, critics have chosen to cling to conventional expectations rather than recognizing the peculiarity of the hermeneutical problem. In so doing they have suppressed the "disequilibrium" of its middle and condemned its ending to make it conform to a preconceived notion of balance, no matter what violence is done to the text itself.

Fortunately, other literary theorists have begun to respond differently to the problem of disequilibrium by raising the possibility of the obvious alternative: contrary to our preconceived notions of order, disequilibrium itself can be the message in a descriptive display text, and not a prescriptive proposition. In this vein, disequilibrium has entered the critical vocabulary as "indeterminacy," and is seen as the aim of such post modern literature. Such a view, is, in the main, proposed by deconstructionists such as Geoffrey Hartman in theoretical works entitled to address the issue directly, works such as *Criticism in the Wilderness* and *Saving the Text*. It is echoed, nonetheless, by nondeconstructionists as well, such as Floyd Merrell in his *Semiotic Foundations*, where he defines the basis of all argumentative discourse as being the "comparative juxtaposition of two or more descriptive messages" (Merrell 1982, 119).

In *El paredón*, Martínez Moreno lays bare the problems of Latin America's dialectical impasse regarding revolution and national identity by reducing it to its barest essential and creating a "comparative juxtaposition" out of the political situations in Uruguay and Cuba in 1959. Leaving the two descriptions in a juxtaposed and unresolved tension, he shows the desired leap of the reader to the prescriptive level to be one of blind faith and not of intellect, one he refuses to make easy out of, from a sense of stubborn

4: *El paredón:* The Ethics of Revolutionary Justice

intellectual honesty—a challenge to the reader's expectations. As Merrell puts it: "This countermessage is what the message is all about. It is the core of the semiotic function of all novel messages in human languages" (Merrell 1982, 126). Notice how appropriate Merrell's choice of the word *novel* is to El paredón as one of Leenhardt's new generic mutations, the "novela ensayística" ("essayistic novel") as a new (novel) novelistic form with a novel and disturbing message. This new message, says Merrell is disturbing to conventional expectations of prose fiction because as a countermessage it is "nonparadoxically conceived. . . . simultaneously" since "all . . . countertexts are sums of differences" (132). The problems is that we, as readers, are "ordinarily not aware of the 'real hole' in our perceptual faculties" as we read ideologically, expecting a preconceived totality (42). This is our "blind spot" that makes it "possible to 'see' what is not there simply because we 'know-believe' that it is supposed to be there" (23–25).

Thus, the leftist readings of *El paredón,* as we have seen, are "blind" to the literal meaning of the novel's title and to its middle section, deforming the novel's interpretation into a simplistic political denunciation instead of accepting it as a complex juxtaposition of two descriptions of reality. A writer such as Martínez Moreno is supposed to hold the same views as those of the novel's protagonist in the novel's first, Uruguayan part. He is not supposed to hold the same protagonist's views nor share his problems regarding revolutionary justice and capital punishment in the second section. Hence, that section is allegorized, its literal meaning suppressed. He certainly is not supposed to endorse the protagonist's *quietismo* at the novel's end. Thus, only that first portion of the novel, the portion in which the critic can imagine direct correspondence between the protagonist and the implied author's messages (an entity they confuse with the actual, extratextual Martínez Moreno himself), is used to create a flat, one-dimensional interpretation of the novel's message. Its difficulties and ambiguities, the changes undergone by the protagonist, indeed, the process of the novel itself is ignored, all in favor of ideological expediency.

However, Martínez Moreno obviously refused to do what he was "supposed" to do with regard to his treatment of the Cuban revolution, in *El paredón*. Rather than blindly assume such an attitude, he takes his protagonist (and, hence, his reader) physically to the setting of Cuba's controversy with both eyes open, refusing to turn a blind eye either to his own country's stagnation or to the ethical problem of justice in revolutionary social change. He honestly submits his protagonist (and the willing reader) to the possibility of "conversion" to Cuba's revolutionary aims, but without deleting any part of the picture for the purpose of proselytizing. As a by-product, in satisfying the need for honest change that is willing to step outside the rigid, stagnant parameters of the *quietista* rhetoric of Uruguayan reality, he takes the reader outside of any such parameters there might be in any other ideology as well. He offers the reader a look from inside and outside Cuban reality as well, with the obvious final results. Merrell describes this process concisely: "To be 'converted' to another religion or to another 'form of life' one must step 'outside' this circle, in order to exist momentarily in that realm where there are other alternatives" (42).

In *El paredón*, Julio Calodoro does just that: he steps outside of Uruguayan society into Cuban reality and back again. He searches for alternatives; he honestly seeks to convert to another way of life both on the microcosmic level in his love affair and on the macrocosmic level in his political opinions. Calodoro is much more than a mere example of typical Uruguayan "quietism." How many true *quietistas* would go so far? Rather, he is an example of the rejection of a hierarch inverted as a solution to false and oppressive oppositions. He signifies an outright rejection of any false hierarchy. His inaction at the end of the novel need not be taken as apathy. Instead, it could also be seen as a statement made by nonparticipation against a political reality that insists on framing itself in either-or terms, one that promises new alternatives but ultimately restates Manichean views in reverse. He rejects the dualism he sees in Uruguay at the novel's beginning, a dualism that dominates every aspect of political and social life, on a scale from the liberalism versus conservatism, at one end, to choice of soccer team, at the other extreme. His experiences in Cuba, however, send him and the reader back to these very same observations as at the novel's beginning. Thus, these experiences with the Cuban revolution prove to have no better intellectual footing than the empty exercise in choosing from predetermined either-or alternatives offered by Uruguayan society. In defining Uruguay's national identity as Manichean and irrelevant to actual change, Martínez Moreno is, in effect, expressing, through his protagonist, the attempt to identify "disyuntivas menos fáciles, menos sentimentales, memos arbitrarias" ("less facile dilemmas, less sentimental and less arbitrary") (8). Julio does not find them

4: *El paredón:* The Ethics of Revolutionary Justice

in Cuba any more than he does in Uruguay. He rejects the world he has inherited, one divided into arbitrary dichotomies:

> Los buenos y los malos, los colorados y los blancos, el antimarxismo y el marxismo, la democracia y el nazismo, la democracia y el comunismo, los pares conflictuales y eternos a través de los cuales él sesuía viendo desplazarse la historia (Martínez Moreno 1963, 16).

> The good guys and the bad guys, the Colorados [members of the urban liberal party] and the Blancos [members of the rural conservative party], anti-Marxism and Marxism, democracy and Nazism, democracy and communism, the eternally conflicting pairs through which he still saw the continual displacement of history.

In seeing history displaced by these habits of dichotomizing thought, Julio observes that what the accepted version of reality amounts to is an actual evasion of it: "El avestruz parecía haber sido desde años atrás el animal emblemático de la política nacional: no hemos querido ver lo que no nos gustaba" ("The ostrich seemed to have become years before the mascot of national politics: we have not wished to see what we didn't like") (23). His aim, then, is to learn to think differently, to insist on looking directly at what people prefer not to see, thereby discovering what converts these habits of mind into national obsessions. Unwilling to stick his head in the sand in Uruguay, he is just as unwilling to do so in Cuba. His revolutionary innocence suffers the consequences. As a colleague of his says to him with respect to Sosa Blanco's trial in Havana, at which both he and Julio have been invited as observers:

> Hay una cosa que un cirujano no debe poder soportar: la parodia de una operación, ejecutada por carniceros. Y ahora sé que hay algo que un abogado no puede sportar: la parodia de un juicio, sobre todo si termina por una condena a muerte (211).

> There is one thing a surgeon should not be able to stand: the parody of an operation carried out by butchers. And now I know that there is one thing a lawyer cannot stand: the parody of a trial—above all if it ends in a death sentence.

Julio, who admits to having come actually in search of a conversion and not really as an impartial journalist or observer, literally loses his appetite—for food and for this kind of change—upon hearing his colleague's statement: "La piedad concreta y la impiedad genérica del abogado le repugnaban por igual" ("The lawyer's real pity and his generic pity were equally disgusting") (212). He is at once and in equal measure repulsed by the double bind in which he finds himself in attempting to justify on another soil that which he would have censured at home. At this point, he truly steps outside the circle of Cuban reality as well. The double bind begins to become clear to him. His inaction at the end is clearly foreshadowed, not as a rejection of a viable course of action, but as a response to an indefensible invitation to yet another evasion that he will not accept as a true alternative. He does not refuse to participate in confronting the reality of *la deca* with activism; he is not a *quietista*. Rather, he sees in Cuba another, even more dangerous form of *quietismo* at work, one that is more than figuratively deadening. This Cuban revolutionary *quietismo* is literally deadening.

An analytical tool that offers a possibility of tracing both the "ethical" moment and this stepping "outside" the ideological bounds of both brands of *quietismo* is provided by Hayden White in his book *Metahistory*.[2] In this study of nineteenth-century historiography, White discovers a relationship between language and ideas that is particularly useful to a literary analysis that seeks to deal with ideological content. In short, White convincingly points to the fact that a close relationship can be found between the literary style of any piece of writing that deals with historical events and the ideological conclusions reached by it. In other words, how one chooses to frame an event in words directly affects what conclusions can be drawn from it. This is a bald affirmation of what we all know in our hearts but usually dare not bring into any analysis: that "objective" analyses are built with very "subjective" craftsmanship, which most of us attempt to embed so deeply in our texts as not to be apparent to the reader, who expects objectivity, and therefore, sees that only. By reading differently, that is, not for the final objective conclusions but for the subjective craftsmanship that builds them, Hayden White is, like Julio Calodoro, refusing to stick his head in the sand. Hence, White's way of reading is extremely useful in dealing with the objective-subjective bind in which the protagonist finds himself at the end of the novel and gives us a new way of looking at his final response to it, one that has received such univocal condemnation.

In delineating the relationship between words and ideas, lan-

4: *El paredón*: The Ethics of Revolutionary Justice

guage and ideology, White builds a model for analyzing the relationship between style and content that is radically unconventional. Rather than see style as subservient to content, he sees the reverse: to him a writer's actual attitude toward a subject matter is contained within his style. Thus, his definition of style is of utmost importance: "a particular combination of a mode of emplotment, a mode of argument, and a mode of ideological implication" (White 1973, 29). Particular modes in certain combinations, then, will produce a certain tendency toward a particular linguistic treatment of an event, a certain predominant choice of tropes. In general, he sees four such combinations to be likely (White 1973, 29; Bonnycastle 1982, 32–33).

According to White, these modes cannot be indiscriminately combined in a given work because they are not indiscriminately compatible. This is especially true in history, which has much invested in systematic and consistent presentation for the sake of credibility. However, in literature modes can be deliberately combined in different ways precisely because flouting is the nature of fiction itself.

Thus, the key to how literary (novelistic) or nonliterary (historically essayistic) a text is can be found in the degree of congruence of its relationships between tropes and modes of discourse. Incongruent points are the points at which one should look for the implied message. If the incongruities are deliberate (and in fiction it can only be presumed to be the case), then whatever the results of the incongruities, they can be seen to reflect the implied author's attitude toward the subject.

This is interesting and relevant to *El paredón* because, as in all of Martínez Moreno's novels, it represents a peculiar marriage of narrative and moral essay of the type Leenhardt has described. This amalgam is what makes *El paredón* difficult to analyze using conventional narratological models, since these are inappropriate to the analysis of its ethical, essayistic aspects.

Hayden White provides a way to treat both aspects—the narratological as well as the essayistic, the stylistic as well as the conceptual—in tandem, simultaneously. The reason is simple: the "ethical moment," the moment in which the ideological judgment is made evident, is the moment in which these aesthetic and cognitive aspects are combined.

These moments, by very definition temporal qualities, can be detected in Julio Calodoro's shifting attitudes toward the past, the present, and the future. Each of these is represented most predominantly and in chronological order by the Uruguayan first part, the Cuban second part, and the final part of Julio's return to Uruguay in part three.

White's modes offer four possible attitudes toward the temporal location of utopian expectations, and each has its own specific ideological implications. These are held by Julio in a temporal or evolutionary sequence that, White claims, is the natural progression of all historical attitudes, making Julio's a concrete case of a universal process, not one merely relevant either to Uruguay or to Cuba, nor only to certain ideological groupings.

ANARCHISTIC   This attitude reflects a desire for a past utopia based on the idea of a loss of innocence that led to a corrupt social state in which one is currently found. The historical apex is found, then, in the distant past. Julio finds himself in this position regarding the Blanco victory in the election of 1958, in the novel's opening pages. He exhibits a clear nostalgia for a Uruguay previous to the ninety-four years of uninterrupted Colorado rule. In his view, the success of his father's party has irredeemably corrupted and stagnated Uruguayan democracy. The first thing we are told about Julio is the degree of his alienation: "Julio Calodoro era, en medio de aquel gentía de ideas encontradas y de entusiasmos tan simples, un ejemplar fuera de serie" ("Julio Calodoro was, in the midst of that multitude of common ideas and simple enthusiasms, an out of place case") (7).

His alienation from Uruguay's "gentío" ("multitude") demonstrates clearly his disenchantment with its own opinion of its "progressiveness." Because of his alienation, he perceives decadence in the present instead of progress, and yearns for the lost opportunities of the past that were afforded his father's generation.

> Hacía noventa y cuatro años que en aquella democracia tan bien dispuesta los grandes partidos no rotaban el poder. Y aunque acaso iban pareciéndose demasiado uno al otro, la fatiga de aquella larga dominación estaba sintiéndose y acusándose en todos los órdenes. (7).

> It had been ninety-four years in that so well-disposed democracy since the great parties had traded places. And although perhaps they had begun to appear alarmingly similar, the fatigue of that great period of dominance was beginning to be felt and to show up in all areas of life.

That "fatiga social" ("social fatigue")—*la deca*—corresponds to the

4: *El paredón:* The Ethics of Revolutionary Justice

loss of innocence perceived, according to White, in the anarchist mode of ideological implication. As for Julio's mode of argumentation at the beginning of the novel, it is clearly episodic and dispersive as far as its treatment of the historical field is concerned, a fact which makes it a formist mode of argument and that one aligned, according to White, with the anarchist ideological mode. The clearest example is Julio's choice of episode to illustrate Uruguay's loss of innocence as far as its democracy is concerned. The episode is the dramatic account of the suicide of Uruguayan President Baltazar Brum in 1933. Despondent on being left to stand alone against an attempted military coup, he calls a press conference and makes the ultimate statement: committing suicide before the entire press corps (15). This act, to Julio, was the direct consequence of yet another clear episode that had determined Uruguay's present stagnation: the death of José Batlle y Ordóñez, Uruguay's great reformer. "Políticamente, el reloj de su padre estaba detenido en la hora de aquella muerte" ("Politically speaking, his father's watch had stopped ticking the hour his mentor died") (29). For that reason, the descendants of that "único revolucionario" ("unique revolutionary") had become "conservadores" ("conservative"). Julio seeks a way to restore that lost sense of revolution (25).

That search ultimately is one of self-identification, which gives rise to the novel's dynamic of romantic emplotment (the mode of emplotment White aligns with anarchism) and makes it the story of Julio's odyssey through all four of White's stages. At the novel's outset, Julio reflects upon himself and his relationship to the grand scheme of things as intolerably nonheroic.

> Tení ahora cuarenta años y el tiempo se le habí ido en viajes, Universidad, y periodismo. . . . [N]o había hallado aún el rincón en que un hombre pueda retirarse a madurar a solas. . . . El tiempo pasaba sin heroicidad sobre esos usos que su cuerpo le daba (8).

> He was now forty years old and his time had flown by him with travels, college, and journalism. . . . He still hadn't found that niche to which a man can retire to mature alone. . . . Time was going by him without heroism, spent on those uses his body could find for it.

As for the dominant tropes of the novel's beginning, metaphors for the Uruguayan condition abound; the metaphor is the trope White corresponds to Anarchism as well. In addition to the metaphor of Uruguay as an "avestruz" ("ostrich") with its head in the sand, another metaphor of evasion refers to the country as a "parque de diversiones, lejos por igual del peligro, de la ón, y de la muerte" ("amusement park, equally removed from danger as from salvation and death") (7). Many more tropes, heroic and self-identifying references to romantic emplotment, and episodic historical arguments make up the bulk of this first chapter, all of which point to a clear, direct implication of Julio who is anarchistic with regard to his country's conservative nature. The remainder of the novel's first part uses a series of social observations and childhood flashbacks that serve to underscore this original characterization. This characterization takes a fundamental turn, a radical one, as it were, when the protagonist is confronted with the fact of having been invited to Operación Verdad (104). With that invitation, he is shaken from his anarchistic nostalgia to confront the radical possibility of utopia in the immediate future, and the activism such a possibility would demand. Julio is reluctant to face such a modification in his worldview. This reluctance is linked to his desire to "mature" as an individual on the microcosmic level, facing his personal responsibilities with his longtime girlfriend Matilde as well as with his political, revolutionary responsibilities: "En varias etapas fundamentales . . . yo me he sentido como (un) . . . adolescente . . . no quiero dar el próximo paso que está convenido que dé. No me lo pidan" ("At various fundamental stages . . . I've felt like an . . . adolescent . . . not wanting to take the next step expected of me. Don't ask that of me") (105).

Yet he accepts the invitation, resigning himself to it as his fate. such a move already constitutes a switch to a tragic mode of emplotment and mechanistic mode of argument, elements that themselves lead, according to White, to a radical mode of ideological implication.

RADICAL This attitude reflects a desire for a utopia in the immediate future where it perceives the historical apex to be located. This is the position to which Julio attempts to move as he anticipates his trip to observe the Cuban revolution firsthand. On the third page of the second part, a fellow passenger on his plane to Cuba asks him, "Eso, la revolución. ¿Le gusta?" ("That revolution thing—you like it?") To which he responds, "Voy sin ningún prejuico, como observador" ("I'm going as an observer, without prejudice"). But internally he admits to himself the contrary: "No iba como observador, sin embargo; y mucho menos aún podía decirse que fuera sin prejuicio" ("He was not going as an ob-

4: *El paredón:* The Ethics of Revolutionary Justice

server, however, and much less could he say that he was going without prejudice") (114).

The dominant trope one should look for in the process of radical ideological implication is metonymy or, as Hayden White defines it, "name change. The part of a thing may be substituted for the whole. . . . Connecting things with neighbors in time and space" (White's table is reproduced on page 202 in the notes). A shift to metonymical tropology is seen most clearly in the account of Fidel Castro's speech that initiates Operación Verdad and, next to Julio's later observation of the night executions at the *paredón* itself, is the high point of the novel's second part. Julio tries to identify with Castro's rhetoric: "El Himmler de nosotros es Ventura. Los Goerings son los Tabernilla, Pilar García, Chaviano, El Hitler de nosotros es Batista" ("Our Himmler is Ventura. Our Goerings are the Tabernillas, Pilar Garcías, and Chavianos; our Hitler is Batista") (131).

From this series of name changes, Castro goes on to describe a view of the state of affairs that reveals a tragic mode of emplotment based on a mechanistic, or, as White puts it, "reductive search for causal laws determining outcome" (see table, p. 202). This mode indicates that the whole is equal only to the sum of its parts. Any attempt to change the whole must come from the elimination of parts, since tragic resignation to the revelation of limits precludes any hope of transcending them by any other means. Thus, Castro justifies his executions: "Estamos fusilando a los esbirros, para lograr la paz; y estamos fusilando a los esbirros para que en el día de mañana no nos asesinen" ("We are executing the henchmen in order to achieve peace; we are also executing the henchmen so tomorrow they will not murder us") (132).

Until his actual encounter with the *paredón*, Julio attempts to maintain expectations of adopting Cuban radicalism completely, as a true conversion process. He mentally defends Fidel's politics as he listens to an American journalist react to Castro's speech.

> Las ideas de Mr. Pordage sobre comunismo parecían ser muy sumarias y sintetizarse así: Comunismo es todo lo que se nos coloque enfrente a combatirnos con el pretexto del progreso. (135).
>
> Mr. Pordage's ideas on communism seemed to be very summary and could be synthesized thus: Communism is anything that could come in our path and confront us with the pretext of progress.

Julio thinks to himself, "No podemos entendernos con esta

gente" ("We cannot possibly come to an understanding with these people"), meaning North Americans. He believes his degree of alienation toward them is directly proportional to his ability to identify himself with the revolution. He entertains the notion, fed to him by his Cuban colleague and lover, Raquel, that "En Cuba, todos tenían derecho a preguntar, a hablar . . . luego de los . . . años del terror" ("In Cuba everyone had the right to ask questions, to talk . . . after . . . the years of terror") (138).

This initial enthusiasm is somewhat dampened as he attends the trials of those whom Castro wants to eliminate, making them a more concrete entity than the metonymical abstractions to which Fidel had referred in his speech.

CONSERVATISM   This attitude views the present as utopia and desires the progressive elaboration of institutional structure that currently prevails, taking the present to be the best of all possible worlds. The emphasis is on the present; the message is to promote the more perfect adherence to the status quo. It locates the historical apex in the present. This is the position in which Julio finds himself shortly after arriving in Cuba and finding things not to be as clearcut as he expected. Change is over with; the revolution is in the process of entrenching itself. In using the *paredón* to do so, journalists' ability to convince themselves to propagate more perfect adherence to the status quo is sorely tested.

> Calodoro no pensaba así. No es que desintiera en el caso de Ernesto De la Fe. Pero en general presentía lo peligroso del juego, y los extremos a que ese juego iba a arrojarlos. (148)
>
> Calodoro didn't think that way. It wasn't so much that he dissented in the case of Ernesto de la Fe. But in general he had a premonition of the danger of the game being played and the extremes to which this game was going to hurl them.

From this point on, Julio begins to listen to Cuba's radical, mechanistic arguments with different ears. His driver tries to convince him of the logical validity of the *paredón*.

> En esa situación, la muerte surge como el término de una ecuación, como uno de los períodos de esta equivalencia matemática: venalidad es igual a muerte. . . .
> Se detuvo a esperar objeciones, pero no vinieron. Calodoro estaba pensando en la exuberancia verbal con que hablaban los cubanos y en

4: *El paredón:* The Ethics of Revolutionary Justice

la estirpe nacional inevitable de todos los razonamientos que estaba escuchándoles en estos días. (149)

> In this situation, death becomes a term in an equation, like one of those periods in this mathematical equivalent: venality equals death. . . .
> He paused expecting objections, but none came. Calodoro was thinking with the verbal exuberance with which Cubans spoke and in the inevitable national heir to all the arguments he was hearing from them these days.

Yet, Julio does not totally reject the radical vision he has tried to embrace until the sordid spectacle of the Sosa Blanco trial. Held in a basketball stadium, it is little more than a kangaroo court. The legal procedures of the "people's tribunal" bring him to some conclusions about the radical appeal to the masses as their justification for such actions.

> La masa marchando silenciosamente es una abstracción en las especulaciones de los ideólogos. . . . Esa masa disciplinada y consciente . . . sólo existe en los libros . . . El pueblo verdadero tiene ese costado indesprensible de alegría obscena, de pesadez, de candor bestial, y de impureza. . . .
> Estra era la audiencia del tribunal, éste era el público del juicio sumario, ésta era Cuba. (158–59)

> The silently marching mass is an abstraction belonging to ideological speculation. . . . That disciplined and conscientious mass . . . only exists in books. . . . The true people have another undeniable side to them consisting of obscene joy, annoying clumsiness, beastly candor, and impurity. . . .
> This was the audience at the trial, this was what filled the gallery at the summary trial, this was Cuba.

Julio has now shifted to a synecdochical tropology; i.e., the mentioned qualities of the part (the mob) stand for the presumed qualities of the whole (Cuba), This is the trope of conservative, not radical, ideological implication. Close reading of Julio's attitudes at this stage of his development reveals a desire to go no further. For him, the revolution's triumph prior to the mass executions is the best of all possible worlds. He believes that nothing can be accomplished by such actions but alienation and destruction of the present utopia. He finds himself arguing for the conservation of the present state of affairs, making the organicist argument that the elimination of individuals on the microcosmic level will have consequences far beyond that on the macrocosmic level.

It becomes difficult for Julio to see a revolution that pursues the policy of mass execution as the best of all possible worlds or even as a good one at all, which brings him to his next ideological stage of development, and the one for which the novel's ending has been soundly condemned: that of a liberal, the position with which he broke at the novel's beginning.

LIBERALISM This is an attitude that hopes for a future utopia, but as a structure in the remote future, in such a way as to discourage any effort in the present to realize it precipitately, by radical means. It therefore locates the historical apex in the remote future. Julio reluctantly finds himself adopting this position by default at the novel's end, which ironically takes him back to the position that caused the corruption he bemoans at the novel's beginning.

The seeds of this ultimate liberalism in Julio can be seen by his conversion to ironic tropology at the approximate mid-point of the novel's second half. The issue is the novel's very theme: the oxymoronic nature of revolution and justice under the present conditions. A lawyer and observer of the mass trials asks Fidel: "¿Ve usted entonces una antinomía entre Derecho y Revolución?" ("Do you now see a contradiction between Law and Revolution?") The answer: "No es antinomía sino renovación. El Fénix jurídico, si así puede decirse, resurge de las cenizas. Pero ya es otro asunto" ("It isn't a contradiction but, rather, a renovation. The judicial Phoenix, so to speak, rising from the ashes. But that is another matter") (194).

Julio's internal reaction is the "negation on the figurative level of what is meant on the literal level" (see table on p. for White's definition of irony): "Palabras, palabras, palabras . . ." ("Words, words, words . . ."). Julio makes reference to the infanticide of the Holy Innocents, "Es la política de Herodes" ("It's the politics of Herod") (195). He begins to notice more cynical attitudes around him toward the revolution than he had before: "todo esto acaba por hacernos cínicos" ("all of this ends up making us cynical") (211). A colleague refers to it as "este pic-nic faccioso sobre toda la isla" ("'this mutinous picnic around the whole island'"), and declares the legal procedure they are there to observe a "parody" of a trial (212). As has already been mentioned earlier in this chapter, Julio is particularly sensitive to this last observation

4: *El paredón:* The Ethics of Revolutionary Justice

on the part of his colleague. It sours his taste for sampling what the revolution has to offer in any serious sense, and turns him, for the remainder of the second part, to a personal hedonism that concentrates on himself and his Cuban lover, Raquel. Close scrutiny of his lover's past, akin to his own self-scrutiny in the Uruguayan first part, reveals personal, ulterior motives for her participation in the revolution that somewhat undermine the idealism she originally espoused. These are sexual motives, a selfish desire for gratification that runs contrary to the espoused motive of utopian altruism to which she had originally laid claim. Julio observes satirically: "Estaban engañándose piadosamente" ("They were piously deceiving themselves") (270). The sexual motif is ingeniously joined with the death motif of the *paredón* (and the foreshadowing of Julio's father's death in part three) by the second part's last sentence, in a way that announces definitively the death of any idea of Julio's taking the revolution back to Uruguay. His failure on the microcosmic level with Raquel is linked with his macrocosmic failure, just as his quest was linked with his need to mature in his relationship with Matilde in Montevideo. As the morning of his last day in Cuba dawns, Julio hears a cock crow. In an obvious intertextuality with Peter's denial in the passion of Christ, Julio reacts to the sound with a rush of remorse.

> (E)l gallo oficiaba de comedido verdugo . . . Apartaba a los amantes, los marcaba en la frente y—en vez de darles muerte—los lanzaba a vivir otra vez sus dos vidas, desasidos, inocentes, remotos (279).

> The cock was acting as the discreet undertaker. . . . It separated the lovers, branded them on the forehead and—instead of killing them—cast them out into the world again to live their two disengaged, naive, and remote lives.

The "dos vidas" (two lives) that end up being "desasidos y . . . remotos" ("disengaged and . . . remote") could be seen allegorically as the two realities Julio has tried to link by ideology; i.e. that of Uruguay and that of Cuba in 1959. The balance of the third part, the novel's shortest part, is dedicated to Julio's experiences with death, that of his father, who dies of cancer upon his return, and at the execution he personally observed one night back in Cuba. It is telling that the graphic, guilt-ridden description of that night, in several pages, is the last scene presented before that of the novel's condemned last line,"que todo siga como está" ("may everything go on as it is"). He gives his summary of his emotions regarding that night: "Lo más cruel e inverosímil de toda la escena era la gratuita sensación de nuestra impunidad, ese abismo de impunidad y de certeza que nos separaba del hombrecito" (The most cruel and unimaginable thing about the whole scene was our gratuitous sense of impunity, that abyss of impunity and certainty that set us apart from the little man) (302).

What we see in this, the actual *pardeón* of the novel's title, is Julio's confirmation as one who now embraces what he found abominable at the novel's beginning. He has become a liberal, in the sense defined by White. His attitude is decidedly contextualist, since what he objects to most in what he has observed is the power of certainty exercised by the revolutionary executioners. Thus, the scene best represents the theme of the novel: the alienation of Julio from the world in which he tries to find a place. The dynamic of Julio's development is his progressive alienation from the systems he samples. His inability to identify fully with anything he finds, either in Uruguay or in Cuba, pushes him through all four of White's modes in quick succession, and then back to the beginning . As White says of alienation:

> What is progress to one is decadence to another, with the present age enjoying a different status, as an apex or a nadir of development, depending on the degree of alienation in a given ideology. (White 1973, 27)

Thus, the key to Julio's interpretation of the "progressive" value of the Blanco election (Uruguay, 1958) as really decadent is due to his degree of alienation from it. The surprise in the novel, which leftist criticism has refused to accept, is the degree of his alienation in Cuba. As he goes from anarchist to liberal in his ideological odyssey (i.e., his fundamental shifts in attitude about past, present, and future utopias), the social consequences of his alienation grow ever broader. At the beginning of the novel, his alienation is mostly related to his father, a defeated Colorado party functionary. Hence, it is totally microcosmic. This alienation expands to include his lover, Matilde, when we find him open to an affair with a revolutionary comrade during his trip to Cuba. From here, he proceeds to break his solidarity with his Latin-American peers and journalistic colleagues regarding the issue of the *paredón*. At the novel's end, his father dead, Julio's alienation upon return to his own country becomes complete—he breaks with his Cuban lover, he has broken with his peers and colleagues regarding Cuba, and yet he refuses to reenter his home society with the consequences of these changes, somehow remaining be-

4: *El paredón:* The Ethics of Revolutionary Justice

tween realities. His withdrawal from society is both specific (with regard to Matilde and the idea of marriage) and general (with regard to social change as a whole), as can be seen in his final decision: "Que todo siga como está" (May it all go on as it is).

Julio does not come to this decision because he literally finds the status quo agreeable (as the conservative position would hold), but because he finds all other positions inadequate as bases for action—the liberal/contextualist position. His trip to Cuba and his encounter with the *paredón* have deconstructed his ability to believe in revolution and just social change as compatible concepts in practice. He is unwilling to commit either personally (by marrying Matilde) or politically (by espousing conformity with Fidel's Cuban practices) to positions that just as unreasonably require him to assume the *quietista* pose of the *avestruz (ostrich),* with head in sand. His travel outside Uruguay in search of "alternativas menos disyuntivas" ("less disjunctive alternatives") has resulted in finding the same dichotomies abroad, only in reverse emphasis and on a grander scale. Uruguay and Cuba insist on limiting the political discourse to a duality: conservatism versus radicalism. When in Uruguay (using White's positioning of ideological modes), Julio finds himself marginalized on the Left of the political spectrum. In Cuba, he finds himself marginalized on its Right. Finding himself marginalized and disenfranchised in both instances, and unable to find a true third option, Julio simply refuses to play. This depiction of the need for true "tercerismo" ("thirdism") in "tercer mundismo" ("third world-ism") as it confronts *la deca* is the actual message in *El paredón,* and not some mere denuciation of *quietismo* on the Right alone. To Martínez Moreno, it was just as necessary to avoid *quietismo* on the Left. His deconstructive honesty bears out his intellectual integrity. *El paredón* deserves better than it received critically for the way in which it anticipated this impasse in leftist ideology. It demands a rereading by anyone concerned with universal issues of ethics and social change, today as much as it did over a quarter century ago.

5
La otra mitad: Know Thyself

The reception of this third novel by Carlos Martínez Moreno, *La otra mitad* (The other half) (1966), is an interesting follow-up to the political scandal of *El paredón* (1963), his novel set partly against the background of the Cuban revolution. In *El paredón*, Carlos Martínez Moreno used Castro's Cuba as a backdrop to highlight Julio Calodoro's futile attempt to apply Manichean solutions to ambiguous problems of national and personal identity. Though his use of the Cuban revolution was incidental to the broader point of his character's search for an authentic identity, from the outset this point was obscured by a critical debate over whether the novel was "pro" or "anti" Castro. Its open ending regarding the matter went totally ignored.

In *La otra mitad*, Martínez Moreno attempts to reopen the issue of the search for authentic identity in the era of *la deca* in a less public and political domain—that of a man's love life. However, though *La otra mitad* is a politically safe novel due to its highly intimate nature, it unlike *El paredón,* was censored in Spain. Apparently, Franco's censors would have none of Martínez Moreno's investigations into *la deca* when it was brought down to more personal proportions, and Seix Barral could not consider it for its prestigious prize. In contrast, despite all the controversy surrounding it, *El paredón* tied four times with Vargas Llosa's *La ciudad y los perros* (known in English translation as *Time of the Hero*) for the Premio Seix Barral before Martínez Moreno lost to the Peruvian wunderkind a little more than half his age. *La otra mitad* lost its chance even to compete because it committed a worse moral sin, at least in the eyes of the Franco regime, than that of possibly espousing communism: it depicted an adulterous affair with tenderness and from the male point of view, two qualities that made it unacceptable to fascist arbiters of morality seeking to protect the institution of marriage.

However, *La otra mitad* is a unique novel for reasons that go

5: *La otra mitad:* Know Thyself

well beyond those two thematic qualities. It is a highly complex and experimental novel in its narrative strategies as well. Its beginning leads the reader to expect a conventional crime novel, if not exactly a full-fledged detective novel. The opening scene should be familiar to anyone acquainted with the first cardinal convention of the genre: a description of the victim(s) and the scene of the crime. However, on the very first page, this convention is somewhat altered by the unusual identity of the novel's "detective," for he is not a detective in any normal sense of the word. Instead of being an objective observer, Mario Possenti is a very subjective one, almost a participant in the crime itself, for he shared what one could call a decadent arrangement with the victim as her secret, adulterous lover. Mario is a literature professor, onetime lawyer, and sometime writer. His lover, Cora has apparently been murdered by her husband, who, it seems, has turned his gun on himself after shooting his wife.

Thus, from the outset, Mario's function in the novel is to discover the truth for himself while guiltily concealing it from others. Along with uncovering the truth regarding the motive for the crime, he and only two other friends know his secret, and it is Possenti alone who is obsessed by the fear that Carlos may have discovered Cora's "other half" and secret life, her love affair with Possenti.

This is only the first of many contradictions that Mario—and the reader—must juggle during the course of the novel. Mario must lie about his relationship to the victims as he seeks the truth about the crime's motive. Though it certainly complicates the conventional detective's role, that very fact is the initial entanglement that spurs the reader on in hopes of something new. The question is not *whether* Mario will discover the truth behind the bloody death described in the novel's first chapter. Rather, it is *how* he will do so without giving himself away. This adds another dimension to the normal challenge inherent in any detective's characterization, a dimension that is the enigma that leads the reader into *La otra mitad*.

However, having obligated the reader to expect the conventions of the detective genre—albeit expectations somewhat complicated by Mario's own identity—Martínez Moreno proceeds to delay, defer, and finally, deny the reader a satisfactory resolution to the enigma of the *deca* situation depicted in the novel. The failure to reconcile Mario's two opposing roles in the development of *La otra mitad* has led most critics to comment on its interesting complexity and contradictory nature without venturing to interpret its unresolved ending.

Fernando Ainsa, in his critical analysis "Las tensiones de Carlos Martínez Moreno" (Carlos Martínez Moreno's tensions) came closer to addressing this problem directly than any of the other, very few, critics whose attention was drawn to the novel in the first decade following its publication.[1] Other studies either allegorized its ending, as is the case with Rodríguez Monegal's "Oedipal" reading, politicized it, as in Delgado's and Benedetti's readings, or produced highly technical analyses of its complex narrative structure that avoided commenting on the ending altogether, as is the case in Joan Rea Green's detailed but disappointingly inconclusive 1976 study.[2] Ainsa's study is different with respect to its careful definition of the problem inherent in analyzing a novel that flouts the conventions of a popular genre, raises a myriad of contradictions, and then seems, at the end, to have had no clear purpose for doing either. He attempts to use Robert Penn Warren's New Critical approach, with its emphasis on "paradox," but in an amazingly honest long footnote on critical methodology at his article's outset, he admits it is ill-suited both because of its origins in poetry and, more importantly, its almost exclusive preference for *resolvable* paradoxes, unity, and what some critics today call the "ideology of totality."[3] At the end of this footnote, which, incidentally, risks undermining his entire essay, he vaguely displays a hope for a new way of analyzing such open-ended texts, mentioning Carlos Fuentes as a possible source of a new poetic of prose because of his role both as author and critic of such experimental fiction.

What even Ainsa overlooked, however, is that the key to understanding the problem posed by the novel's problematic ending lies in the novel's name both for itself and for its protagonist. The novel repeatedly defines itself as a "policial metafísica" ("metaphysical detective story") (34). This should not be taken lightly, for the novel begins with a crime scene that raises reader expectations that it is a detective story. Yet by the end, it seems to be quite far from such concrete, conventional considerations. Instead, it operates extensively on the abstract plane of existential issues typically raised in Martínez Moreno's treatment of *la deca* throughout his novels. These issues—issues such as alienation, death, and the individual's struggle to forge a meaningful identity for himself in the face of their mysteries—pose problems truly metaphysical in nature. The meaning of the text's ending and the identity of the protagonist are inextricably linked to these problems by

5: *La otra mitad:* Know Thyself

his function as detective of this policial metafísica's" investigation. Whatever discoveries are made in the course of this investigation are not produced by a clue found at the scene of death (the fact that the couple's wedding bands were removed and lying together on a dresser before the killings), but, ironically enough, by the "broma celeste" ("heavenly joke") of a nickname, "Planeta Neptuno" ("Planet Neptune"), given to the protagonist by his lover (18). Over three-fourths of the way through the novel, once all other leads have come to nothing, the protagonist realizes the serious implications of this joke not only as descriptive of his own identity, but also of his affair and his whole endeavor to find meaning in it, and in life, after his lover's death. Thus, by a riddle, the novel as detective story is deconstructed, and its contradictions, though never resolved, become meaningful to the reader rather than merely a source of frustration.

Martínez Moreno's notion of *policial metafísica* brings to mind a term introduced into literary criticism by Michael Holquist, the *metaphysical whodunit* (Holquist 1971, 135–36). It also brings to mind the best Spanish-language example of this relatively recent subgenre, *Los albañiles* (The bricklayers) (1964), a novel by the Mexican Vicente Leñero, since the two have much in common. In both, logical method is applied to a crime with the surprising result that, far from narrowing the possibilities for explaining it, it increases them to the point that, as far as solving the mystery is concerned, the detective protagonist utterly fails. As a further surprising by-product of the failure to resolve conflict with logic, both Munguía in *Los albañiles* and Mario in *La otra mitad* come to question the most bascially assumed facts at the novel's outset. In Munguía's case, his failure to resolve the case leads him—and the reader—to question whether the crime ever occurred at all. Mario does not come to the point of questioning the actual existence of the crime in *La otra mitad*, but he does question the validity of his relationship with Cora, becoming unsure to the point of switching roles with Carlos from cuckolder to cuckolded. In both cases, such questioning leads to a breakdown of the worldviews of the respective protagonists. However, here we find the two novels in sharp contrast. In the metamorphosis of Munguía from a logically dispassionate stereotype like Sherlock Holmes to a failed ex-detective, we can see a humanizing process, since he acquires an identity more like those of the novel's other characters. In Mario's situation, by reaching the point of questioning the basis for his investigation—what he had believed at the novel's outset to have been his close relationship with Cora—

he loses all motivation for continuing in his role as an investigator into her death. In his inability to reach any hard truth in his investigation, he becomes alienated. Munguía, at the end, shakes hands with a man who, quite possibly, could be the caretaker whose alleged murder he had wasted his career in trying to solve. Though frustrated, his handshake is a symbol of solidarity, one of participating in the world as a peer and not as a superior and distantly analytical godlike figure. Mario is also humanized, but in a negative sense. Becoming human, for Mario, means accepting alienation after solidarity (with Cora), whereas with Munguía, a sense of human interdpendence is what follows the alienating investigation the detective has so unproductively conducted. For Mario, becoming humanized means having to accept the effects, on the most intimate area of his life, of his denial of *"la deca."*

The transformation of Mario from grieving lover to a recognition of his identity as a man driven and alienated from himself and others by *la deca* shows two extremes in his characterization. Those extremes are bridged by an emphasis on *process* in the novel, in this case, the *policial metafísica* process. Such a process is perhaps best traced by means of following what Roland Barthes has called the encoded "texture" of the text (Barthes 1977, 19). According to Barthes, the codes of a *récit* are the "voices off-stage" in a narrative that, "converging" in "stereographic space" (the written text), are interwoven. This interweaving of that which is always just barely absent or "offstage" (e.g., Mario's "otra mitad," Cora) with what is present in Mario's world (his clues to her and the meaning of her life and death to him) is what constitutes the textural process of the novel. Given this circumstance, Barthes' procedure of textual, or "texture-al," analysis is most appropriate to a tracing of its "threads" toward its surprising outcome. The "tracing of threads" in Barthes's criticism is an exhaustive study of the "codes" of a text, and is best exemplified for our purposes here by his analysis of a short story by Edgar Allan Poe, the inventor of the contemporary detective genre, according to Holquist. (Barthes 1977, 1–12)

The codes I find useful in the present analysis explain the transformation of Mario Possenti from the role of detective, investigating the motives and actions of others into a character who questions his own motives, identity, and relationship to *la deca*. Since identifying all the codes of the entire *récit* would be unwieldy, I intend to limit myself, as critic John Brushwood has in his Barthesian study of *María* only to such codes as pertain to the characterization of the protagonist.[4] Therefore, unlike Barthes's

5: *La otra mitad:* Know Thyself

own study in *S/Z* and in his article on Poe, I will use only connotative codes, and only those relevant to Mario's process of characterization and the change in emphasis that produces his transformation in much the same manner as a change in thread can transform the texture of a tapestry from one color or pattern to another. The codes used will be adapted to *La otra mitad* and the needs that arise from its reading. The consideration that arises in the case of *La otra mitad* is that the *cultural code* plays a particularly important role. It is so constantly emphasized that it merits a brief discussion.

The *cultural code* is defined by Barthes in *S/Z* as a "reference to a science or a body of knowledge." (Barthes 1977, 5) This definition suffices in the case of Balzac's text, studied by Barthes in *S/Z*, but in the case of *La otra mitad* it is necessary to define it even more specifically. Thus, for the purposes of this study, let us divide the cultural code into two parts, and name the second the *reflective subcode,* leaving *cultural code* free to signify the conventions of the genre we know as the popular detective novel. Since from its first scene the novel is encoded with this cultural code so as to give readers the expectation of a conventional detective story, we must trace it as a separate code from the reflective one in order to understand the play between the two and the transformation of convention that affects the characterization of Mario.

To understand the analysis of this "flouting" of a popular genre for metaphysical effect in Mario's characterization, the folklore of the conventional product of this subgenre—the conventional detective character—must be understood. Michael Holquist defines it well in his historical study of the subgenre and its recent transformation:

> The basic clichés of the detective story especially should be clear. . . . It is not, as is often said, the character of great detectives which accounts for their popularity. If character means anything, we must admit that most of them have very little of it. Take Sherlock Holmes, for example. He does not really exist when he is not on a case. The violin, the drugs merely keep him in a state of suspended animation until the inevitable knock on the door comes, announcing a new problem. He does not solve crimes, he solves puzzles. There is no death in his world—only the statement of riddles. . . . This is a metaphor for what happens in all the stories. Nothing really happens, but it is therefore curious. Holmes is less a detective than a mathematician; he is his function. Therefore other people simply are not people for him. . . . The degree to which Holmes is pure mind may also be seen

in the official iconography of him; in the later illustrations he is all nose and bulging brow. (142–43)

The flouting of the establishment of a character as a "function" is the essence of Mario's humanizing transformation since he, unlike any conventional detective like Holmes, does experience a death in his world and has to face the fact that he has been trying to see himself and others not as people, but as functions of himself. Death reveals the lie in this *deca* view of the world. His attempt to find meaning in his life after Cora's death by creating a "function" for himself in her death as a *metafísica policial* fails. As a consequence, he comes face to face with *la deca*, and must accept the pain of recognizing that his denial of it has caused him to waste the opportunity a relationship afforded him to transcend it. With that recognition comes the awareness of an alienation from himself and others that he refused to see until it was too late.

Before coming to an analysis of that moment of recognition in the novel, however, we must analyze the "function" of the codes in the novel by which Mario tries to create a "function" for himself, however doomed that endeavor might be. In doing so, in a larger sense, one may perceive a parallel frustration of "function" in the reader, and in the frustration of the reader's genre expectations. In the end, the larger purpose of such a deliberate frustration by the implied author of the novel's themes and messages will have to be addressed as well.

The following codes will serve for this analysis:

CULTURAL CODE   The specific body of generic knowledge of the conventions of the fictional detective story.

REFLECTIVE SUBCODE   The nonfictional body of knowledge that pertains to the inquiry into the nature and meaning of knowledge itself and its origins, its philosophical implications for self-knowledge and the knowledge of others, etc.

SOCIAL CODE   The behavior of each individual to the other, be it Mario to Cora or to those he interrogates to obtain knowledge about her death.

The social code can be divided into two subcodes:

POWER SUBCODE   The hierarchical conventions of society that privilege certain relationships over others (i.e., marital relationships over all others.

5: *La otra mitad:* Know Thyself

ASSOCIATION/ALIENATION SUBCODE   The encoding of the process of affirmation and negation that produces the transformation, the study of which is the purpose of this analysis.

Because the best application of these codes can be seen in an extremely close reading, it is best to display their function in a limited segment of the text rather than attempt to demonstrate them in a close reading of the entire text's 343 pages.

The rationale for this is not simple expediency. The structure of *La otra mitad* is such that upon reaching the novel's climax, the reader is forced to return and reread the opening scene in which the novel's crime is presented. In that rereading it becomes evident that all the clues to the novel's resolution (which is not the solving of the crime) were contained in the first chapter and that reader expectations based on a conventional reading of the cultural code lead to a misreading up to the climax, with less than one-fourth of the novel remaining. Thus, the climax is the "navel" of the text from which the deliberately encoded conventional misreading offered by the implied author is unraveled or deconstructed from the beginning up to that point, providing a new reading that offers a context for the interpretation of the novel's otherwise elliptical and enigmatic unresolved ending.

> Por favor, dígame exactamente cómo los encontró. (9)
>
> Please, tell me exactly how you found them.

This statement, which opens the novel, establishes all the cultural code by directly encoding the expectation that this will be, above all, a detective story. It is the first rule in the detective genre that the crime be committed either before or outside the *récit,* and that the reader clearly identify the enigma from the outset by knowing of the existence of a victim (or victims). In short, a murder is needed for a murder mystery. In this opening statement, the reader is succinctly supplied with both. The opening scene continues:

> Más cerca, detrás de la cabeza de la mujer, reía . . . gente barrosamente . . . en las lindes de mi campo visual, como en una toma *floue* del cine, cuando director y fotógrafo quieren que el espectador sólo se ocupe de cuanto ocurre en primer plano y los fantasmas que paradojalmente lo distraen transcurren en una niebla de espacio lechoso (9).
>
> Closer, behind the woman's head . . . people were laughing darkly . . . in the outer limits of my field of vision, as in a *floue* shot in film

when the director and the cameraman want the spectator to bother himself only with what is happening in the foreground and the phantoms that paradoxically distract him pass by in a fog of milky space.

Carefully read, this sentence, also from the novel's first paragraph, can be seen as paradigmatic of the implied author's narrative procedure throughout the novel. The narrator introduces himself in the first person, thus establishing the cultural code referent to the detective genre. The reader is pointedly told that the novel's focalization will be primarily from the narrator-protagonist's viewpoint. By the same token, the reader is also editorially made aware of the handicap of such a limited point of view. Thematically, this encoding is of utmost importance, since it represents both the procedure and the problem of the novel: Mario can only see, try as he may, his own *mitad* (half) of things clearly. The *otra mitad* (other half) haunts him as a vague awareness of "fantasmas" ("phantoms"). Mario's clear view, therefore, is limited to his first person *primer plano* (foreground). Others are seen as "borrosamente localizable" ("sketchily identifiable") and as inhabiting a *niebla* (fog). By this last description, the social code is introduced in its alienating subcode form. Though Mario (deceptively employing the power subcode) pretends to be a investigative reporter and therefore entitled to the information he seeks, his vision is depicted as already limited in both scope and depth to a single plane, as well as being somewhat distracted by *fantasmas* that blur, as it were, in his limited lens. Thus, from the outset, we see that the cultural detective code is established, as well as somewhat undermined, by the concurrent conflict of other codes. Ultimately, the introduction of planes of vision brings the reader to suspect that reality will be presented in the novel as occurring on different levels at once.

> Yo me había presentado como Mario Possenti, periodista, mezclando lo verdadero del nombre a lo mentido del oficio. (9)
>
> I had introduced myself as Mario Possenti, journalist, mixing the truth of the name with the lie of the job.

The reflective subcode is introduced at the same time as the narrator-protagonist's identity, establishing their link. Mario is a man in search of a function, one attempting to assume what Holquist described as Sherlock Holmes's abstract detachment from a painful experience (the death of Cora, his lover) by attempting to play the role of investigative reporter. Of course, this last fact

5: *La otra mitad:* Know Thyself

involves the use of the power subcode. Mario must assume that function not only for the purpose of overcoming his own subjective grief over her death, but also in order to be socially entitled to the information he seeks. But the reflective subcode remains of primary importance here; Mario is introduced as having the problem of proceeding with not only a vision distracted by phantoms, but also a conflicting mix of truth with falsehood *within* his own identity. Thus, from the novel's first page we learn of Mario's limited focus and divided fielf of vision, one divided between objects in focus and the others that blur in his frame, the "other half" of which he is aware but which he is unable to see with clear resolution. Simultaneously, we see that his vision is not only clouded in terms of viewing the *outside* world, but also is "mixed up" (clear, unclear; true, false) with regard to his own *internal* identity.

> . . . según decían las crónicas policiales que yo había leído y tenía . . . para releerlas. (10)

> . . . according to what was said in the crime section of the paper, which I had read and kept . . . to reread.

Here we find the cultural code brought to bear in that although he does attempt to follow his self-scripted role by following the "crónicas policiales" ("crime section") we now know our detective admits only to playing at satisfying the requirements of detective genre conventionality.

> —Bueno—dijo (y ustedes habrán observado cómo la gente de poca elocuencia empieza a hablar partiendo siempre de una palabra recapitulatoria; yo, como profesor de letras, vivo corrigiéndolo en mis discípulos)—Ahora fui yo quien . . . empleé la palabrita:—Bueno, ¿y? (10)

> "Well," he said (and you may have observed how people with little eloquence begin to speak always using a word that will serve to recap; I, as a literature professor, spend my life correcting this in my students) . . . Now I was the one who used the little word: "Well, so?"

This exchange reveals much about our main character. First, we find out his real identity—he is a literature professor. The initial expectations regarding our protagonist as a detective are diminished in the conventional sense. However, his analytical mind is revealed by his reaction to the use of a single word, showing the use of the power subcode: he believes that he has a superior command of language. This notion, too, is immediately blurred somewhat; the professor transgresses himself even though he knows better. The associative code is revealed in the use of direct address that links the protagonist's own limited point of view with the reader's.

> . . . habían simplificado los *prolegómenos* del hallazgo. (11)

> . . . they had simplified the *prolegomena* of the discovery.

Any reader educated in the most basic texts of metaphysical philosophy will recognize the reference to the title of Emmanuel Kant's most famous work, *Prolegomena to any Future Metaphysic*, an example of the cultural code as reflective subcode. It is worth noting here that the connotations of that word reverberate even more with meaning as in the near textual future (in another twenty-three pages), we are presented with the text's self-definition as a "policial metafísica" (34).

Lastly, the narrator's observation that "they" (the writers of journalistic and police accounts of Cora's death) had "simplified" the event implies that his function will be to bring out its larger implications in a manner contrary to "their" narrative method.

> . . . como si el *techito* de estas . . . *palabras* fuese su roca de *resguardo* sentimental en toda esta historia. (12)

> . . . as if the *little roof* of these . . . *words* were his rock of sentimental *shelter* in this whole story.

Implying that language is a shelter for the emotions rather than a vehicle for their expression. Mario pretends that, because of his analytical powers, he, like Holquist's Holmes, has no need for it. This is the lie that has reinforced Mario's defense mechanism in the same way that "arquitectura mental" ("mental architecture") underpinned Robledo's characterization in *Cordelia*. Stubborn adherence to these defense mechanisms, even when facing the death of a loved one, is what most clearly defines Mario and Robledo as *deca* characters. In Mario's case, the self-deception of his implied claim to superiority is made painfully evident. Later in the novel, he cracks Cora's linguistic code in the nickname she had given him and discovers it to be the remote "Planeta Neptuno." In the end, by solving her riddle he dissolves his own identity, adding irony to her "heavenly joke."

5: *La otra mitad:* Know Thyself

> ... yo—en otra de mis estúpidas rachas rememorativas—le pregunté:—El teléfono, ¿ya estaba bien, entonces? (13)

> ... I—in another of my stupid streaks of remembrance—asked her: "The telephone—was it already fixed, then?"

In this statement, we see the power subcode come into play. Mario's vulnerability is exposed in his falling prey to a slip of the tongue. He had assumed he could successfully detach from Cora and her death by virtue of his superior control of language. However, if he really were the disinterested researcher he is trying to play, he would not know such an intimate detail from a time prior to the crime. Cora's phone was out of order because they had ripped it out so that their lovemaking would not be interrupted by a call from her husband, Carlos, when he was away on business.

> Si dormía en el momento en que la mataron, como parece haber indicios de que ocurrió, ¿cuál fue su último sueño trunco, el sueño roto o perpetuado por la muerte? ¿Estaría yo en el? (14).

> If she had been sleeping the moment she was murdered, as the clues seemed to indicate happened, what was her last aborted dream, the dream broken or perpetuated by death? Would I have been in it?

No detached detective would ever attempt such a feat as reading a sleeping mind—not even Sherlock Holmes. Mario's *policial* and the cultural code it represents is shown to be truly metaphysical in that it tries to piece together the ethereal, a broken dream.

> ... los anillos ... ¿ hecho de habérselos quitado esa noche significa algo? (14)

> ... the rings ... did the fact that they had taken them off that night mean something?

Mario may be able to uncover his lover's last thoughts if he can decipher the meaning of this clue—provided it is a clue and not a casual red herring. The enigma surrounding this piece of evidence is maintained until the end of the novel, when both Mario and the reader finally learn that it is false. The maintenance of such a conventional enigma, so as to spur the novel's reading, reinforces the emphasis on the detective genre cultural code. The myth of convention is exploded with the revelation that the clue on which we have been counting is false. Along with it is exploded the myth that this extramarital affair was as conventional and casual as Mario might have wished to believe.

> En la realidad, empiezan y acaban así los interrogatorios que rinden tanto en los libros . . . esos interrogatorios eslabonados y de hermosa simetría mental que tejen las tramas de las novelas policiales (15).
>
> In reality, that is how all those interrogations they write about in books so much really end . . . those multilayered interrogations constructed with such beautiful mental symmetry woven into the plots of detective novels.

Obviously, as the first chapter draws to a close, the cultural, detective genre, code is again reinforced in a manner recalling the "arquitectura mental" of Robledo in *Cordelia*. Mario is shown reflecting (reflective subcode) on his interview with Cora's maid and its relationship to the "novela policial." He yearns for the clear symmetry of fiction, something he does not enjoy in his muddled world of "policial metafísica." While aware of other possible *mitades*, no method seems to lead him toward an answer to his question regarding Cora's thoughts during the last night of her life. He has wasted his time with Cora in role-play and allowed her truth to slip through his fingers just as Robledo did with Susana in *Cordelia*.

> . . . los tabúes destinados a envolvernos en misterio . . . a prevenir la intrusión de los otros en *nuestro* mundo. (15, emphasis in original)
>
> . . . the taboos destined to should us in mystery . . . to prevent the intrusion of others in *our* world.

Mario's reflection on that role-play, a game that had kept him from truly knowing Cora fully, is displayed in his examination of the associative/alienating subcode. Mario and Cora had protected their relationship from discovery by observing certain rules of conduct, or "tabúes," in their illicit affair. These "tabúes" were central to maintaining their relationship and were grounded in the denial characteristic of Martínez Moreno's *deca* characters. The irony of observing "tabúes" in that which is itself socially taboo—adultery—is of profound significance to *La otra mitad*. One could argue that this double bind of ironies is the pathetic message of the novel itself. The double irony of that message is made most clear when Mario discovers that those "tabúes" did not really serve the purpose of protecting their relationship from discovery.

5: *La otra mitad:* Know Thyself

The more important function of those "tabúes" seems to have been to shield each of them from the other, from discovering each other. They each hide an "otra mitad" that they try to keep concealed by fashioning a system of "tabúes." Such discovery in a relationship cannot be avoided forever, no matter what taboos are put in place. Mario suffers the discovery, like most of Martínez Moreno's characters, too late, and too alone.

> —Porque tengo que escribir sobre el asunto . . .—le dije. (15)

> "Because I have to write about the matter . . ." I told her.

On the most literal level, Mario lies to the maid he interviews here, because he intends to make her believe that his interest in investigating is purely professional and that he is a journalist and/or private investigator for an insurance company (he's a bad liar and confuses his own cover story). Thus, on this level, he is involving a power subcode, privileging himself through false hierarchical claims. But on a more figurative level, Possenti is not lying, but rather, making a metafictional reference (reflective code) to the process of the novel as a whole. Unable to find meaning in his lover's death through normal grieving conventions because of his taboo relationship with Cora, he has to create meaning and a context for her death on paper. Having denied *la deca* in their relationship too long, it is his only viable response. Thus, it is imperative for him to resort to writing as a substitute for living—in this case, living out his grief openly.

> En un mundo en el que Cora ya no existe, yo también estoy dejando capciosamante de existir. . . . Mi condición de deudor cuajaba frente un solo ser humano y esa deuda ya ha sidao cancelada, ese ser ya no existe (18).

> In a world in which Cora no longer exists, I also am ceasing insidiously to exist. . . . My debtor's condition squared with only one human being and that debt has now been cancelled, that being has now ceased to be.

This twist on Descartes reveals the metaphysical underpinning for the entire detective enterprise of the novel. Mario, in light of society's taboos, cannot rightfully acknowledge an intimate relationship with Cora; he therefore cannot mourn her death. In her presence, Mario had no existential problem. Although society denied their right to affirm their relationship, it provided them a system of "tabúes," a role-play that shielded them from that denial of an important part of their lives. However, social convention provides for no role to play in death. Mario has no way to react to the loss of this relationship, since he could not seek recognition of its existence. He could expect from society even less recognition of and sympathy for his loss. Because he doubly broke society's taboo with regard to adulterous relationships—he not only committed adultery but also took it seriously and did not just treat it as a sexual misadventure—he is doubly lonely. As the novel develops, it becomes more and more obvious that, as Mario's frustration with grieving the loss of a "nonexistent" love grows, the emphasis on the cultural code and power code will diminish. The "investigation" loses it purpose as he loses his will to go on. Instead, predictably the reflective and alienating codes gain prominence. Mario tries and fails to find a social mechanism by which to give meaning to and make some sense of Cora's death.

> ¿Es para esto—pienso, mirando las baldosas que corren perezosamente por debajo de mí,—fue para esto que Cora inventó la broma celeste de llamarme su Planeta Neptuno? (18)

> "Was it for this," I wonder, watching the tiles run lazily beneath me, "was it for this that Cora made up the celestial joke of calling me her Planet Neptune?"

At the novel's beginning, "Planeta Neptuno" seems to be only an odd nickname. Yet this odd nickname, not the removed wedding rings, turns out to be what could be called the naval of the text. The "heavenly joke" ultimately is not on the cuckolded husband but on the adulterer left behind to the double irony, both in life and in death, of the conditions on his relationship to his beloved that he tacitly accepted. Though Mario exhausts all other possibilities before coming to this realization, at the novel's climax he returns to his identity as Cora's "Planet Neptune." It is far from the revelation that Mario, or the reader, expects from his search for meaning in Cora's death.

Twenty chapters of shifting through false clues passes before Mario realizes the significance of "Planeta Neptuno." When he cracks the meaning of his own nickname rather than trying to find the answer in the Other, he comes to recognize himself and his own withholding of commitment as both the mystery and its solution. In so doing, he recognizes himself as a man who has

5: *La otra mitad:* Know Thyself

fallen victim to *la deca*. In the interim, he searches for a clue that could help him maintain the defenses that he and Cora shared against that recognition. He speculates as to what Cora's last dream might have been. In the second chapter, he remembers his first meeting with Cora and sharing with her his amusement at a friend's insistence that she could read her cat's mind even as the cat was lost among the shelves of her bookstore. Her response inspired him to consider it as a topic for a short story. He discards the idea now, but does not see the analogy in his attempt to read his dead lover's mind in search of her last dream, although the reflective subcode here is evident to the reader. In chapter three, he experiences the indignity of not being able to claim his lover's remains because of the illicit nature of their relationship. The power subcode here at work vicitimizes him by maintaining the privilege of the institution of marriage. Even with Cora in her grave, their adultery inscribes the alienating code in his character.

Following this indignity are two chapters describing the only trip their taboos ever allowed them to take together. Their escapade took place on a weekend when Cora's husband was away on business. Mario's detailed recollections of it produce no clues, but rather much guilt and sadness, reinforcing the alienating code inscribed in his character upon his failed attempt to claim Cora's remains. Chapter six returns him to the narrative present and a trip to the coroner. The coroner happens to be an old schoolmate of his, which raises Mario's hopes that, as an old friend, he may be willing to circumvent normal procedure and share information with him that could be of consolation. However, this proves not to be the case, not because of any unwillingness on the part of his friend, but because, apparently, there is no information to be had.

Mario's disappointment only intensifies his inner turmoil and self-doubt, and he returns to search his memory for the key to the way out of his suffering. This time he remembers the letters he received from Cora during their three-month separation as she accompanied her husband on a trip to Europe. The detective cultural code is reinforced by Cora's comment that his appearance as he bade her farewell at the airport (in disguise) reminded her of an Interpol agent. He compares that separation to his present sense of loss and remembers the "huella talismánica de su amor" or "trace of [her] love" on his body.

Mario's diminishing faith in that trace of love now reflects a growing emphasis on the alienating subcode. Their shared readings of Simone de Beauvoir and Graham Greene (the former a metaphysical reading, the latter a detective one) offer him little solace. He begins to doubt his memory's accuracy, and his confidence of her feeling for him is shaken. His desire for some objective, external sign of his internal reality is reflected in his recollection of Cora's prophecy that someday there would be an "amorímetro," an instrument that could gauge emotions with clinical precision just as a thermometer measures temperature. He yearns for such an objective instrument as his faith in his analyatical and recollecting faculties begins to fade.

Returning to the narrative present, the reader is presented with Cora's funeral, a spartan affair poorly attended due to the circumstances of her death. Her burial reminds Mario of three stories he once told Cora when he used her as a sounding board for his fiction writing. Now, in lieu of an objective *amorímetro*, he tries to gauge her reactions to his stories in his memory of them. It becomes apparent to him now that the common theme of all three stories is love and loneliness, and that each of them narrates the literal or figurative death of the woman in the relationships they describe. Mario is unable to say whether he shared his present analysis at the time or not. He can recall no clue to Cora's feelings on the subject either, which brings home to him the extent to which they went to hide their feelings from one another.

He does remember, however, that he once told Cora that the figure of a love relationship should be a chiasma. He named this chiasma "Amorequis." In his description of it to Cora, he had described one of its lines as descending, the other as ascending. The descending line, he had said, represented the man's decrease in desire over time, while the ascending line represented the woman's increase in desire. Now he bitterly reflects upon his facile cynicism at the time, in which he was willing to boast of an acceptance of love as only a momentary intersection of wayward emotions. In the narrative present, the figure comes to represent an X instead of an intersection, representing the erasure of an identity, a relationship, a world, a figure of *la deca*. Thus, "Amorequis" also clearly represents a decreasing emphasis on the positive aspects of the cultural and social codes at work in the novel, and an increasing emphasis on their negative aspects. This shift in emphasis marks yet another step in Mario's progress toward breaking Cora's cryptically encoded clue as to his identity, "Planeta Neptuno," that puzzled him in the novel's first chapter.

As Mario constantly shifts between past and present, between external and internal reality, for clues—in addition to the dynamic of his chiasmic "Amorequis" analysis—he begins to lose control

5: *La otra mitad:* Know Thyself

over his previous notions of reality, and his recognition of *la deca* in his relationship increases. This loss of control becomes most evident in his professional life. Simultaneously with his investigation into Cora's death, he has been teaching a class as well as doing research for a book on the Uruguayan poet Delmira Agustini. Agustini is almost as well known in Uruguayan literary history for her lifelong adulterous love affair and tragic death as she is recognized for her poetry. Mario's secret life begins to slip out of his control as, both in class and in his writing, Agustini's identity becomes confused with that of Cora. The result is a series of slips of the tongue whose root in his emotions can only be evident to himself as he embarrasses himself before his students with hybrid names such as "Delcora" and "Colmira." The same occurs, in less embarrassing form, in his writing. He takes this as a possible sign of hope that a comparison and contrast of the two may render a clue; not surprisingly, he is once again disappointed and returns to his lonely recollections.

The only time in which the novel's focalization extends beyond the limits of Mario's vision is when he narrates Cora's recollections of her father's death when she was a child, as if he were there. His attempt to assume her point of view toward such a traumatic event in her life, of course, is never any more than his own reconstructed version. He becomes even more keenly aware of his inability to objectively recover her sense of the event when he recalls that Cora's sister once recounted their father's death from a totally different point of view. At a loss for any criteria by which to judge the veracity of the versions of the story, Mario comes to realize that in researching the past for the truth he is rewriting it as well.

With this realization as the only fruit of his attempt to reconstruct Cora's biography, he decides, in desperation, to reconsider his own. In so doing he stumbles upon the meaning of Cora's "heavenly joke." He had thought he might use it as a title of his "investigation" (i.e., this novel), and the irony of that does not escape him when he finally realizes the joke's meaning.

> Fue Cora quien inventó lo del Planeta Neptuno. Carlos iba a descubrirme algún día—predijo—como Leverrier a Neptuno, por las perturbaciones en la órbita de Urano. Y Urano era ella con sus cambios, con sus transformaciones desde que me había conocido. ¿Cómo podrían serle invisibles?
>
> En los días en que le empecé, creí que esta historia iba a llamarse Planeta Neptuno. Pero no será el título que en definitiva prevalezca. Sospecho, además, que puede haber varios planetas Neptuno en el mismo juego de tres personajes; y que cada uno de nosotros debería

> haber sido a la vez el Neptuno y el Leverrier de algún otro, debería haber oficiado de descubridor y de objeto descubierto, en una suerte de colisión perpetua. (252)

> Cora was the one who made up that stuff about Planet Neptune. Carlos was going to discover me someday—so she predicted—like Leverrier had discovered Neptune: by its disturbance of the orbit of Uranus. And she was Uranus, what with her changes, all those transformations since she had met me. How could they be invisible to him?
> When I began writing it, I thought this story was going to be called Planet Neptune. But that will not be the title that prevails. Besides, I suspect there could be several Planet Neptunes in the interplay of three characters; each one of us must have been both Neptune and Leverrier at various times as well as playing the roles of discoverer and discovered object in a sort of perpetual collision.

With this realization, Mario comes to understand that the problem of identity is always a three-way struggle among the self, the Other, and the invisible trace of a truth that can never be directly observed but that has an effect on the relationship between the two nonetheless. Though the trace if this truth is invisible to him, Mario realizes that this truth cannot be denied, and yet he sees that up until this point his thinking has been rooted in its denial—in *la deca*.

This haunting sense of *la deca* drives home the importance of the scene that opens the novel. In that scene, we have a sense of Mario himself as a character operating solely on a "primer plano" ("foreground"), aware of "los fantasmas que paradojamente lo distraen (y que) transcurren en una niebla de espacio lechoso" ("the phantoms that paradoxically distract him and that pass by in a fog of milky space") (9). With the inclusion of another plane to his perception of reality, many truths now become evident to Mario.

Most important of all, of course, is the truth regarding *la deca* and his relationship with Cora. Rather than continue to feel that he haunted Carlos the cuckold, Mario begns to feel haunted by the possibility that he himself might have been cuckolded by the *otra mitad* of Cora, the part of her he refused to see in her marital relationship. His "policial metafísica" has degenerated into the story of a world without a stable metaphysical system, in which nothing is certain anymore. He tries to return to the idea that he can treat the problem of *la otra mitad* as a detective's case, but he has no more external certainties to which he can turn as clues.

5: *La otra mitad:* Know Thyself

He has made his discovery, and it has overturned his philosophical apple cart.

> Siempre comprendí lo que Sartre destruía y todo lo que filosóficamente afirmaba. Entiendo la eficacia de la conducta polítca y social que propone, pero hasta ahora no le he visto afrontar el escueto destino individual. (310)

> I always understood what Sartre destroyed and all that he affirmed philosophically. I understand the efficacy of the political and social conduct he proposes, but until now I have not seen him face up to the unadorned facts of individual human destiny.

The final chapter begins with what is the shortest but, perhaps, the most revealing sentence of the whole novel: "Lloré, sí" ("Yes, I cried.") (322). Mario's world has finally come unraveled; he sheds tears for having lived in an illusion, a life of "insidiosa mediocridad" ("insidious mediocrity"), a life dissolved in *la deca*. Life was, as he had once flippantly observed, truly no more than

> Una policial metafísica, como creo haber ya dicho; una policial metafísica cuyo centro somos nosotros, cuyo objeto de piedad somos nosotros, cuyo tema de pesquisa somos nosotros, cuyo asesino—*develado no a la última sino en todas la páginas*—somos nosotros. (68, emphasis mine)

> A metaphysical detective story, as I believe I've already said; a metaphysical detective story whose center was ourselves, whose object of pity was ourselves, whose topic of inquiry was ourselves, whose murderer—*revealed not on the last but on all the pages*—was ourselves.

This new revelation, born of the rereading forced by the crux of the novel—his understanding the "heavenly joke" of "Planet Neptune"—aptly describes the analysis applied to the novel in explaining the texture of its codes. Thus, the key to the novel's interpretation is truly to be found not in a final resolution, but in an unusual degree of attention to the process of its reading, both on the part of its narrator-protagonist as well as on the part of the reader. The novel leads both—one in fiction, the other in reality—to return to the novel's beginning for its ending.

With Mario's revelation as to the meaning of "Planeta Neptuno," the possibility of resolving the bipolar contradictions terms is inhibited by the final recognition of an internal triangular struggle in addition to the external one that is most obvious one in the novel's central conflict. Retracing the novel's transformations in the character of Mario Possenti, we are able to see that the conflict between its elements, the perceptions that Mario, Cora, and Carlos may have of one another, is also a sign of a similar conflict within the elements themselves.

In Mario's case, this struggle within is a struggle among the self, the perception of the Other, and the elusive truth of the porousness of the boundaries of identity, which poses a challenge that must be undertaken if one is to have a truly meaningful relationship—a recognition of *la otra mitad*. The consequence of denying *la otra mitad* is, in this novel, Martínez Moreno's message regarding the personal effects of refusing to deal with *la deca:* it results ultimately in the dissolution of individual identity. The recognition of this deconstructive principle is at work within the novel from its first page. The statement it makes about the question of identity by showing rather than telling, (i.e., by display rather than by explanation) seems to support a statement made by Barbara Johnson in her book *The Critical Difference* to the effect that theory describes what literature has already intuited (Johnson 1980, chap. 7.) In its deconstructive treatment of *la deca* at life's most intimate level, *La otra mitad* displays an originality that explains, at least in part, its undervalued position in the canon of the Latin-American boom: it is a novel whose ideas were ahead of its time.

6

Con las primeras luces: The Darkness before the Dawn

Con las primeras luces (By dawn's early light) (1966) is not, by any means, Martínez Moreno's most appealing work. It has very little action, and it provides no sympathetic characters with whom the reader can identify. Martínez Moreno's works tend to bridge two poles: what John Brushwood calls the "intimist," and its opposite, the social. In *Luces*, Martínez Moreno does not mitigate the intimist tendency with a dynamic setting such as the Cuba of *El paredón* or Bolivia and Rome in *Los aborígenes* or a dramatic situation such as the murder-suicide of *La otra mitad* or the cocaine trafficking of *Coca*. *Luces* stands apart from his novels in the depth with which the novel spirals into *la deca*, in the lonely awareness and impotence before it that is depicted, in a manner extreme even for Martínez Moreno's canon.

This distinction may be due in part to the circumstances in which it was written. According to its author, it came about as a last minute substitute for the Spanish publisher, Seix Barral, upon the censorship, under Franco, of *La otra mitad*, a novel he had been working on for most of his writing career. Just as he was about to board an ocean liner in Spain for Montevideo, he received a newspaper clipping from his mother informing him of the death of a distant relative in the same circumstances as those of Eugenio, the protagonist of *Luces*. Hence the seminal idea for this novel of *la deca* of the fictional Escudero family. Martínez Moreno, whose personal history contained the reconciliation, by marriage, of two of Uruguay's rival elite families, sought to explore the exhaustion of such past historical arrangements and grounds for some third way out of tired dualisms, a way he called *tercerismo* (thirdism).[1] *Con las primeras luces* is the product of the author's four weeks in solitude aboard ship, with that idea. He himself never gave it much importance when discussing his own works, choosing instead to dismiss it for its status as a substitute for *La otra mitad*, which he considered his best novel. For the student of Martínez Moreno's thought as reflected in his novelistic canon, however, it is the most naked and direct exposure to be found of his attitude toward the individual and time, values inherited from the past and their value in the present and for the future, and the subject of change and denial—*la deca*.

The earliest reviews of Martínez Moreno's third novel, *Con las primeras luces* (1966) differ sharply from the novelist's own appraisal of its importance, praising the novel by analogy with others. H. Ernest Lewald says of it in *Books Abroad*:

> An outstanding novelist of Uruguay today, Martínez Moreno has in this new effort departed in technique and structure from his previous ones. . . . The almost obvious parallel to Faulkner's *As I Lay Dying* exists here on two levels: similarities in structural technique and the creation of a novelistic texture dominated by a personal, intimate conception of man's illusions, needs, and failures. . . . The power of the novel lies in the evocation of a past that is still shaping the present and is being restated in all its immediacy by the dying narrator with all the symbols and motifs of his futile existence. . . . What unites the descendents of this Uruguayan House of Thebes is their sullen refusal to grow into a world full of struggle, responsibility, and challenge. . . . Only his final agony offers him the possibility of seeing his (Eugenio's) insufficiency, to atone in time for his sin against life. (Lewald 1967, 324–25)

While the similarity in structural technique that Lewald mentions is altogether accurate, it is more important that he makes a point of mentioning the novel's texture. That texture, as he says, is "dominated" by a "personal, intimate conception." As Addie, the protagonist in *As I Lay Dying*, puts it, it is a conception dominated by characters "each with his and her secret and selfish thought." That thought is dedicated to the belief, instilled in her by her father, that "the reason for living was to get ready to stay dead a ling time" (Faulkner 1987, 155).

This view of life from the vantage point of what Martínez Moreno calls in his works the *sobremuriente* ("as-good-as-dead survivor," literally the neologism "sur-dead-or"; see my comments on *Los aborígenes* in the first chapter of this study) is essential to the theme of *la deca* that is a current throughout his canon. In *Luces* we find its most profound elaboration. In fact, the term *la deca* itself appears in the novel with frequency until its climactic pages (if the novel can be said to have a climax at all), where it appears

6: *Con las primeras luces:* The Darkness before the Dawn

italicized seven times. It is not surprising, then, that *Luces,* with its almost total thematic dedication to *la deca,* should represent what Lewald calls a dramatic departure in technique and structure as well. Nor should it be surprising that Faulknerian analogies should be drawn from such an experimental novel about dying.

Twenty years after the publication of *Luces,* however, the importance of Faulkner, both thematically and stylistically, to the Latin-American novel of the boom has been stated (and sometimes overstated) to the point of nearly losing any precise significance.[2] For the purpose of this study it can be made more precise by drawing on its importance to a cardinal work of the boom canon, a novel to which *Luces* has also been compared, *La muerte de Artemio Cruz (The Death of Artemio Cruz).* Both Faulkner's retrospective narration and his multivocity serve as a clear foundation upon which Fuentes builds his now-famous yo-tú-él (I-you-he) narrative shifts and analeptical treatment of time. Fuentes's thematic treatment of the moral decay following the Mexican revolution parallels Faulkner's own depiction of the post–Civil War South. *Luces* follows suit on both counts. As Jorge Campos pointed out, when *Luces* appeared:

> Es inevitable la comparación del esquema argumental de la novela con el de otra publicada no hace mucho: *La muerte de Artemio Cruz* del mejicano Carlos Fuentes. En las dos se pinta la agoní de un hombre, y durante ella la evocación de su pasado y en él el paso de todo un país caminando al mismo tiempo que el protagonista. (Campos 1966, 11)

> The comparison of the plot scheme of this novel with another published not too long ago is inevitable: *The Death of Artemio Cruz* by the Mexican Carlos Fuentes. Both paint a portrait of a man's dying agony. Each man's dying moments evokes a past which encompasses the passing of an entire country walking in step with the protagonist.

By the same token, however, he aptly points out a basic difference between Fuentes' novel and *Luces:*

> Al observador de las letras de la América hispana le alegra precisamente la coincidencia por las divergencias que le es posible considerar: en las dos novelas un hombre se muere y el novelista pinta con ello el fin de una generación o el declinar de una clase. Pero en México, en el caos de Artemio Cruz, lo que muere es la clase de aquellos que hicieron la revolución y luego la traicionaron y se entregaron al enriquecimiento y la vida cómoda. Gentes de acción todavía ellos mismos.

> Aquí, en cambio, nos encontramos con que la historia del Uruguay ha marchado por un derrotero muy distinto. País de vida tranquila. . . . País en que más generaciones han vivido la existencia de una nación próspera con una estructura política aún decimonónica, y cuya decadencia se pinta aprovechando el lastimoso y funesto accidente del hombre alanceado en la verja. (11)

> The observer of Spanish-American letters is delighted by the coincidence precisely because of the divergences it makes it possible for him to consider: in both novels a man dies and, with his death, the novelist portrays the end of a generation or the decline of a class. But in the chaos of Artemio Cruz, what dies is the class of those who made the revolution happen only to betray it by selling out to wealth and the comfortable life. Yet they themselves had been men of action.
> Here, however, we find ourselves facing the fact that Uruguayan history has taken a very different path. A country of tranquil living. . . . A country in which generations have lived the life of a prosperous nation within a political structure that still belongs to the nineteenth century and whose decadence is portrayed from the vantage point of the painful and unfortunate accident of a man speared on his fence post.

Fuentes's *Cruz* depicts, in retrospect, a man who exchanged one form of action for another. He is corrupt, he is decadent, he is dying, but he has been decisive. He has been capable of immense change, at least on the personal level, even if that change has been aimed at cultivating corruption and blind ambition. Eugenio, the dying protagonist of *Luces,* shares Artemio's blindness in life as well as his lucidity in death, but neither he nor the generation he represents could be accused of sharing Artemio's ambition. His is a generation that clings to the "estructuras decimonónicas" ("nineteenth-century structures") to which Campos refers. They go far beyond being merely political structures, however, they are a dinosaurian way of seeing the world, inadequate to the realities in which they live, much like Primitivo's "genteel barbarism" in *Los aborígenes.* Hence, a quiet, nondramatic, self-conscious passivity pervades *Luces,* as it does all of Martínez Moreno's works.

This is *la deca,* and *Luces* is the work Martínez Moreno most dedicates to it, to decadence and decay. Juan Carlos Onetti, his contemporary, best depicted it in the rusted machinery of *El astillero* (The shipyard), an allegory, on the social and philosophical level, of a society in which decay is a given condition and not one into which the characters themselves slide. In *Luces,* Martínez Moreno personalizes that allegory, making it more intimate. The shipyard of *El astillero* is exchanged for a dilapidated family man-

6: *Con las primeras luces:* The Darkness before the Dawn

sion, once the *quinta* (country estate) of a general who is in some ways similar to Artemio. The *quinta*, formerly a retreat for a nation-building man of action, is now an anomaly that has been engulfed by the twentieth-century suburbanization of progress. It stands now not as a retreat for plotting a nation's future, but, rather, a place of retreat from both nation and future. The general's descendents, Eugenio Escudero and "Bob," his cousin, have turned it into a family mausoleum for the living.

This retreat from the world is more a product of Bob than of Eugenio, the novel's protagonist. Bob, in inverse manner to Artemio Cruz, is decisive in his inaction. Far from building a revolution, Bob has devoted his life to perfecting banality, as his ludicrously out-of-place Anglicized name implies. Eugenio is the one who feels the pull to abandon the claustrophobic world of family relics and venture into the changing world outside. Yet he never makes up his mind, remaining tied to the decaying house, Bob, and *la deca* as if by an invisible umbilical cord to the past that he refuses to suffer cutting. It is for this reason that he ends up in the predicament at the novel's outset. It is for this reason, as well, that he realizes, as the novel's opening line states, that "Ahora sí que me jodí del todo" ("Now I am definitely totally fucked").

This predicament gives rise to an even more personalized form of allegory. According to contemporary literary theorist Linda Hutcheon, "fence-sitting" is the quintessentially painful symbol of the postmodern condition.[3] If that is so, then Martínez Moreno's *Luces* is a novel depicting the agonizing results of this condition beyond any other, for in it the protagonist literally perishes of inertia—of fence-sitting. He has tried to have it both ways (inside/outside, past/present), to divide himself between worlds without committing himself, and he has done so once too often. It is fitting, then, in an extremely perverse way, that the fence itself, in a sense, should rise up and put an end to its use as artificial boundary between two worlds. Herein lies a message that seems to be implied in the novel's allegorical symbol, the text's controlling image of the agonizing Eugenio, dying slowly, pierced through the groin by a spike in the family mansion's fence. A fence is not a ground for being any more than it can be a retaining wall against change. In *Luces*, fences insist upon becoming prison bars for those who would enclose their worlds in them, as in the case of Bob. Fences straddled can become instruments of unwitting suicide—in this case, Eugenio's.

In the introduction to her recent study of Faulkner, Gail L.

Mortimer states that "the need to cling—to deny loss—is a central emotional reality underlying his fiction" (Mortimer 1983, 2). As my study of *Cordelia* has established, this is also true of Martínez Moreno's fiction. In *Cordelia*, Robledo refuses to accept his daughter's death just as he refused to accept her mother's death years earlier, preferring instead to cling to an identity based on that denial. In *Luces*, we have a very similar character in Eugenio, except that here the accidental death that confronts his system of denial is his own. As Eugenio learns, denial of change such as death is quite another matter when that death is one's own. Too late, he is bitterly confronted in that final goodbye with the fact that his denial of loss, his clinging to the past, has left him without much of a life to leave behind. He realizes too late the paradoxical relationship of life and death, gain and loss, in which change is the constant that cannot be denied. As a result, as Ravazzani states in her study of *Luces*, he realizes that he and his family, contradictorily, "son suicidas por miedo a la muerte. No han salido al encuentro de sus problemas mas estos los ahogan" ("are suicidal in their fear of death. They have never sallied forth to confront their problems even though their problems are suffocating them") (Ravazzani 1981, 59).

Luces is built around this paradoxically suicidal fear of death, which generates a series of further paradoxes: past/present, absence/presence, animate object/inanimate object. All of these paradoxes lack fixed poles, representing instead points of contradiction, a flux that Eugenio and his family tried to avoid. Eugenio has always played the role of one who speaks of change but always puts the responsibility for it in the hands of others. Most often, it is in the hands of his cousin Bob, a strategy that affords Eugenio a degree of self-righteous superiority, but that effectively only provides him with an excuse for perpetuating his own stagnation, with Bob as his scapegoat.

Bob is the architect of the family's *deca* in this generation, something revealed slowly throughout the novel's flashbacks and that becomes overt in the account of his reaction to his own mother's death, the death of the last of a long line of family matriarchs from whom the boys learned their values. Eugenio has always struggled, within himself, with *la deca* as he feels its destructiveness operating upon his life, but he has always projected onto external events the power to break its hold on him. He expects much from the death of Bob's mother, which took place a short time before his own accident:

6: *Con las primeras luces:* The Darkness before the Dawn

> Eugenio empezó a sentir que se movía en un mundo abolido, en un mundo sin salidas, en un mundo de oprimentes presencias muertas: Mariucha antes que nadie, Tío Jaime, Tía Rosina, los abuelos. . . . De un momento a otro la verja de la quinta iba a caerse y ellos saltarían por encima de sus lanzas depuestas. (Martínez Moreno 1966, 151)
>
> Eugenio began to feel as if he was moving through a world that had been abolished, a world with no exit, a world of oppressive dead presences: Mariucha above all, Uncle Jaime, Aunt Rosina, his grandparents. . . . From one moment to another the fence around the estate was bound to fall down and they would all leap over its deposed spearheads.

Rather than free himself, however, Eugenio has awaited some sort of miraculous Jericho experience, when the fence would come falling down of its own accord. His final, fatal jump is a rude awakening from this infantile fantasy upon which he has based his life's dreams.

As for Bob, his resolve to depend on the fence that separates him from the outside world of change is not weakened. Because of his mother's death, he clings to it all the more. In a flat declaration that echoes Julio Calodoro's last words in *El paredón,* Bob refuses to grieve for her or to allow anyone else (Eugenio, in particular) to effect any change in the mansion's monotonous routine as a response to her death: "todos nos debemos a un orden ya hecho. La vida tiene que seguir como hasta ahora" ("we all owe ourselves to an already established order. Life must go on as it has till now") (159). Bob makes this declaration while fully aware of the consequences of such inflexibility. It is as if, in a sense, Martínez Moreno picks up with Bob where he left off with Julio. Bob chooses to justify his denial by interpreting causality with regard to *la deca* in the manner most convenient to him—that is, in reverse. To Bob, *la deca* is not a product of his inactivity; his inertia is solely a product of *la deca,* as if it were an external condition that has imposed itself upon him from without, causing his internal ruin. By objectifying *la deca* and making himself its product, Bob objectifies himself. His comments upon the death of his mother, the last of the family matriarchs, is a significant example of the tendency of the characters in the novel to equate themselves with objects:

> ¿Por qué no te casás, por qué no te vas a vivir al centro, por qué no tomás la iniciativa de liquidar este caserón que se viene abajo solo? . . . Pues queridos—la palabra era dicha en el tono más

frígido— . . . tal vez sea porque el caserón ya se ha derrumbado hace años dentro de mí. . . . Debo estar lleno de escombros por dentro, un tipo de escombros que no se ve. (174, ellipses in original)

"Why don't you get married? Why don't you go live downtown? Why don't you take the initiatve and sell this old run-down house that's already falling down all by itself? . . . Well, dearies," the word was uttered in the coldest of tones, ". . . perhaps it is because this old house already fell down inside me years go. . . . I must be full of rubble, the kind of rubble you can't see."

Yet even as *la deca* results in an ossified characterization, flux is the nature of the novel's structure. From that juxtaposition, that opposition of fluid structure to static characterization, comes the meaning of the novel, which is in the novel's contradictory experience, its indeterminacy, rather than in any literal, didactic declaration on the part of the narrator. It is the purpose of the novel's complexity, which would otherwise be tedious and gratuitous. Thus, it is the reader who is able to sense the contradictory relationship between the novel's characterization and its structure who will most be able to benefit from its reading. It is a demanding novel, requiring that the reader witness the attempt of a character to redeem a life, through its narrative reconstruction, that has been a series of absences of life in living, a "sinvivir" ("nonlife"). A life lived in the manner described by Eugenio means a life in which time—the stuff of life itself—has been treated as a static object rather than an uncontainable flow. As he lies dying, Eugenio realizes with increasing clarity how he has objectified himself, treated himself and his world with little distinction between thing and person, and that such a "thingifying" is actually not life but death.

En esta quinta es todaví posible la ilusión de que ese tiempo no ha cesado de transcurrir, porque aquí . . . se vive todavía el nivel del tiempo de las cosas, y todo existe sobre un fondo detenido, grávido, de peso muerto, hecho de tiempo y de objetos, de presencias corporales, como si el tiempo fuera una gran sala vacía y las cosas . . . representaran su mobiliario, sus flotadores a través de las edades. (26)

On this estate it is still possible to entertain the illusion that that time has not ceased to pass by, because here . . . one lives life still at the level of the time frame of things, and all things exist as if against the backdrop of a still-life, heavy, deadweighted, made up of time and objects, of corporeal presences, as if time were one great big empty

6: Con las primeras luces: The Darkness before the Dawn

room and things . . . represented its furniture, its ball-floats across the ages.

He finds himself bleeding to death next to an empty milk bottle set out for the milkman and imagines himself found in the morning by him, drained of blood, an empty container just like the bottle: "que el lechero madrugue y llegue hasta la botella y aquí, tendido como otra botella, como otra botella y sin nada me encuentre" ("that the milkman should get up in the morning and get to this bottle and find—set out like another bottle, empty—me") (12). This analogy is far from an isolated occurrence of this strategy in the novel: it pervades it. As Ana-María Ravazzani observes:

> Sigue el narrador describiendo objetos, hechos, y personajes que formaron parte de la estructura de un mundo cerrado, en el que el presente no tiene cabida. Al hacerlo va uniendo los objetos a los seres ya muertos y los fija en un tiempo quieto, sin marcha, como ellos mismos. Todo queda convertido en cosas, iguales en su significado vital. (Ravazzani 1981, 69–70)
>
> The narrator goes on to describe objects, actions, and characters who formed part of the structure of a closed world, a world in which the present has no place. In so doing he links objects with those already dead and fixes them in a quiet time, a time without motion, like themselves. All are transformed into things, each equal to everything else in its vital significance.

This strategy can be found in Faulkner's works as well, and is one whose significance is no different from that in *Luces*. Faulkner

> uses images of containers and absences to convey his characters' anxiety in the face of loss: by focusing on what has just been, by creating images of emptiness and then only partially filling them, by playing with the notion of crossing forbidden boundaries (conceptual, social, narrative). (Mortimer 1983, 8)

In the particular Faulknerian novel to which *Luces* has been compared, *As I Lay Dying*, the coincidence is so close as to be uncanny. Mortimer says of *As I Lay Dying* that "the obscuring of the boundary between animate and inanimate pervades this novel about death" in which a main character, faced with Addie's death, expressed the desire "to hold Cora (his loved one) like a jar of milk in the Spring" (Mortimer 1983, 61–62; Faulkner 1987, 132) To her, this "perception of objects as containers has the effect of forestalling loss by insisting upon the substantiality and boundedness of something that threatens to go away" (Mortimer 1983, 88). As Mortimer further explains, this perception can extend to the very language used to describe the world. Language becomes emptied of its organic qualities, and becomes a lifeless substitute for reality. Instead of being animated signs pointing ways to penetrate reality, words have the contrary effect: rather than gateways through the boundaries separating one from the Other, they become the boundaries themselves. Words become agents of absence, not presence; instead of being vehicles for intimacy, they become obstacles to drawing nearer to others.

> Among the boundaries, the dead things in Addie Bundren's world, the most conspicuous are words. "Love, he called it . . . that word was like the others: just a shape to fill a lack. . . ." Once again, we recognize the paradox of a shape "filling" another shape, or the concentricity of empty, bounded things. . . . To put it differently, words do not simply fill lacks in peoples' lives, they replace them. When you have words, you cannot have the absent entities to which they refer. . . . The absences in peoples' lives are filled either by words or by doing, mutually exclusive possibilities. (Mortimer 1983, 89–90)

These last words paraphrase Eugenio's bitter realization in *Luces*. He realizes that his life has been dedicated to filling absences and denying losses through a self-serving discourse embodied in the term *la deca*, instead of using each absence as a loss that presents a new opportunity for action. If he had it to do over, he resolves, he would muster the courage to endure emptiness and not attempt to fill it, to do away with it artifically.

> yo pienso que si uno supiera que va a morirse en pocas horas más el mundo se le vaciaría de golpe, se vaciaría de gestos convencionales . . . que son la obra de la rutina de la muerte y no de la rutina de la vida. (61)

> I believe that if one knew that one was about to die in a few hours the world would suddenly become empty for him, devoid of the conventional gestures . . . that are the work of the routine of death and not of the routine of life.

He remembers the "rutina de muerte" ("routine of death") with which every death in the family was treated, an ironic ritual of filling gaps with words.

6: *Con las primeras luces:* The Darkness before the Dawn

vienen con rollos de papel y a veces hasta con trozos de diarios y rellenan los huecos que siempre quedan entre los flancos de un cadáver y su caja, los rellenan con páginas de telegramas o de crímenes y obligan al señor tan previsor a irse cargado de noticias que ya no le interesan, que al final de los tiempos van tal vez a quedarse pegadas a sus huesos. Así yo ahora . . . quisiera . . . aprovechar el tiempo restante sin falsas piedades ni falsas ceremonias, porque si a un muerto le llenan los huecos del ataúd de papel de diario es porque un muerto ya no es más que una cosa y un diario es otra cosa. (62)

they come with their rolls of paper and sometimes even with their pieces of newspaper and fill in the hollow that is always left between the flanks of a corpse and its coffin; they fill it in with pages of telegrams or the police pages of the newspaper, full of crime news, and force the prudent genttleman to a send-off all loaded down with news in which he is no longer interested, which, in the end, is perhaps bound to end up joined to his very bones. That is why I now . . . would like . . . to take advantage of the remainder of my life without false piety or phony ceremony, because if they fill in the hollow spaces of a dead man's casket with newspaper it's because the dead man is no longer more than a mere thing and the newspaper is just another thing.

Every death in the family has been met by the living with that attitude, one of "filling in" or covering up the lack, rather than recognizing it and adapting to it as change. Eugenio's dying reminiscences reveal to him, and to the reader, the inadequacy of a static treatment of life to its almost imperceptible flow of change. He tries to rewrite his life, as it were, from the moment in which it outgrew his static notions of it.

Casi nunca es posible saber a qué hora exacta de un día justo comenzó un hecho, así se trate del hecho más nítido. . . . Y si no se trata de un hecho tajante sino de una situación, menos que menos: la decadencia de una familia, digamos. ¿A qué hora empieza, en qué día se consuma, qué signos, qué señales la marcan?
Lo que entonces cada uno puede hacer es elegir una imagen. (147)

It's almost never possible to know at what exact hour of what precise day an event began, be it even the clearest event. . . . And if it isn't a matter of a definitive event but, rather, of a situation, even less so—the decline of a family, let's say. At what time does it begin, on what date is it consummated? What signs, what signals mark it?
What everyone must do for himself, then, is choose an image.

He goes about the business, in his dying moments, of stringing together the images to which each member of his family has clung in order to try to create some overall narrative that will explain his final predicament: when hard times first come upon the family because of his uncle's gambling, and the English tea garden goes to seed; the time the reality of suburbia's press upon them makes itself grotesquely evident by the appearance of a fetus in the family's mailbox; the selling of the family Panhard (an automotive status symbol); and finally, under Bob's regime, the auctioning of the family furniture. At every turn, he had watched as these events were explained as the result of some external force, *la deca*, as if it were forced upon them from without. Eugenio had positioned himself in his family as if he were an observer and not a participant of this process that had them in its clutches. He lived by pointing his finger at them silently, assuming—mistakenly, as Bob's later candor reveals—that they were unaware of the truth within:

> esta gente va a arruinarse (como si él no fuera uno entre esta gente), esta gente va a arruinarse y esa ruina por suerte no va a alcanzarte, no va a arrastrarte, no va a degradarte como a Bob. (94)

> these people are going to be their own ruin (as if he himself were not one of these people), these people are going to be their own ruin and, luckily, that ruin is not going to reach you, is not going to drag you with it, is not going to degrade you as it has degraded Bob.

Even so, however, as the objective narrator's parenthesis here suggests, Eugenio senses that his posture is a false one: "Pero era—lo sabía muy bien—un falso consuelo, un resguardo vacío" ("But it was—he knew it very well—a false comfort, an empty defense") (94). He has lived in a fantasy of Otherness: "Muchas veces quise o pensé cambiarme por otro, fútilmente" ("Many times I wished or planned to change myself into someone else, uselessly") (113). By that denial, by pretending and not acting, he has ended up, as Ravazzani states, literally stuck in time. Eugenio is himself impaled by the family *quinta's* boundaries: "Los personajes centrales están clavados en su sitio, uno postrado por el sueño y la borrachera (Bob) y el otro desangrándose" ("The central characters are nailed in place, one prostrated by a drunken sleep [Bob] and the other bleeding to death") (Ravazzani 1981, 67).

The implication that this oxymoronic stasis-in-motion has for the narrative as a whole, however, is perhaps the most interesting

6: *Con las primeras luces:* The Darkness before the Dawn

aspect of the novel, next to the grotesque image of the agonizing Eugenio himself. As it displays the characteristics of Eugenio's life and death in its very structure, it is a narrative that does not move in a linear fashion. Indeed, it does not go anywhere. As Ravazzani puts it:

> No es un relato lineal. Deteniendo el lente en distintos objetos nos va haciendo partícipes de todos los pormenores de esta familia. . . . Nos encontramos así en medio de una yuxtaposición de tiempos. (Ravazzani 1981, 67)
>
> Is is not a linear narrative. Lingering with its lens on different objects it gradually makes us participants in all the foibles of this family. . . . We find ourselves, thus, in the midst of a juxtaposition of time frames.

The result is a difficult narrative in which setting and characterization both have a deliberately equivalent quality: objects, persons, and words have no hierarchical value. Time, past and present, is also causally meaningless. The novel's structure goes from object to person to words themselves, in the past and present, with a maddening circularity that is finally revealed to be the evolving figure of *la deca* itself. This clue to finding the novel's meaning in its structure is given to the reader by way of Eugenio himself, who observes that "todo el mundo parece suponer que las espirales tan sólo subieran . . . la espiral de la deca desciende, taladra, penetra" ("everyone seems to suppose that spirals only go upward . . . the spiral of *la deca* descends, drills, penetrates") (148).

Ravazzani betrays a sense of this spiraling dynamic in her study of *Luces*. Although she does not recognize it as the novel's overriding structure, the fact that she detects it in its language alone underlines the consistency with which Martínez Moreno maintains this motion-in-stasis on the novel's every level. As she says of Eugenio's final monologue:

> las ideas se van entremezclando y se salta del presente al pasado, de un momento a otro, simulando un torbellino que cada vez girara con más y más fuerza. De pronto, la calma se siente como algo tangible. . . . La muerte se acerca. (148)
>
> ideas intermingle, jumping from the present to the past and from one mment to another, simulating a whirlpool spinning round with ever more force. Suddenly, a tangible calm can be felt. . . . Death draws near.

Here, one finds that the many useful correspondences to be drawn between Mortimer's Faulkner in *As I Lay Dying* and Martínez Moreno's *Luces* end. Martínez Moreno has incorporated the strategies of Faulkner, whether knowingly or not, and carried them beyond anything hinted at in *As I Lay Dying*, refining them to an overall relationship of character and setting to a structure that goes beyond anything achieved in Faulkner's novel. As a result, Martínez Moreno has not written a novel about *la deca*, he has written a novel that *is la deca*, from its most comprehensive structural level down to its most subtle use of language.

Ravazzani has summarized the novel's organization:

> Desde el punto de vista externo, la novela se divide en treinta y dos cuadros, seis de los cuales son monólogos interiores en el que el 'yo' es Eugenio Escudero. Si numeramos estos cuadros, tenemos que los monólogos están colocados en orden I, IV, XI, XVIII, XXVI, y XXXII. (Ravazzani 1981, 55)

> From the external point of view, the novel is divided into thirty-two scenes, six of which are interior monologues in which the first-person narrator is Eugenio Escudero. If we number these scenes, we find tht the monologues are placed in order I, IV, XI, XVIII, XXVI, and XXXII.

In between these monologues, she observes,

> un narrador omnisciente se entretiene paseando su cámara ciematográfica por los distintos ambientes de la vieja quinta y hablándole directamente al lector. (Ravazzani 1981, 66)

> an omniscient narrator amuses himself by running the lens of his movie camera through the various rooms of the old estate while addressing himself directly to the reader.

The effect of these shifts between the limited intradiegetic focalization of Eugenio in his monologues and that of the passages between them is that

> permite dar credibilidad a lo dicho por Eugenio en su desvarío agónico. . . . Eugenio distorsiona los hechos en un intento muy humano de autojustificación. . . . [E]sta falta de imparcialidad se corrige con los comentarios de ese narrador que, desde lo alto, se interna alternativamente en el pasado lejano, en el inmediato, y aún dentro de Bob. (Ravazzani 1981, 72)

> it permits him to lend credibility to the words of Eugenio in his agonized ramblings. . . . Eugenio distorts the facts in a very human

6: *Con las primeras luces:* The Darkness before the Dawn

attempt at self-justification. . . . [T]his lack of impartiality is corrected by the commentary of that narrator who, from on high, penetrates into the distant past, the immediate present, and even inside Bob.

Yet, though Ravazzani clearly ennumerates the elements that make up the narrative, she does not recognize the overall figure that his monologue/narrative juxtaposition produces. As each "autojustificación" on the part of Eugenio attempts to put forward a reason that would give meaning to his admittedly absurd life and death, it is corrected in a way that returns it to its beginning and demands that he dig deeper, penetrate himself, for another.

This painful process produces a reader identification with Eugenio as he or she experiences a frustrating process parallel to Eugenio's own: a race against time to find a justification for this predicament as the wound, the trace left by the fence spike, bores itself more and more deeply into him, emptying him of life as the novel is consumed by the reader. As Eugenio describes it, the experience of death as a spiral, a screwlike boring into something—the motion of *la deca*—becomes one with the sensation of the spike that has penetrated him in the groin. This is the subject of his monologues. His body has become an object penetrated by that contradictory motion of dying, of becoming static. As Eugenio tries to create a context from each of his memories, a container for creating meaning around his imminent death, it is emptied by the omniscient narrator's objectivity, forcing Eugenio to try again as he sinks closer to oblivion. In addition to comparing himself to the milk bottle beside him, he speaks of his bleeding as maddeningly static: "dejándose chorrear hacia abajo, como la gota de resfrío balanceándose en la punta de la nariz en mi cara de chico, así gotea . . ." ("letting it dribble down like a drop balanced on my sniffly nose when I was a kid; that's how it drips away . . ." (8, ellipsis in original). This oxymoronic static motion of Eugenio's death is highlighted as his monologues are followed by descriptions such as that of the portrait of the family patriarch, General Escudero, which is also slowly and quietly decomposing on the other side of the door against which Eugenio lies bleeding. The portrait, an inanimate object, also appears at first glance to be intact, but is really, on closer investigation

> deteriorándose y como afantasmándose, amalgamándose en una apacible mancha confusa, dejándose ganar por una impudicia anacrónica . . . en que viborean las venitas del tiempo, esa delicada muerte varicosa. (14).

deteriorating and becoming phantomlike, blending into a placid, confused stain, allowing itself to be won over by an anachronistic impudence . . . in which the little veins of time snake in a delicate, varicose dance of death.

The careful parallel in language, both on the overall and immediate levels, is amazing. The verb "viborean" ("snake") evokes the spiral motion of the novel itself just as "las venitas del tiempo" ("little veins of time"), Eugenio's own hemorrhaging, denotes a "delicada muerte varicosa" ("delicate varicose death").

This sort of self-conscious monologue appears six times in the novel. Thus, it could be said that, structurally, the novel is a spiral consisting of six circles, pointing toward a seventh that represents death. It is a six-part attempt at the recreation of a life, with rest,as in Genesis, on the seventh "day." The obvious irony is, of course, that this recreation of a life is really the preparation for death, the final rest. Yet the Genesis analogy holds if one remembers the ironic hope in the novel's title, *Con las primeras luces*. It is a negative Genesis, mirroring hopes of a positive one to come.

It is particularly interesting that Martínez Moreno should use the figure of the spiral in *Luces* to illustrate the process of *la deca*. As Martínez Moreno is a transitional figure from modernist conceptions of history toward a more postmodern conception, it is possible that *Luces*, in 1966, augurs the advent of a movement in philosophy that conceives of reality in a way similar to that portrayed in Eugenio's agony. In the work *Margins of Philosophy*, a book that many point to as a signpost of the passage from structuralism to poststructuralism, Jacques Derrida coincides with Martínez Moreno in the figure he chooses for his critique of philosophy: a spiral. The first essay of his book, "Tympan," announces its purpose to be "To tympanize—philosophy." The translator of the text adds the note that "in French, *tympanisesr* is an archaic verb meaning to criticize" (Derrida 1982, x, footnote 1). As a novelist of Uruguay's *Generación crítica*, one could argue that to "tympanize" is also Martínez Moreno's purpose, to "tympanize" the view of reality that has resulted in *la deca* and, in *Luces*, to its most grotesque manifestation.

Furthermore, alongside his "tympanizing" of philosophy, Derrida juxtaposes in the margins a long text by Michel Leiris that consists of variations on spiraled objects that occur in nature. This supports the idea that Derrida, as he developed his argument, follows the spiraling structure of philosophical thought itself, boring, penetrating into it like an "earwig" (Derrida 1982, xiii). A

6: *Con las primeras luces:* The Darkness before the Dawn

further observation he draws from the word *tympan* is the dual role as boundary and conduit played by the tympanum, the ear drum. Thus, he draws from his word *tympan* ironies similar to those Martínez Moreno draws from Eugenio's situation. *La deca* is a spiral. Eugenio's agony is a six-layered spiral of monologues and narration moving downward toward a death not actually portrayed in the novel. The fence that served as a boundary, as protection against the outside world, kills him. The true meaninglessness of his life's philosophy bores into him by its agency as he dies, "deconstructing" his life as he awaits death. Derrida speaks of deconstruction as the "systematic unity of a spiral" that never ends. Likewise, one could speak of Eugenio's death as an agonizing deconstruction. Not only is it a deconstruction of the denial that has led the Escudero family to ruin, it is, by extension, a deconstruction of the "genteel barbarism"—also seen in *Los aborígenes*—to which they cling, the nineteenth-century modernist nations of linearity and localizing of enemies without that keep them from realizing, until too late, that their *deca* is a descending spiral of unpredictable twists and turns within them—not a controllable, predictable line of decline in the outside world upon which they can plot their irresponsibility so as to avoid its consequences in their own generation.

The passing of Eugenio implies the need for a new way of thinking that at least recognizes the nonlinear relationship of past to present and the localizing of *la deca's* malaise as an internal condition, not an external one. The novel holds Eugenio and his family up as negative examples of how *not* to respond to *la deca*. For those willing to learn those examples' painful lessons there may be, as the title imlies, a new day. But such optimism can only be derived from the shared experience of Bob's long night of agony, a possible allegory of Ihab Hassan's declaration, only five years later, that

> the postmodern spirit lies coiled within the great corpus of modernism . . . gnawing at the nerve of certain authors, diverting others into mad experiments. It is not really a matter of chronology. . . . It may be rather a question of "Terrorism" . . . a sense that literary language can no longer carry the burden of consciousness, an intuition that culture can neither mediate nor contain. (Hassan 1971, 139)

It is not going too far to suggest that Martínez Moreno, in the case of *Luces*, wished to represent some sort of hope in that the process of *la deca* can serve as a coiled spring to propel the reader toward new postmodern modes of thought. But converting the static spiral of *la deca* into a dynamic spring with which to launch into the future implies tripping a trigger, a release—releasing old habits of thought before it is too late. Martínez Moreno's "terrorism" lies in maintaining before the reader the agony of a man killed by his own clinging to the constructs he inherited from a previous generation, a view he had not built himself in his own lifetime, and which he recognized, too late, as inadequate for describing his reality.

7
Coca: Cupid, Cocaine, and Military Corruption

After plumbing the depths of *la deca* in his experimental novel of 1966, *Con las primeras luces*, Martínez Moreno comes forth with a much more accessible novel in his fourth effort, *Coca* (1970). In contrast to *Luces*, which had no structural subsidivions at all to guide the reader through its spiraling monologues and flashbacks, *Coca* (Cocaine) is a relatively transparent synthesis of elements seen individually in his previous novels. It resembles the structure of his novella *Cordelia*, fragmenting the narrative's focalization chapter by chapter, giving each of its characters a chance to narrate his or her version of the central event, the arrest of a Bolivian diplomat, in Montevideo, for drug smuggling.

This diplomat, the novel's protagonist, is himself of the age and mentalityy of a character seen before in Martínez Moreno's novel *El paredón*. In *El paredón*, Julio Calodoro is a young man whose life has been molded for him and who seeks to assert himself in a search for some alternative only to decide, at the novel's end, "que todo siga como está" (that everything should go on as it is). *Coca*'s protagonist, known only to the reader as the Captain, could be said to be a Julio Calodoro with whom events have caught up. A passive survivor both of a revolution and an unhappy arranged marriage, the Captain's *quietista* (quietist) approach to life fails him when he finds he has allowed himself to drift to the center of a cocaine smuggling ring and is caught in Montevideo on his first trip in that trade.

If we have seen the Captain's *quietismo* before in *El paredón*, we are also reminded of other Martínez Moreno characters as well. The Captain is also much like Primitivo, the elderly, self-exiled diplomat in *Los aborígenes* in his nationality and status as a diplomat estranged from his country. Primitivo, like the Captain in *Coca*, is a man at a loss to find a role for himself in the course of

Bolivian history—specifically, the Revolution of 1952. As a third party's retrospective investigation into a crime involving a love triangle, the novel itself bears some similarity to *La otra mitad*, although here the third party, the couple's lawyer, is much less involved than was Mario Possenti, whose involvement with that novel's female protagonist influenced its central event.

Yet even as the novel's craftsmanship reveals a synthetic sophistication on the part of a novelist confident of being at the peak of his powers, it nonetheless lacks the depth of his previous efforts. However, the author admits that such is the case. According to Martínez Moreno, in the case of *Coca* he set out, for the first time in his career, to write "un entretenimiento latinoamericano al estilo de Graham Greene . . . una obra distensiva . . . contar una historia por la historia misma" ("a Latin-American entertainment in the style of Graham Greene . . . a distended work . . . to tell the story for the story's own sake") (Ravazzani 1981, 122). The result is, as reviewer Wolfgang Luchting put it, a novel that is "circumstantially about what is probably the least likely trio of 'dope-pushers' that ever wandered through reality or fiction," one that is a "very civilized novel" and "a pleasure to read" (Luchting 1971, 488–89).

It is, of course, more than that. Even in turning from heavy experimentation to entertainment in the novel form, Martínez Moreno does not abandon his major theme, *la deca,* and its attendant treatment. In fact, one could possibly argue that *Coca* is the author's most effective novel, were it not for the unfortunate epilogue, which mars the novel's ending. In this epilogue, it appears as if Martínez Moreno, in a highly uncharacteristic instance of didacticism that does not display his usual respect for the reader, felt the need to add on an explicit message to his carefully crafted entertainment.

Still, as Luchting observes, *Coca* is "an admirable display of narrative techniques" in which "the shifting point of view is superbly handled and, above all and in contrast with so many recent abuses of it, always organically justified." In addition, he writes, "as always in Martínez Moreno's writing, the psychological subtlety is remarkable, the language is supple, the humor unobtrusive" (Luchting 1971, 488). Even as slightly flawed entertainment, *Coca* is an enviable piece of work.

The "psychological subtlety" to which Luchting alludes applies to a cast of characters larger than the two or three found in any of Martínez Moreno's previous novels. Here we have a cast of twelve characters, each of whom merits the dedication of at least

7: *Coca:* Cupid, Cocaine, and Military Corruption

one of the novel's twenty chapters to him or herself. Foremost among the dozen, of course, is the "unlikely trio" central to the novel's plot: the Captain, the novel's cocaine-smuggling diplomat; Marie-Louise, his mistress and accomplice; and Marcel, a chronic fugitive and smuggler who is at once their co-conspirator and Marie-Louise's ex-husband by common law.

Of the three, the Captain is the most important to the novel's plot and thematic development, and yet he is the least preisely characterized of all. As Ana-María Ravazzani puts it, "para recalcar la nebulosidad de este personaje, el autor ni siquiera le da un nombre" (in order to underscore the nebulous nature of this character, the author doesn't so much as give him a name) (Ravazzani 1981, 147). This lack of definition is what marks him as the novel's most truly *deca* character.

Like Eugenio in *Luces,* the Captain is a man who allows his life to be guided by the decisions of others. As a youth, he was passive in the selection of a career: "había elegido—o dejado que madre y tío eligieran por él—precisamente la carrera de las armas" ("he had chosen—or allowed his mother and his uncle to choose for him—precisely a career in the military") (Martínez Moreno 1970, 20). Entering the military at that moment of Bolivian history, as popular discontent built up toward the Revolution of 1952, was not a situation for the sheltered and noncommitted. His genteel naiveté is disrupted by a rude awakening to the polarized conditions under which the country lives:

> [E]l joven y tierno aspirante a soldado se sinitió sobrecogido de que tan cerca de él y de todos los suyos, envolviéndolos sin que se dieran cuenta, ocurriesen hechos que merecieran frases tan impresionantes. . . . ¿De modo que el país se dividía trágicamente en dos partes, los que debían matar y los que debían morir? . . . Todo parecía a un país que él nunca había llegado a conocer bien. (20)

> [T]he young and tender aspiring soldier felt overcome with the fact that, so close to him and his and enveloping them without their even knowing it, events were taking place that deserved such impressive phrases. . . . So the country was tragically divided in two halves—those whose duty it was to kill and those whose duty it was to die? . . . Everything looked as if it came from a country that he had never gotten to know all that well.

Nonetheless, even though his experiences as a cadet reveal to him the extent of his alienation from the forces at work in the society around him, this awareness brings about no decisiveness, no act or even sense of commitment from him. Instead, he attempts an impossible feat of passivity—that is, to avoid compromising circumstances in a moment of turmoil. Passivity has its price, however, since as a member of the military his attempt to remain untouched by the events around him is akin to one attempting to find shelter in the eye of a hurricane. Before long, he is literally caught in the crossfire upon each other in the capital, for reasons he never understands and which are never revealed to the reader. He is wounded, and the resulting limp serves from then on to remind the reader of the fragile absurdity of the Captain's attempt to live a life of passivity in a politicized military:

> herido a los veinte y siete sin estar convencido de que debiera haber dado el cuerpo ni la vida por nada o por nadie . . . tenía por dentro otra historiq que aquélla que narraban los hechos del país. (21)

> wounded at the age of twenty-seven without ever having been convinced that it was his duty to give his body or his life for anything or anyone . . . he carried within him a history different from that which narrated the events of the country.

Career, however, is not the only major area of his life that he leaves to the discretion of his family: his marriage is arranged as well. Like Primitivo in *Los aborígenes,* after a "noviazgo colonial" ("colonial courtship"), the Captain submits dutifully to a marriage of convenience to an aristocratic daughter of the oligarchy, "no consultado acerca si quería u odiaba lo que estaba una vez más por imponérsele desde afuera" ("not consulted as to whether he loved or hated what was once again about to be imposed on him from without") (21).

Though politically noncommitted, married into the aristocracy, and a member of the military, the Captain, despite one's plausible expectations to the contrary, is no amoral Machiavelli; this is not a stereotypical tale of military corruption, as one might expect from a novel about a cocaine-smuggling Bolivian army officer. Both cocaine and the politico-military events of the novel are incidental to what operates beneath the surface of the novel's main characters: a profound sense of alienation from conflicts that impinge upon them. Against these superimposed role definitions, the protagonists seek a secet revenge by way of entering the drug trade; only incidentally do their personal actions gain political significance as well.

In such bold characterization against type lies the key to Martínez Moreno's masterful sense of irony, which he is able to bring

7: *Coca:* Cupid, Cocaine, and Military Corruption

to all of his social and/or political situations. In the conclusion to her study of *Coca*, Ana-María Ravazzani notes and astutely summarizes the intermingling of personal and sociopolitical levels achieved in the work:

> el autor ha logrado su propósito: utilizar el concepto de destilación para presentar algunos de los graves problemas que aquejan a la sociedad como si fueran rasgos personales o una peripecia circunstancial. (Ravazzani 1981, 148)

> the author has achieved his purpose: to use the concept of distillation to present a few of the serious problems that trouble society as if they were personal traits or a matter of a sudden, circumstancial change of fortune.

Martínez Moreno does this so effectively that the reader, in the process of reading *Coca,* may be led to question ever having had any other hypothetical explanation of how social problems are caused. The novelist's ability to bridge personal and social aspects of reality in his works is the most distinguishing characteristic of his canon. That ability in evidence in *Coca,* just as it was, for example, in *El paredón*. However, in the case of *Coca* as well as that of *El paredón,* criticism has adhered more closely to sociohistorical approaches to Martínez Moreno's works. Consequently, more attention has been devoted to the analysis of the historical situations depicted in his novels than to an analysis of the disturbingly complex characters with whom readers are confronted.

The result is an analysis that gives short shrift to Martiínez Moreno's careful, incisive, psychological portrayal of characters struggling with the sociohistorical implications of *la deca* as human beings, and not as types. In *Coca,* the Captain is a character who bears the external characteristics that fit stereotypical definitions of the "prototipo de la oligarquía" (prototype of the oligarchy), as Ravazzani describes him. Nonetheless, the internal aspects of his characterization far transcend such easy stereotyping (Ravazzani 1981, 148). This is not to say that the novel is meant to be a vindication of characters such as those represented by the Captain and Marie-Louise, his lover and accomplice in crime. There can be no question, however, that Martínez Moreno meant, as he tells us through Marie-Louise, that he, like the character of the narrator, has meant to "escribir sin tocarnos, dejándonos ilesos. 'Ilesos e ilusos,' bromeó usted esa vez" (write without touching us, leaving us unhurt. 'Unhurt and deluded,' you had once joked) (219). That he does. Rather than deliver "prototipos," he does on a smaller scale something similar to what Mario Vargas Llosa did in a novel only a year earlier, *Conversación en la Catedral* (Conversation in the cathedral): he shows how actions with tragic sociopolitical consequences can be rooted in very complex personal motives, hidden both to the apologist and the armchair moralizer.

Thus, the author pares judgments regarding his characters down to their basic elements, and deals with stereotypical situations in the same way. By using a fragmented narrative, he requires the reader to reconstruct the "rasgos personales" ("personal traits") and "peripecias circunstanciales" ("sudden, circumstancial changes in fortune"). As the reader does so, the reader is in the unusual position of being party to the construction of a challenge to his or her own expectations. If that challenge includes having to accept sharp contradictions between the external and internal elements of the Captain's characterization, Martínez Moreno reminds us that it is human nature to behave in ways that are often illogical and contradictory. As *Coca*'s narrator, a character Martínez Moreno admits was based on his own role as a defense attorney in Montevideo, puts it when interrogating a minor character implicated in the Captain's arrest for cocaine smuggling:

> Usted me pregunta si lo encuentro lógico, yo contesto que no y usted supone que mi respuesta lo absuelve. Y ahora podría preguntarle yo: ¿usted está seguro de no haber hecho jamás algo ilógico en su vida? . . . ¡Contésteme! (154)
>
> You ask me if I find it logical. I reply that I don't and so you suppose that my answer absolves you. And now I could ask you: Are you sure you've never done anything illogical in your entire life? . . . Answer me!

As he did with his deep psychological portrayal of Julio before the complexities of the Cuban revolution in *El paredón*, in *Coca*, Martínez Moreno sets out, once again, to take a politically-charged setting and character situation and bridge its personal and social significance. Thus, in spite of the important part political events play in the novel's development of its characters—particularly in the development of the Captain—this novel is not primarily political. Political events serve as a polarizing backdrop, an external set of historical conflicts that bear little relevance to the internal agendas of the protagonists. They are not mere vil-

7: *Coca:* Cupid, Cocaine, and Military Corruption

lains but rather characters who are frustrated in their weak attempts to deal with the corrosive influence of *la deca* upon their lives.

This characterization is just as true for Marie-Louise, the Captain's mistress and main accomplice, as it is for him. As the Captain is still essentially a body who has refused to grow up to a world of arbitrarily divided suffering for which he is expected to accept responsibility, Marie-Louise is essentially still a frightened child seeking to forget an intimate experience with horror. As an adolescent, she lost her first love and closest friend to Gestapo torture in France, during World War II, and took comfort in escaping with the first man who showed an interest in her. In her haste to flee the horror of the war, she discovers—too late—that she has actually married herself to it. Her lover is a Nazi-sympathizing war criminal. By aiding his escape, she has doomed herself to living with the very memories she sought to leave behind. Eventually, her life in the underworld leads her to the Captain and the Bolivian drug trade.

The circumstances of the Captain's journey to that same point are different, but his motives are the same. He falls into disgrace and prison on his very first bumbling attempt to extract any advantage from his position as a privileged diplomat. Furthermore, as the reporting of his own innermost thoughts reveals, he himself recognizes that he is incapable of such clever manipulation, because of mere incompetence if for no other reason. At the novel's climax, he is hiding in a public toilet, clutching his packet of cocaine while a police dragnet circles around him in the streets. He then realizes that he has always suffered from a "lucidez tardía . . . que le permitía juntar las piezas del rompecabezas cuando otros ya lo habían sacado y abandonado" ("late lucidity . . . that permitted him to put the pieces of the puzzle together only when everyone else had solved it and left") (123). The Captain is interesting as a character precisely because, although corrupt, he is very bad at being corrupt.

Thus, the Captain and Marie-Louise are joined by the fact that both have a deep need to redeem themselves by betraying those whom they have passively obeyed. They share a desire to break the bonds of relationships in which they have consistently betrayed themselves by allowing others to define them. Cocaine and the military, society and politics, are clearly secondary to the personal purpose of their crime. As Marie-Louise comments to the narrator on the novel's last page:

> Usted me dijo un día . . . lo recuerdo muy bien, que la verdadera mercadería que nosotros dos habíamos contrabandeado, en toda nuestra historia, no era tanto la coca sino, inconfesablemente, el amor. (220)
>
> You told me one day . . . —I remember it very well—that the actual merchandise that we two had smuggled in all our story together was not cocaine but, unspeakably, love.

However, their love is not one born so much out of desire for each other as out of a mutual need to escape the personal circumstances that they have tolerated too long. The Captain seeks to escape his wife and the responsibilities of the oligarchy she represents; Marie-Louise seeks to escape Marcel and the guilty association he represents for her. Too late, they both come to see that their externalized rage was misdirected: their failure is an apt fulfillment of a destructive self-loathing created by a tendency toward passivity. As Marie-Louise tells the lawyer-narrator after her arrest, that propensity to deny responsibility for her own identity was there even before her childhood friend's untimely death. When they played games, she would impose upon them "una extraña condición de participar sin sentirlo" ("a strange condition of participating without feeling it") in much the same way the Captain attempted to conform to his family's career plans for him without commitment or conviction of his own. Too late, she recognizes that such an (in)action

> empieza haciendo la generosidad y hasta una forma del amor y termina siendo la hipocresía y la antipática pasividad en nuestra vida de adutos. . . . Porque pienso que, de entonces a hoy, he seguido del mismo modo otros sueños que no eran míos y que no han sido siquiera tan inocentes . . . y he trabajado en escenarios que yo no he elegido y me he prestado a gestos, movimientos y palabras que imperceptiblemente me han sido dictados por un apuntador egoísta y monstruoso, o dictados no por una determinada persona sino por todas, por las circunstancias, por el instinto femenino de avenirme a otros gustos como si fuesen los míos. (191)
>
> begins with generosity and even a certain form of love and, in our adult lives, ends in hypocrisy and passive resentment. . . . Because I believe, in the very same way, that from that day till now I have followed dreams that weren't mine and that weren't even all that innocent . . . and I have worked on stages I haven't chosen and lent myself to gestures, movements, and words that were being imperceptibly dictated to me by some monstrous and egotistical prompter, or dic-

7: *Coca:* Cupid, Cocaine, and Military Corruption

tated to me not by any person in particular but by everyone, by circumstances, by the feminine instinct of reconciling myself to other tastes as if they were my own.

The mistaking of this mutual need for actual love was foreshadowed from the very moment Marie-Louise and the Captain cuckolded their respective spouses and began their illicit adventure. When they declare their feelings for each other, Marie-Louise's love is framed in terms of helping, of aiding the Captain in some way that isn't even clear to her at the time.

> ¿Por qué dijo "ayudarlo"? Se lo preguntó después muchas veces, pero la elección del verbo había sido tan repentina como infalible: ayudarlo porque él era el más débil . . . ayudarlo porque . . . era la forma en que ella concebía el amor y nunca le habían dejado practicarlo. (57–58)

> Why did she say "help him"? She asked herself that later many times, but the choice of verb had been as sudden as infallible: help him because he was the weaker one . . . help him because . . . it was the manner in which she conceived of love and no one had ever let her practice it on anyone before.

Indeed, what had attracted Marie-Louise to the Captain in the first place had been what she perceived as a need, a vulnerability in which she might be able to find a useful role for herself, something she had not been able to do with the secretive, war-hardened Marcel. She admires the "estructura casi aniñada de ese cuerpo" ("almost childlike structure of that body") as well as the childlike quality of his voice, "llena de una titubeante escoria infantil" ("so full of an infantile, tottering residue") (50). To her, the Captain represents a contrast to a man with whom she has lived in silent obedience, a man who has always treated her as if she were a child, never making her party to either his plans or his feelings, a man who arranged an abortion for her and beat her almost mechanically so she would remember to never become pregnant again.

Just as quickly as she attains the role she seeks with the Captain, however, its attraction becomes somewhat tarnished for her. He is, indeed, a contrast with Marcel; from a chauvinistic father-figure, she has gone to the other extreme. As the consequences of their affair become clear—the Captain loses his diplomatic commission as retaliation from his powerful wife—he responds with a typical passivity that begins to earn him her contempt. In the same way that he allowed his marriage to be arranged for the convenience of others, he doesn't even participate in his own divorce proceedings, allowing the ambassador at his post in Buenos Aires to mediate for him like a "señor feudal" ("feudal lord") (63). With unemployment and the Captain's divorce drying up their funds, Marie-Louise begins to see the Captain's endearing meekness for what it really is: an unwillingness to assume responsibility. Her attitude toward his passivity turns sour. When Marcel realizes what is happening between her and the Captain, he drops his aloof demeanor only once to comment upon the man to whom he was to lose his passionless arrangement:

> hizo un comentario de los que nunca hacía; dijo que el Capitán era un tipo de esos tantos nativos triviales que en América Latina pueden llegar a generales o doctores, y que en Europa no podrían estar al frente de una panadería. (52)

> he made the kind of comment he never made; he said that the Captain was one of those many trivial natives who in Latin America can become doctors or generals and who in Europe wouldn't even be allowed near the front counter of a bakery.

When events force her to recast her image of the Captain, Marie-Louise comes to the same conclusion regarding his character. Unfortunately, rather than confront him about it, an act that could allow the possibility of some sort of change, she attributes it, as Marcel did, to racial characteristics, a sort of hereditary fatalism based on cultural stereotypes that, ironically, absolves him of responsibility yet again: "El Capitán, como buen sudamericano, prefirió siempre que Cada Día fuera Cada Día" ("The Captain, good South American that he was, always preferred that Every Day be Every Day") (64).

There is a further irony here in that the criticism dealing with *Coca* seems to have ignored the fact that this is the first instance of a constant recourse to cultural stereotype in the novel. The recourse to cultural chauvinism is used by each character in turn, attempting to absolve him- or herself from guilt. In his ironic portrayal of this chauvinism, Martínez Moreno seems to call for the assumption of personal responsibility rather than the use of what he calls in the novel "sociología de bolsillo" ("paperback sociology") to explain it away. However, criticism on the novel—even though it is largely based on a sociohistorical hermeneutic—seems to choose to take it literally, ignoring its ironic use. Ravazzani writes of the couple that "ambos se lanzan a vivir la aventura

7: *Coca:* Cupid, Cocaine, and Military Corruption

que les depara el destino. El, en forma apática, típica de la idiosincrasia de su raza" ("they each launch out to live the adventure that destiny would prepare for them. He, apathetically and typically, given the idiosyncrasy of his race") (Ravazzai 1981, 141). Given that Martínez Moreno parodies such an explanation for his character's actions in the novel, such a critical appraisal of their motives is difficult to defend. The character who offers such an analysis of the motives for the novel's crime, "El Abogado de Buenos Aires" ("The Buenos Aires Lawyer") is portrayed as an unprincipled attorney. His only interest is to curry favor with the story's narrator, the Captain's defense attorney, so as to distance his client, the Captain's smuggling patron and boss in Buenos Aires, General Ichazo, from the cocaine smuggling operation. Thus, it is difficult to see how his "sociología de bolsillo" (paperback sociology) could be taken as a literal appraisal of the characters' motives.

> Usted sabe cómo es esta gente, no son como nosotros . . . nunca van más allá del día en que viven. . . . Allá la vida vale menos que la muerte. . . . Aunque nosotros, en el Río de la Plata, tengamos que hacer un esfuerzo de abstracción para pensar seriamente en América Latino como un todo del que seamos parte . . . porque somos más complejos. (194)

> You know what these people are like. They're not like us. . . . (T)hey never see beyond the day in which they are living. . . . There life is worth less than death. . . . Although we, in the River Plate, have to make an effort of abstract intellect to think seriously about Latin America as a whole of which we are a part . . . because we are more complex.

Such patent snobbery is in no way meant to be taken seriously, particularly when the lawyer sums up his argument to absolve his client of any responsibility in the matter by appealing to his "indiosincrasia" (literally, the neologism "indiosyncrasy") (194). It should be obvious that any "esfuerzo de abstracción" ("effort of abstract intellect") he actually makes use of serves to abstract his client from the damning facts, and not in any way to reach an understanding of the motives underlying the crime that has taken place. The irony here is intended to portray how both Europeans and Latin Americans, both damned by their own actions, point to external factors such as cultural differences to explain away their actions rather than to internal factors that would require them to accept personal responsibility. As Bob admits in

Con las primeras luces, la deca is a matter of an internal "derrumbe" (collapse) that occurs when one's ossified denial system, a clinging to inherited preconceived notions, is forced to concede to the pressures of a changing reality which it cannot withstand.[1] Cultural stereotyping permits the characters to persevere in their beliefs that their mistakes are not their own, but products of forces beyond their control, even though they never make any effort to challenge those forces themselves. Instead, they prefer to be vindicated by their self-fulfilling prophecies, even when those prophecies result in self-destruction. Such rationalized denial is central to *la deca*, in Martínez Moreno's characters from Robledo of *Cordelia* on; it is no different here, except that the denial here appears defined in culturally chauvinistic terms.

Such chauvinism is used to show how the characters attempt to mask what the novel itself terms the "bovarysmo de Marie-Louise" ("the Bovary-ism of Marie-Louise"), a woman always searching for that magically-emancipating partner, and the passivity of the Captain himself, who drifts through life on the current of *la deca* in a way no different from what Eugenio did in *Con las primeras luces* (56). Like Eugenio, however, the Captain comes to a moment of self-recognition that forces him to reflect upon his life and its failures, not as a result of external forces, but as a result of an internal one: cowardice. Like Eugenio's moment, this moment of self-recognition comes too late and is depicted as absurd and grotesque, though not quite as grotesque as the image of Eugenio stabbed in the groin by his own carelessness. Here, the moment occurs as the Captain hides with his package of cocaine in a public restroom, literally defecating from fear.

> Entró al retrete . . . el Capitán en lo oscuro, el Capitán en lo sucio, el Capitán en lo maloliente, en lo amoniacal, en lo lóbrego, sujetándose los faldones de la camisa, sintiéndose chicoteado en el rostro por las puntas de su corbata, acucurrado, atento a las feroces explosiones de su vientre. (132)

> He went into the restroom . . . the Captain in the dark, the Captain in the filth, the Captain in the stench, reeking of ammonia in the gloom, holding on to the tails of his shirt, feeling the tips of his tie whip him about the face, squatting, attentive to every one of the ferocious explosions of his bowels.

In his demeaning position, the Captain comes to recognize that this, "cagado de miedo" ("shitting himself with fear"), is the controlling pattern of his life. He realizes, as does Marie-Louise in

7: *Coca:* Cupid, Cocaine, and Military Corruption

her explanation of her childhood games, that he has always been willing to play a part in someone else's plan rather than to devise some plan of his own for his life, all for fear of what others might think of him if he made decisions that ran contrary to their expectations. He reflects back on key points in this pattern of cowardice, and, remembering another time when he had had a case of diarrhea out of fear when he was a cadet, he devised a symbol for himself—a rooster. Every explosion of his bowels on that day had been punctuated by the crowing of a rooster nearby, a comedy that had set a local girl to laughing at him, much to his chagrin. As he crouches in this public lavatory in Montevideo, years later, he feels he can hear the rooster crowing again, and knows that he will not do the sensible thing—discard the evidence of his crime, the cocaine, down the toilet—for fear of being laughed at by Marie-Louise. He also remembers that when he was wounded in the crossfire of the revolution he was in front of the "Gallo de Oro" ("Golden Rooster"), a restaurant in La Paz. When he leaves the package of cocaine with an unwitting pharmacist later on and returns to reclaim it, he realizes that his paranoid manner "era como dibujar otro gallo" ("was akin to another sketch of a rooster") (141). He is, by his own definition, what one could vulgarly term a "chickenshit."

Yet he also recognizes that this condition is not his alone; he is part of a generation of disenchanted elite who, rather than face their disillusion and reassess their failures, would rather hide behind a mask of fatalistic and decadent postures, blinding themselves to the consequences. As he sits on the public toilet, he remembers a story, told to him many times by the ambassador, of the death of the Peruvian poet, Abraham Valdelomar. Valdelomar was an Oscar Wildeish character who was a favorite guest at cocktail parties in Lima due to his polished repertoire of decadent poses; he died at one of these parties, victim of a rotten outhouse seat.

> —Ahogado en la mierda vestido de frac,—concluía siempre el Embajador, como si fuera un versículo ritual, al final de un apólogo, la alegoría del destino de nuestros países o del destino de los poetas y de los intelectuales en nuestros países. (136)

> "Drowned in shit, dressed in a coat and tails," the Ambassador always concluded, as if it were a ritual verse at the end of an apology, the allegorical destiny of all our countries or the destiny of all the poets and intellectuals of our countries.

To the Captain it is "como si esa historia de retretes fuera una cifra simbólica de esa pobre América pobre en que él vivía" ("as if that story of restrooms were a symbolic cipher of that poor, poor America in which he lives") (134). In *Los aborígenes,* Martínez Moreno had written of Primitivo, the novella's protagonist, and his desire to write of "el drama de las clases cultas, el aislamiento y la incomunicación de las élites en esta nuestra América Española" ("the drama of the cultured classes, the isolation and the lack of communication of the elites in this our Spanish America") (58). In his novels written since that speculation, that is in part the problem to which he addresses himself: the drama of the elite, aware of its own outmoded ideas and its own decadence, confronted with the need for alternatives. In *Coca,* he develops his image of an elite in distress as finally drowning in its own excrement.

The novel is centered around that grotesque scene structurally as well as thematically. This scene, which appears in the eleventh of the novel's twenty chapters, is central to explaining the motives of the Captain and how he and his small ring of smugglers came to be in the predicament in which they find themselves as the novel opens; i.e., under arrest for drug trafficking. In the ten chapters leading up to this scene, Martínez Moreno has described the Captain's drifting passage through Bolivia's military academy, his passive consent to an arranged marriage, and the detachment from events in the Revolution of 1952 that resulted in his getting caught in a crossfire and wounded. His need for physical therapy has led, by the influence of his wife's powerful family, to an appointment in Buenos Aires as a superfluous military attaché. In like manner, the chapters preceding the central scene in the toilet in Montevideo supplied the reader with a summary of Marie-Louise's life before her involvement with the Captain. In those chapters, Marie-Louise describes in her own words, presumably written down by her defense attorney, the story of how she met Marcel, the fugitive war criminal and smuggler who leads her into an underground life in Río, Chile, and with whom finally came to live in Buenos Aires, where she meets the Captain. The story of the couple's affair and its consequences is narrated in great detail. It develops from a chance acquaintance at a swimming pool, where the Captain is exercising to rehabilitate his wounded leg, to the point at which they each abandon their respective partners. Marcel, a hardened man of little feeling, easily relinquishes his hold on Marie-Louise and is willing to help in arranging the cocaine-smuggling deal through Montevideo. The

7: *Coca:* Cupid, Cocaine, and Military Corruption

Captain's wife, on the other hand, is not so indifferent to being spurned, and retaliates by having him relieved of his commission, again by the intervention of her family in Bolivia. It is in these circumstances that Marie-Louise, having long observed the smuggling trade in her years with Marcel, decides to take matters in her own hands. She decides upon the ill-fated business with cocaine which results in the Captain's predicament in Montevideo.

What folllows the Captain's chapter in the toilet is a series of chapters representing, in various voices, depositions given to his lawyer, the Martínez Moreno character himself, all with the secondary characters' views of the events of that same day. All of these depositions intersect as the novel, in its next to last chapter, winds its way back to the narrative present depicted at the novel's outset; that is, the scene of the couple at their trial. Such a circular course takes the reader back to the novel's beginning, where the lawyer-narrator's own ruminations prefigure the course the novel has taken. As he shuffles the paper of the file on the case, the lawyer observes: "Vuelvo a las hojas del expediente, donde toda esta historia ya sabida y escrita da lentas, lentas vueltas, como en un vientre mitológico de ballena" ("I return to the pages of the file where this whole already known story lies written in its slow, slow turns, turns like the inside of the stomach of a whale") (14).

To the knowledgeable reader of Martínez Moreno's canon, this return is particularly significant, because as he or she mirrors the lawyer-narrator's observation on the story's movement, the pattern resembles one seen before in Martínez Moreno's fiction: the Derridean spiral of *la deca,* last seen in *Con las primeras luces.* In that novel, Eugenio's reflects on his life as he awaits death. Those reflections are structured in six descending spirals as he follows a dying deconstruction of his life to its morbid conclusion. In *Coca,* the novel's twenty chapters have, in the end, related in twelve versions the background and motives behind one man's moment of truth. On a "retrete" ("toilet") in Montevideo, the Captain, like Eugenio, sees the cowardly nature of his life flash before him, as the narrator states, in "lentas, lentas vueltas" ("slow, slow turns"), like the proverbial turns of the screw, and he sees no other recourse but to step forth and pay the consequences.

The resolution of those "lentas, lentas vueltas" is alluded to self-referentially as the trial scene of the next to last chapter progresses. The lawyer-narrator describes the judge's task regarding the different versions of the crime as a "trabajo estético de adecuación . . . de componer el puzzle, para luego mandar moler las piecitas y empezar otras historias" ("an aesthetic labor of adequation . . . of putting together a puzzle so as to send the pieces later to be ground down into bits and construct other stories") (202). When he has finished, the lawyer-narrator concludes: "Esta era la historia, según la quería cada uno, y así tendría en el tiempo que ser contada" ("This was the story as each one had wanted it, and this was how, in time, it would have to be told") (210). Martínez Moreno even indulges in a little self-congratulation as his fragmented "entertainment" comes to a clean resolution. As the chapter ends, the judge remarks to the lawyer-narrator: "Esto salió bien" ("This turned out rather well"). To which the lawyer-narrator adds, implying that said comment goes for the story itself: "Y no aludía al progreso judicial del asunto" ("And he wasn't referring to the judicial progress of the matter") (211).

Ravazzani has most aptly observed that here is where the novel should have ended. Martínez Moreno chose instead to include an epilogue, which contains a letter received by the lawyer-narrator from Marie-Louise eight years after the trial's conclusion. In the letter, Marie-Louise writes from yet another self-imposed exile in French Africa, after completing her prison sentence in Montevideo. The Captain has left her, she suspects, to return to his wife. Her letter expresses concern over an issue that was never raised in the course of the novel: the Bolivian drama of Che Guevara and his band of guerrillas, who were killed by the Bolivian military in 1967. The novel had addressed the role of the Bolivian military in that country's political life repeatedly, but being set in 1959, the revolution with which it dealt was that in which the Army had participated, the Revolution of 1952. It is never made clear how concern over Che Guevara relates to these issues. Ravazzani comments:

> Martínez Moreno no puede sustraerse a la tentación de clarificar el mensaje social y para hacerlo pone en la boca de la protagonista palabras que no cuadran con la sicología de Marie-Louise. . . . La Marie-Louise del epílogo es la antítesis de la del libro, para quien el Che o Debray no representan absolutamente nada. Nuestra heroína no ha vivido ninguna experiencia, por lo menos dentro de los límites de la novela, capaz de despertar su conciencia social. . . . [H]a ahondado un poco en el problema existencial de la soledad, . . . el amor, . . . [y] la comunicación. . . . El final lógico de esta búsqueda será la soledad, no una reacción contra el capitalismo. (Ravazzani 1981, 146–47)

7: *Coca:* Cupid, Cocaine, and Military Corruption

> Martínez Moreno cannot resist the temptation to clarify the social message and to do so he puts words in the protagonist's mouth that do not correspond to Marie-Louise's psychology. . . . The Marie-Louise of the epilogue is the antithesis of the one in the book, the one for whom Che or Debray represent absolutely nothing. Our heroine has not lived any experience, at least within the confines of the novel, that could have awakened her social conscience. . . . [S]he has delved a little into the existential problem of loneliness, . . . love, . . . [and] lack of communication. . . . The logical conclusion of this search is solitude, not a reaction against capitalism.

Martínez Moreno's ending does have its defenders, most notably Wolfgang Luchting, who has contended:

> Objections have been raised against the inclusion of the guerrilla-theme. I find them unfounded. . . . It seems to me to give a better insight into the state of affairs . . . than many of those novels that deal centrally with the guerrilla theme. (Luchting 1971, 488)

Nonetheless, to this reader it is regrettable to see that Martínez Moreno should choose to jeopardize such carefully balanced characterization. His surprisingly crude attempt to link his characters with current events by linking them with the death of Che Guevara violates the premise upon which his characters are based: i.e., their tendency to withdraw from events surrounding them and to behave as children. It violates the novel's most distinguishing characteristic, also seen in *El paredón,* which is to venture a treatment of one of Latin America's most controversial issues without catering to stereotype. That distinction in his novels leads them to offer, almost without exception, an analysis of human problems in Latin America that transcends conventional forms of political and social protest. Midway through *Coca,* Martínez Moreno comments, by way of the Captain's Ambassador, on the artificiality of persisting in false dialectics in order to force resolutions. He clearly conveys a message that such "purificación" ("purification") for the satisfaction of one's preconceptions is itself a factor in bringing about *la deca.*

> Mire: la tragedia de nuestra Revolución ha sido la falta de una verdadera purificación, . . . esa purificación que sólo se consigue de modo dialéctico, chocando con el enemigo. . . . Hemos tenido que inventar la oposición. . . . Bueno, y después la corrupción precoz. (164)

> Look: the tragedy of our Revolution has been the lack of a true purge, . . . the kind of purification that can only be obtained in a dialectical

manner, clashing with the enemy. . . . We have had to make up our opposition ourselves. . . . Well, then comes the precocious corruption.

By introducing a sudden concern for Che Guevara and giving cause for speculation on the part of the reader as to the possible involvement of the novel's protagonist in his death, the author seems to contradict his own assertion. This is an assertion common to all of his previous novels, and one which holds for *Coca* in every chapter until the epilogue. It is almost as if Martínez Moreno decided at the last minute that the "enemigo" ("enemy") necessary for that dialectic (Che) had appeared after all. By including him as he does in the epilogue, it would seem that he vainly attempts a "purificación" himself, one of the kind the novel generally condemns. Unfortunately, to use its character's own words, it comes to the same end, a "corrupción precoz" ("precocious corruption") of an otherwise extremely effective novel. It would not matter were it not for the fact that nineteen of *Coca*'s twenty chapters represent something that, until its publication, might have seemed impossible to achieve: a sustantive "entertainment" depicting, once again, the complexity of the individual's struggle against the "deca's" glacial erosion of Latin America's hopes for the future.

8
Tierra en la boca: Decadence, Death, and a Decent Burial

Tierra en la boca (A mouthful of dirt) (1974) is significant to Martínez Moreno's canon not only because it is his last novel; it is also his only "post" novel. With regard to his other novels, it can be said to be "post-*deca*." Its original title, *Alguien tiene que enterrarnos* (Someone will have to bury us), bears even more direct witness to the novel as a swan song for Uruguayan society and Martínez Moreno's Cassandric depictions of it in his previous novels. The ailing democracy, whose mascot Martínez Moreno had said in *El paredón* (1963) should be an ostrich with its head in the sand, was now beheaded. *La deca* in Uruguay finally had reached its horrifying, sad, and inevitable conclusion in 1973, with its dissolution of the country's long-standing democratic institutions by military intervention.

The manner in which the coup took place was bitterly ironic in the light of Martínez Morono's writings. It almost could have been deliberately conceived along the lines of Martínez Moreno's view of *la deca* as seen in Primitivo's *sobremurientes* ("sur-deadors") in *Los aborígenes* or Eugenio's slow agony in *Con las primeras luces*. After years of dramatic clashes among students, police, the military, trade unions, intellectual leftists, and the Tupamaro guerrillas, on June 27, 1973, Uruguay's democracy went out with a whimper rather than a bang.

In the year 1974, the year *Tierra en la boca* was published, life continued to imitate art in Martínez Moreno's world. In its first year in power, the country's de facto military dictatorship lashed out at the literary community in a way that pitted it against Martínez Moreno both as lawyer and as literary figure. As it consolidated its hold on the country, the dictatorship specifically targeted those associated with the weekly journal *Marcha*.

Martínez Moreno had been a writer for *Marcha* since it was

founded by his close friend Carlos Quijano in 1939. The jury of *Marcha*'s 1974 literary prize, a jury that included Uruguay's most eminent cultural treasure, Juan Carlos Onetti, was faced with the dilemma of whether or not to confer honors upon a controversial short story, *El guardaespaldas* (The bodyguard), by a young writer named Nelson Marra.[2] Deciding not to bow to intimidation, the jury awarded first prize to the story, whose title referred to a known figure in the government. The consequence was immediate arrest for all members of the jury, Onetti included, as well as for the story's author. Martínez Moreno was retained as the group's defense attorney; the case was seen as the dictatorship's attempt to strike at the heart of the intellectual community. The author and lawyer found himself playing center stage in Uruguay's "drama of the elites," a drama he had satirized in his novella *Los aborígenes* (1960).

Martínez Moreno managed to obtain Onetti's release in short order on humanitarian grounds. The eminent author's legendary alcoholism produced symptoms frightening even to the dictatorship's hardened jailers. Onetti's immediate flight into exile in Spain upon release meant the permanent loss of Uruguay's greatest literary figure to those who opposed free artistic expression.

The other members of the jury, including critic Jorge Ruffinelli (later founder of the Mexican journal *Texto crítico*) and poet Mercedes Rein, were released later and also fled into exile. However, in a courtroom defeat that Martínez Moreno himself claimed was his life's only regret, Nelson Marra was convicted and sentenced to several years in prison.[3] *Marcha* itself was closed after over thirty years of operation, a remarkable record for any Latin-American journal of its kind.

Likewise, 1974 marked the end of Martínez Moreno's practice as Public Defender in the Criminal Court of Montevideo, a position he had held for twenty-five years, since 1949. He had proved as stubborn a civil libertarian in deed as his commentary in *El paredón* had implied in word. He argued before the country's supreme court for eighteen months challenging the legality of the dictatorship's application of military law to civilians. When all indications seemed to show that Martínez Moreno's arguments had prevailed, the government simply dissolved the court before it could render its decision.

In the years following, his legal practice was to deteriorate considerably. Eventually, as documented in the last pages of his final novel, *El color que el infierno me escondiera* (The color hell would hide, translated as *El Infierno*) (1981), Martínez Moreno served as

8: *Tierra en la boca:* Decadence, Death, and a Decent Burial

the person the government contacted anonymously when it wished to return the body of a torture victim to his or her family. A bomb blast at his home in 1978, followed by a tip from an officer within the government who begrudgingly respected Martínez Moreno's integrity, finally drove him into exile in Mexico. Ironically, within a few years he found himself next-door neighbors with Carlos Quijano, his old friend and the founder of *Marcha*, who revived the publication abroad. Neither of them was ever to return home.

In expressing a new set of concerns quite distinct from those of the novels of the boom in the 1960s, *Tierra en la boca* is one of the earliest of what is now called the postboom Latin-American novel. *Tierra* is a novel that shows itself to have moved beyond the boom not only chronologically and thematically; it also bears characteristics shared with other novels that many have pointed to as definitive sylistic qualities that identify a break with the predominant novelistic form of the boom. In its broadest context, however, *Tierra en la boca* raises questions regarding the definition of what is theoretically termed the *postmodern* in its approach to depicting humanity and human problems, reflecting a worldwide change in attitudes toward art and its relationship to society.

The first thing the reader of *Tierra en la boca* may notice that distinguishes it from all other Martínez Moreno novels is its choice of character and setting. Ever since the novella *Los aborígenes* in 1956, Martínez Moreno had dealt effectively with what he calls in that book "el drama de las élites en la América Latina" ("the drama of the elites in Latin America") in his concern for how they dealt—or, rather, refused to deal with *la deca* and the urgency of finding new ways of thinking in order to deal with it. At times his setting was the microcosmic one, for example, that of family relationships in *Cordelia*. Usually, however, such microcosmic concerns were paired with macrocosmic ones as well, as in the masterful juxtaposition of Julio Calodoro's family problems with Uruguay's response to the Cuban revolution in *El Paredón*. Nonetheless, in all of his previous novels, Martínez Moreno had depicted with great psychological depth the twilight struggles of an elite, which recognized, albeit often too late, the need to abandon passive acquiescence to old models of thinking in favor of forging new ones.

In *Tierra en la boca*, he turns from the "lumpen aristocracy" (to use a turn on Marxist terminology) to the opposite end of the socioeconomic spectrum the lumpen proletariat. The characters of *Tierra en la boca*—Font, Isabel, Ramos, and Luján—are dwellers of Montevideo's "cantegriles," or slums, and are the real casualties of *la deca*. Unlike Eugenio of *Con las primeras luces* (1966), who lives clinging to the relics of the past in a patrician mausoleum, Font is a grave-robber who cannibalizes history for such relics (plaques, monuments, etc.) in order to feed himself in the present. Isabel is the daughter of a scrap-metal dealer, who ekes out a living selling such scavenged objects. Ramos and Luján are their cohorts in a world in which, in contrast to previous Martínez Moreno novels, there is no past to escape to for comfort, and little future for which to hope.

Those are the conditions that set the novel's plot in motion. Font and Ramos, men with little faith in the present order of things, decide to supplement the meager fruits of their labor by committing a burglary, a theft in the world of the living, instead of only robbing graves. They borrow a revolver and decide to rob a butcher shop in the barrio. Their plan goes awry immediately, when a night watchman they hadn't accounted for interrupts their heist. They panic and kill him, almost before they know what they are doing.

The rest of the novel deals with the aftermath of the murder. They are careless with clues to the crime, turning the gun itself over to a bartender—and hence, to the police—as a deposit for liquor. They do little to save themselves or to escape, preferring instead to walk on the beach discussing soccer games, go to dances and to bars with their women. They put up little resistance to the dragnet that, as they are aware from newspaper and radio reports, is closing in on them. Ultimately, Font jumps under the wheels of a train in order to avoid arrest, Ramos goes to a relative who is a policeman and turns himself in, Luján is turned in as accessory to murder after the fact by her father, and Isabel, also a fugitive as accessory after the fact, is left to fend for herself, pregnant with a child conceived with Font in the crime's aftermath.

Criticism on the novel has dealt almost exclusively with the social and political implication of Martínez Moreno's choice of this subject matter. In an article dedicated entirely to the novel's language, Avenir Rosell has commented extensively on its realistic reproduction of the dialect of Montevideo's "cantegriles." In fact, he considers the novel's language to be so realistic that his article provides a glossary for the reader not versed in the slang of Montevideo's underclass.[4] Liz Salisbury-Ginsburg, in her study *Downfall of a Democracy: Carlos Martínez Moreno and the Uruguayan Experience*, asks:

8: *Tierra en la boca:* Decadence, Death, and a Decent Burial 149

But why does the author devote a whole novel to a senseless homicide, and thereafter, to the aimless meanderings of the perpetrators? The answer lies, on closer inspection, in the recognition that the novel's drama is, in microcosm, a reflection of the time period when dictatorial takeover in Uruguay became inevitable. The execution represents that unspecified moment in which the Uruguayan democratic system received its deathblow, virtually assuring that the road could not be closed to the inauguration of some type of despotic regime. It is in this context that the murder has a more expansive meaning, "como si fuera el resultado de una fuerza que ellos hubieran desatado y echado a andar y contra la cual ahora no pudiesen nada ("as if it were the result of a force that they had unleashed and set in motion and against which they could now do nothing") (140). (Salisbury-Ginsburg 1982, 147–48)

One could hardly disagree with the reading of *Terra en la boca* as a reflection of its time period, as Salisbury-Ginsburg suggests. However, like all of Martínez Moreno's novels, *Tierra en la boca* reflects its time period in more than politics. It is my belief that *Tierra en la boca* offers something unusual to criticism as a whole, and not only to criticism that might be interested in specifically Uruguayan political concerns. The question Salisbury-Ginsburg poses about this "post-*deca*" novel also provides a unique opportunity to observe concrete relationships between the specific development of a particular novelist's canon and two more general developments: the historical concern of the postboom, and the theoretical concern of postmodernism.

Considered in this context, *Tierra en la boca* takes on expansive meaning indeed. It acquires not only political significance, but significance as a landmark in the recent history of the Latin American novel. Furthermore, it links this history to universal theoretical concerns, such as those represented by the contemporary interest in postmodernism as a watershed in Western thought. *Tierra en la boca* may well represent a case in which criticism is able to establish a relationship between a specific political event, literary history, and a theoretical turning point in the novel. It may represent an unusual case in which one can argue, with pinpoint accuracy, for a moment in which postmodernism inserted itself into a society's intellectual history. It may serve to reveal an unusually clear causal link between a political event, with its social implications, and the emergence of a new way of dealing with such an association artistically and intellectually.

Uruguay's *deca*, the recurrent theme of Martínez Moreno's canon, ended on 27 June 1973, the date of the country's military takeover; Uruguay's "post-*deca*" therefore begins on that date. If one can establish a relationship between Martínez Moreno's treatment of the "post-*deca*" in his subsequent novel and postmodernism itself, then one will have established a unique link between historical and theoretical concerns that can perhaps provide considerable insight into other instances of postmodern thought in literature.

Such a possibility leads one to look for indicators of change other than those of choice of character, the distinguishing feature mentioned by Salisbury-Ginsburg. Aside from his choice of *non*-elitist characters, the most immediately notable change to be noticed is in the presentation of the novel's *récit*. The first chapter is called "La víspera," or "The Eve," meaning the eve of the crime. The novel's four subsequent chapters are merely the numbered days following the murder until the foursome breaks up, each to face his or her individual fate. Such deliberate adherence to simple, diachronic chronology is highly unusual for Martínez Moreno, a writer so well-known for his mastery of the experimentally fragmented and synchronically retrospective narrative he had produced during the boom, in novels such as *Con las primeras luces* (1966) and *Coca* (1970).

The significance of *Tierra en la boca*'s departure from experimental form can best be understood in a broader context. Angel Rama, in his book *Más allá del boom: literatura y mercado*, claims that the political, social, and economic market conditions that gave rise to the boom were exhausted by 1972, a fact that would lead one to expect some subsequent fundamental change in the novel (Rama 1981, 85). Though he does not mention Martínez Moreno by name, literary historian John Brushwood suggests that the sea change forecast by Rama is in evidence in the novels published the same year in which *Tierra en la boca* appears, 1974. The distinguishing features Brushwood pinpoints as clues of a watershed in the Latin American novels published that year can be found in *Tierra en la boca*. Such a coincidence suggests that *Tierra en la boca* may reflect a general shift in the Latin-American novel as a whole:

> Para 1974 . . . autores que habían establecido sus carreras con novelas complicadas y altamente exigentes para sus lectores . . . publican novelas que sólo un novelista muy seguro de su arte podría publicar; la sencillez aparente en algunas de estas narrativas es una característica de producción en plena madurez. (Brushwood 1984, 322)

> By 1974 . . . authors who had established their careers with novels

8: *Tierra en la boca:* Decadence, Death, and a Decent Burial

that were complex and highly demanding for their readers . . . publish novels that only a novelist who is very sure of his art would dare publish; the apparent simplicity of some of these narratives is a characteristic of a literary production in full bloom.

Michael Holquist, in an article published in 1973, had anticipated such a change in the novel genre, using Latin American authors as indicators of that change. His comments explain Martínez Moreno's choice of "sencillez" ("simplicity") to which Brushwood points in the novels of that year. They also serve to explain his particular choice of the crime story as well as having broad implications. He states:

> what the structural and philosophical presuppositions of myth and depth psychology were to modernism . . . the detective story is to postmodernism. . . . If such is the case, we will have established a relationship between two levels of culture, kitsch and the avant-garde, often thought to be mutually exclusive. (Holquist 1971, 135)

Holquist's comments, when applied to *Tierra en la boca*, suggest an interesting analogy between Martínez Moreno's break in the ordering of the *récit* (from his *deca* novel to his "post-*deca*" novel), and a break observed between modernism and postmodernism. They also offer an explanation for Martínez Moreno's choice of the crime novel to represent this rupture. Holquist says of modernism that

> the moulders of the modernist tradition sensed . . . that Christianity was losing its power to console and explain, to flood a hostile world with meaning. Such masters as Joyce and Mann sought to fill this religious void with different symbols, more often than not taken from mythical systems older than Christianity. . . . Modernism had dual roots in psychology and myth. . . . Modernist novels essentially take place in a country of the mind, inside. (Holquist 1971, 145)

Manifestations of this modernist country of the mind are easy to identify in Martínez Moreno's previous works. In *Los aborígenes*, Primitivo's Bolivia is nothing more than a distant memory in his self-exile in Rome. Eugenio's Uruguay in *Con las primeras luces* amounts to a country of the past that can be evoked by the symbolic objects of the family mansion, which his relatives have attempted to preserve against the changes in external reality.

Further manifestations of a modernist treatment of reality can be found, Holquist says, in the treatment of time. He says:

their time is Bergsonian, not chronological. Thus, these works are marked by an emphasis on recurring patterns of experience, those paradigmatic human occasions that seem to happen outside of time. (Holquist 1971, 146–47)

Martínez Moreno's previous, retrospective narrative is almost solely dedicated, in its characters' introspective analepses, to the discovery of such patterns and paradigms in order to explain their particular circumstances in the general *deca*. The most obvious example is to be found in Eugenio's flashbacks as he agonizes in *Luces:*

> Casi nunca es posible saber a qué hora exacta de un día justo comenzó un hecho, así se trate del hecho más nítido. . . . Y si no se trata de un hecho tajante sino de una situación, menos que menos: la decadencia de una familia, digamos. ¿A qué hora empieza, en qué día se consuma, qué signos, qué señales la marcan?
> Lo que entonces cada uno puede hacer es elegir una imagen. (Martínez Moreno 1966, 147)

> It is almost never possible to know at what exact hour of what precise day an event began, be it the clearest event. . . . And if it is not a matter of a definitive event but, rather, of a situation, even less so: the decline of a family, let's say. At what hour does it begin? On what day is it consummated? What signs, what signals mark its passing?
> All each of us can do, then, is choose an image.

In contrast to that novelistic mode, says Holquist, is the postmodern mode, which, he says,

> can best be understood as springing from a different view of man, and therefore a different view of art from that which obtained in modernism. It has at its heart the exact opposites of the two tendencies which define modernism. The aesthetics of postmodernism is militantly *anti*-psychological (if that word is taken in its usual meaning) and radically *anti*-mythical. (Emphasis in original.) (Holquist 1971, 148)

He then explains the detective story's role in embodying that postmodern aesthetic:

> Now, if . . . you are interested in disestablishing the mythic and psychological tendencies of the tradition you are defining yourself against, what better way for doing so could recommend itself than that of exploiting what had already become the polar opposite of that

8: *Tierra en la boca:* Decadence, Death, and a Decent Burial

tradition in its own time? Detective stories had always been recognized as escape literature. But escape from what? Among other things, escape from *literature itself,* as we emphasized above in the dichotomy between the detective story with its exterior simplicities and modernism with its interior complexities. (Emphasis in original.) (Holquist 1971, 148)

Tierra en la boca demonstrates these qualities, not only in a subject matter and choice of form and chronology that break with Martínez Moreno's previous, arguably modernist works, but also in its characterization. In *Luces,* Eugenio confronted his death, as we have noted, by psychologically reviewing his life and groping for an explanatory image. In *Tierra en la boca,* as Font likewise faces death, he pointedly does not seek such symbolic explanations. Instead, as he walks toward the train tracks to commit suicide, the narrator observes:

Un hombre que va a morir es un hombre que va a morir. No hay comparación posible en el mundo, con ninguna otra situación. Un hombre que va a morir es un hombre que va a morir y se acabó. Sin deseos, ya sin mensajes para nadie, sin pensamientos, sin edad, sin infancia. Otros llenan el tiempo que les queda con recuerdos, con nostalgia, con la fanfarronería de los amores vividos. El con nada. No porque no haya tenido esos amores, no porque le hayan faltado una niñez, la juventud, historias. La vieja, Isabel. Y el hijo, si desde anoche viene. Pero ahora ellos quedan, no se van con él. Empieza a andar sin ellos, se quita la camisa en la noche, se pone a bajar sin nada. (Martinez Moreno 1974, 193)

A man who is going to die is a man who is going to die. In the whole world, there is no possible situation that can stand in comparison to it. A man who is going to die is a man who is going to die and that is it. He has no desires, no messages for anyone any more, no thoughts, no age, no childhood. Others fill in the time left to them with memories, nostalgia, and the bluster of loves lived. He has nothing. Not because he hasn't had such loves, not because he hasn't had such a childhood, such a youth, such history. Isabel, the old lady. And the kid, if he's still on the way after last night. But now they're staying behind, they're not going with him. He begins to walk without them, taking off his shirt in the night and starting down with nothing.

This passage can be seen as a key to the different view of man presented throughout the novel—an antipsychological view of the kind described by Holquist. Such an approach also provides another answer to Salisbury-Ginsburg's questions as to the purpose of the novel's "senseless homicide" and subsequent characters' "aimless meanderings." It challenges conventional notions of causality with regard to two of the most frightening aspects of the human condition: violence and death. Rather than couch them in a symbolic causality, it strips them down to the bare bones. As Martínez Moreno's character strips himself of all worldly attachments, so his creator confronts the reader with the inadequacy of causal notions in explaining his fate.

Thus, it represents a more chilling and darker view of man than that seen in any of Martínez Moreno's previous works. In the world of *Tierra en la boca,* objects often seem to take a more active role in shaping human destiny than do people. The scene of the murder is described with a curious detachment. There is no enigma as to why it occurs; the presence of the murder weapon itself, a gun, seems to bring about the murder as much as any act of will.

> Ahora el viejo ha conseguido zafarse apenas y articular con claridad "No me maten" (es la *r,* sobre todo, la letra imposible cuando ha querido decir Lárguenme, pero en la súplica No me maten no figura la *r*) . . . y eso marca el momento. . . . [H]an olvidado qué iban a hacer, lo poco que el viejo habría podido contra ellos. . . . Ha vuelto a decir No me maten y en ese justo instante suena el balazo de Ramos sobre el hígado del viejo, un balazo sordo, no demasiado ruidoso, como sofocado y silenciado y envuelto por las ropas que rasga. . . . El No mem . . . ha sido sustituido por un estertor como de asombro, como el estupor de un globo que saliese de la caverna y reventase en los labios del viejo, una burbuja como ésa que encierra las palabras de los personajes en las historietas: no llega a ser un hipo, es el rumor blanduzco de una vejiga que se desinfla y expresa su protesta por el absurdo de desinflarse así, tan sin razón. (42)

> Now the old man has barely managed to slip loose and clearly articulate "Don't kill me" (it is the *r,* above all, that was the impossible letter when he wanted to say Release me, but in the plea Don't kill me the *r* doesn't come into play) . . . and that marks the moment. . . . They have forgotten what they came here to do, how little the old man could have done against them. . . . Once more he's said Don't kill me and at that very instant Ramos' gunshot rings out above the old man's liver; a muted gunshot, not very loud, sort of suffocated, silenced, wrapped up by the clothes it rips through. . . . The Don't kill m . . . has been replaced by a rasping sound like a breath drawn in amazement, like astonishment from a bubble flown up from the depths of a cavern to burst on the old man's lips, a bubble like the ones that enclose the words of characters in comic books: it doesn't quite make

8: *Tierra en la boca:* Decadence, Death, and a Decent Burial

it to hiccup stage; it's just the pale murmur of a bladder that's sprung a leak and registers its protest at the absurdity of being emptied this way, so senselessly.

This minute description is pointedly and deliverately kitsch in its reference to the "historieta" ("comic book") at such a crucial point in the novel's plot. It clearly distinguishes itself by its pointedly antipsychological approach, its exterior, rather than interior, quality. The old man's life does not flash before his eyes. Such clichés tend to attempt to humanize and reconcile death, to bid the character farewell with dignity by fantasizing the luxury of one last private moment, one last run through life, one last thought—all that Martínez Moreno narrator observed previously a dying man does not have. Faithful to his narrator's previous observations of a dying man, Martínez Moreno's description here seeks the opposite effect found in the conventional death scene. There is no dignity, no privacy; instead, we find nakedness, exposure, and absurdity. The night watchman is killed for no clear purpose. By an accident of fate, if such a statement can be made, he simply goes from human being to inanimate object from one instant to the next. At best, he is a two-dimensional cartoon character.

The senselessness seen in the description of the nightwatchman's death, its "tan sin razón" quality, corresponds to a new, dark skepticism on Martínez Moreno's part regarding causal explanations of human behavior. That dark skepticism is seen in what Mempo Giardinelli calls the postboom "género negro." As he notes, novels such as *Tierra en la boca*, in their depiction of impulsive, absurd crimes, seem to reject utopian notions regarding human behavior.

> En la novela policial clásica, el detective nunca se pregunta *por qué*, sino *cómo* se comete un crimen, y el milagro del indicio, que sostiene la investigación, es una forma figurada de la causalidad. Por eso el modelo del crimen perfecto que desafía la sagacidad del investigador es, en última instancia, el mito del crimen sin causa. Esta es una utopía que la novela negra desceña. . . . Sirve para narrar un crimen que se le ocurrió a alguien dos minutos antes de llevarlo a cabo y no el que a los muchachos que apoyan los pies sobre el escritorio les resulta más fácil solucionar o aquel en el que alguien ha tratado de pasarse de listo. . . . Es una narrativa de emergencia, y por ende, de conflictos, de pasiones. De ahí la violencia como característica de lo negro. ¿Y qué, acaso no es violento el mundo en que vivimos? (Emphasis in original.) (Giardinelli: 1984, 28)

In the classic detective novel, the detective never asks himself *why*, but, rather, *how* a crime is committed, and the miracle of the clue, which sustains the investigation, is a figurative form of causality. Hence the model of the perfect crime that challenges the sagacity of the detective is, ultimately, the myth of the crime with no cause. This is a utopia that the noir novel disdains. . . . It serves to narrate a crime that occurred to someone two minutes before carrying it out and not the crime that the boys with their feet up on their desks find easy to solve or the kind in which someone has tried to be clever. . . . It is a narrative of emergency and, therefore, of conflicts and of passions. Hence violence as a characteristic of the noir. And, after all, isn't this world in which we live violent?

In Martínez Moreno's case, Giardinelli's last query becomes much more than a rhetorical question. As in *Coca,* one of his criminal cases served as the basis for the plot of *Tierra en la boca.* It was to be one of his last cases as Criminal Public Defender. As he pursued it, struggling to draw twenty-five years of service as an officer of the court to a close with dignity, he could see the path lying beyond *la deca* as nothing but bleak and horrifying. Uruguay's future was no longer the agony of Eugenio in *Con las primeras luces* (1966). Rather, it was a future devoid of even the most basic respect for the human values for which he had struggled so long both in literature and in life.

This vision of the abyss, as it were, is reflected in Martínez Moreno's stark description of the murder scene in *Tierra en la boca.* It is the sort of description that represents what Holquist describes in the postmodern detective story as an exploitation of convention for a larger purpose.

> By exploiting the conventions of the detective story such men . . . have fought against the Modernist attempt to fill the void of the world with rediscovered mythical symbols. Rather, they dramatize the void. If, in the detective story, death must be solved, in the new . . . detective story, it is *life* which must be solved. (Emphasis in original.) (Holquist 1971, 156)

The novelist provides the problem, but does not feel compelled to provide the clues. Life itself is often baffling; why should it not be so in novels as well? *Tierra en la boca* does not even present the reader with a detective upon whom to hinge the murder's resolution. Why should there be one? There is no enigma as to how the crime was committed. There is only the enigma of why it occurred at all, and yet beyond the surface explanation offered in the scene itself, with its "historieta" ("comic book") quality, even the characters themselves cannot reveal its cause.

8: *Tierra en la boca:* Decadence, Death, and a Decent Burial 157

Still, it changes their world, as much as they would like to deny it, just as the events of 1974 had changed their author's world. It devalues them as human beings. In inverse proportion to their lessening humanity the objects of their world become animated, as it were. Walking aimlessly in the night with their women later on, in search of a party, liquor, anything, they confront a sign on a poor café. It announces the special plate of the day: "Hoy buseca" ("Today's special: tripe"). Font reads it aloud differently: "Hoy busca" ("Today's special: searches"). His comrades chide him for it, "No jodas, carajo. No jodas con la verdad" ("Don't fuck around dammit. Don't fuck around with the truth") (59). Isabel erases it, but cannot erase the point made. The sign is, literally, a sign of things to come. "La verdad" ("truth") is going to "joder" ("fuck") with them. The lack of causal explanation for what they have done and, therefore, the lack of causal clues as to what to do next, in no way alters that "la verdad" had entered their world as a central fact—a central void. When that central void in one's life is a murder one has committed, "la verdad" brings a bitter point home about the inadequacy of the human capacity for logic, reflection, and self-consciousness in dealing with such central issues as life and death. Sometimes logic, reflection, and self-consciousness can be of little use in confronting the big issues. In foregrounding this inadequacy, *Tierra en la boca* is demonstrating a quality which, according to Giardinelli, is characteristic of the "género negro" ("noir genre"):

> [E]l delito no es . . . un problema matemático, un crucigrama, un desafío al ingenio. . . . Cada delito es producto de relaciones—malas relaciones—entre los seres humano. No hay, como la ciencia jurídica ha demonstrado, un modelo de criminal como imaginaba Lombroso; lo que hay son circumstancias que llevan al hombre a cometer un crimen. A cualquier hombre. A usted o a mí. (Giardinelli 1984, 28)

> [T]he crime is not . . . a mathematical problem, a crossword puzzle, a challenge to ingenuity. . . . Every crime is the product of relationships—bad relationships—between human beings. There is no such thing, as juridicial science has demonstrated, as a model criminal such as the one imagined by Lombroso; what we do have are circumstances that can carry a man to commit a crime. Any man. You or I.

In the absence of a logical explanation for what they have done, Font and Ramos are unable to reason, to plan what to do. The objects of their world seem to conspire to damn them. Ramos wishes for the exile of a "ciudad dentro de la ciudad, otro mundo dentro del mundo" ("city within a city, another world within the world") in which to take refuge, but knows that the popular myth of an underworld for men such as he is only that—a myth (65). They are alienated from their world that, like the dictatorial Uruguay of 1974 in which Martínez Moreno suddenly had to live, has turned silently hostile:

> empiezan a saber que son dos náufragos, sí, ahora, en lo negro sin luna . . . desorbitados en las tinieblas. . . . Ningún gallo canta. . . . En una ciudad donde estarán desatándose las fuerzas que se han puesto a perseguirlos, este cuarto no los protege. (77)
>
> they begin to realize that they are two marooned people; yes, now in the moonless blackness . . . disoriented in the darkness. . . . No cock crows. . . . In a city in which forces have been unleashed to persecute them, this room is no protection.

Unlike the case of the Captain in the bathroom scene before his capture in *Coca,* the characters in *Tierra* shall receive no warning— no cock, real or imaginary, will crow. Obviously, their crime makes them seem even less deserving of such consideration than *Coca*'s Captain. Yet the thoroughly pathetic nature of the criminals' lives in *Tierra* makes it seem almost cruel. After all, they are no more expecting such a warning to change their eventual fate no more than the Captain expected it to do so. In addition, from the outset, they were born into a world with far fewer choices.

Still, events grind on toward their conclusion with the inevitability of the Passion of Christ. A bottle of wine comes to represent the blood of the victim (81). The radio announces that the revolver has found its way to the police (105). Font goes to the beach and, staring at the garbage floating in the water, "cáscaras de fruta y pedazos de género y suelas de zapatos y condones . . . suciedad de la gente" ("fruit peels, pieces of material, shoe soles, and condoms . . . people's filth"), he wants to join it (111). He recalls the story of another murder years before. The police were unable to identify the victim, and so her dress was put on a mannequin and put on display in the window of a downtown store so as to obtain the public's help in solving the crime.

Such an emphasis on objects and the human inability to transcend them brings to mind the manner in which, Holquist says, other postmodern detective story writers modified them to serve their ends. He cites a Robbe-Grillet essay on the subject:

> You have to keep coming back to the recorded evidence: the exact position of a piece of furniture, the shape and frequency of a finger-

8: *Tierra en la boca:* Decadence, Death, and a Decent Burial 159

print, a word written in a message. The impression grows on you that nothing else is true. Whether they conceal or reveal a mystery these elements that defy all systems have only one serious, obvious quality—that of being there. And that is how it is with the world around us. We thought we had come to terms with it by giving it a meaning, and the whole art of the novel, in particular, seemed dedicated to this task. But that was only an illusory simplification and far from becoming clearer and nearer, all that was happening was that the world was gradually losing its life in the process. Since this reality exists above all in its presence, what we have to do now, then, is to build a literature which takes this into account. (Holquist 1971, 149)

What Martínez Moreno achieves in his modification of the detective story is an inversion of the usual purpose of clues and other objects. They are not there in order to solve the crime; rather, they are clues that enable the perpetrators of the crime to figure out when they may be apprehended. These clues are infuriatingly unreliable, as the criminal, burdened by guilt, cannot discern which are figments of his imagination and which constitute real evidence of causality. The remaining chapters of the novel are framed by daily newspaper reports on the investigation of the murder that become, to their minds, "cartas por el diario" ("letters via the newspaper") (138). On the third day, the newspaper announces that a couple has been arrested—the wrong couple. Ramos sees it as an example of the lack of causality in the world, as he expresses in a colloquial speech based on the premise of the North American colloquialism that "life's a bitch and then you die":

> Se jode el que lo hizo, se jode el muerto, se jode el que no lo hizo ni lo sabe, se jode el que lo sabe y se calla, se jode a la larga el que lo supo y lo bate. Es un infierno: la joda agarra cada vez más gente. (139)

> It's a bitch for the guy who did it, it's a bitch for the dead guy, it's a bitch for the guy who didn't do it and doesn't even know about it, it's a bitch for the guy who knows about it and shuts up, in the end it's a bitch for the guy who knew about it and beat it. It's hell: the bitch always gets more and more people.

"La joda" is Holquist's void, and nothing will fill it for them. It is at this point that Ramos becomes genuinely afflicted with an obsession. As inanimate objects have seemed to turn against them all, a set of animate objects—dogs—seem to pursue Ramos in particular. He hears them in the night; they follow him by day (137). They finally corner him, as it were, in a place so symbolically named that it is bound to bring what Holquist calls "the void" even to the most unenlightened reader's mind. "La Cueva" ("The Cave") is the name of the bar in which Ramos is taking alcoholic refuge from "la joda" when a dog enters and, to his mind, seems to single him out. As he throws his glass at the dog, something breaks within him (172). He loses his mind. The fact that his only thought is the phrase Martínez Moreno first proposed for the novel's title underscores the scene's central importance to the novel's meaningful commentary on void: "alguien tiene que enterrarnos, alguien tiene tendrá que enterrarnos, en este agujero de mierda alguien tendrá (quieras que no) que enterrarnos" ("someone has to bury us, someone will have to bury us in this shithole someone [like it or not] will have to bury us") (201).

The latter half of Marínez Moreno's next book, the nonfiction novel *El color que el infierno me escondiera* (1981) would later shed even greater light on this scene. Martínez Moreno was about to assume a role in the life of his country more akin to that of an undertaker than that of a novelist or a lawyer. In that light, Ramos's words—and the fact that they were first considered for the title of *Tierra en la boca*—are even more soberingly ironic.

As Ramos breaks, so does Font, though with different consequences. Font has decided to commit suicide, to launch himself into the void willfully instead of putting up a futile resistance. He has decided that he has reached a "punto de acorralamiento en que todas las verdades son reversibles, en que las verdades son tan inútiles como las mentiras y como las promesas y como los cálculos" ("point of being cornered in which all truth is reversible, in which truths is just as useless as lies and as promises and as calculations") (183). All points of reference, be they etiological, moral, or psychological, dissolve as he contemplates death, the void. Rosell has said of the manner in which his suicide is portrayed in the novel, without psychologizing it, that the characters

> en el plano meramente material están integrados en la burda materia, en la inmundicia . . . y en lo físico espiritual se sienten impotentes contra el acoso espiritual, y también acaban integrándose a la materia por el suicidio. (Rosell 1977, 92)

> on the merely material level they are integrated with base matter, with filth . . . and in both a physical and spiritual sense they feel impotent against their spiritual hounding, so they wind up joining with matter by way of suicide.

8: *Tierra en la boca:* Decadence, Death, and a Decent Burial 161

The description of Font's suicide scene bears out this analysis:

> Penetrar en la muerte. No permanecerá en aquella altura . . . para arrojarse desde allí. No. Bajará al pie mismo de las vías, esperará que la locomotora se acerque, ras a ras con él. Y desde allí, al mismo nivel, cuando la máquina esté encima se arrojará. O no, ni siquiera se arrojará, dará solamente paso, como si caminara, no subirá a un cadalso, no bajará como a un foso de leones o de serpeintes, simplemente dará un paso y penetrará en la muerte. Penetrará a que la muerte lo envuelva, como quien entre a una cámara de gas, más rápido y más fuerte y más golpeante y allí mismo . . . el resto será sólo la muerte llevándose lo suyo, desinteresada repentinamente de su caza, hecha ella una sola cosa con su presa, arrojándola a un lado, cayendo otra vez en el silencio. (189–90)

> To penetrate death. He won't stay up high here . . . to throw himself down from here. No. He will go down to the foot of the tracks themselves and he will wait until the locomotive draw near, eyeball to eyeball with him. And from there, on the same level, when the engine is right there he'll throw himself under it. Or maybe not. Maybe he won't even throw himself. Maybe he'll just take a step, as if he were walking. He won't mount the scaffold, he won't go into a lion's den or snake pit. He'll simply take a step and penetrate death. He'll penetrate death so it will envelope him as if he'd walked into a gas chamber, enveloping him faster and stronger and more gustily and then there, right there . . . the rest will just be death carrying away its own, suddenly uninterested in the hunt, made one with its prey, throwing it off to one side, falling silent once again.

In grappling with his own imminent death, he rejects any moral arguments to explain the events that set him on a collision course with it: "no es que estaba bien o mal, es que era lo único" ("it's not that it was the right thing or the wrong thing, it's that it was the only thing") (330). He searches for sociological explanations for what Font did with him and has done now alone, and can find none: "Pero nunca, nunca me dijo soy así porque fui así o asá y sufrí tanto y cuanto y pasé por esto o aquello, eso jamás" (But never, ever did he tell me 'I'm like this because I was this way or because I suffered so much or because I went through this or that'—never) (233). The implacability of it all is made more poignant as newspaper headlines announcing his suicide play before his eyes, forming puns with words and letters that seem to mock him, offering no explanations.

Font's suicide marks the disintegration of the little group. Luján takes the bus to her father's shack on the edge of town. On the bus, she follows the accounts of the progress of the murder investigation, and the novel's description of her thoughts turns very "novela negra" ("noir").

> Al hombre del asiento de adelante ya no le interesa aquel crimen tan fácilmente aclarado y sin ningún encanto en las formas, en las complicaciones, en el enigma, en los móviles. Un simple crimen bruto, a cargo de dos brutos. Vuelve la hoja, pasa a los deportes . . . ya no interesa su historia; el destino de cuatro loco en la desbandada final. . . . Un crimen grueso y bruto, sin ningún revoco, sin ningún artificio: a otra cosa (252–253).

> The man in the seat in front of me is no longer interested in that crime that has been so easily solved with no charm in any of its forms, complications, in its enigma, or in its motives. A simple brutal crime, carried out by two brutes. He turns the page, passing on to sports . . . he is no longer interested in the story: the destiny of four lunatics in their final rout. . . . A heavy and brutal crime, lacking a cover, lacking any artifice: on to something else.

When she arrives at her father's house, her own father calls for the neighbors' help and turns her in. Much like the man on the bus, her father isn't interested in her story. She passively submits to his decision.

Meanwhile, Ramos is involved in the scene that goes give the novel its title. Driven by what has now become a delirium about dogs, he has gone to seek refuge with a friend he knows from the world of petty crime. His friend, en Negro Mario, gives him refuge for the night. When Ramos returns the next day, however, he finds the police in the process of arresting his friend for his hospitality. Ramos reaches his lowest point in the novel, both figuratively and literally, as he crawls away on his belly in order to avoid arrest. His previous words, "alguien tiene que enterrarnos" ("someone will have to bury us"), return to haunt him:

> Tierra en la boca. Tierra en la boca, como si el mundo estuviera subiéndosele encima, ¿enterrándolo? . . . gusto de tierra en la boca. ¿Ha estado arrastrándose con la boca abierta, jadeando a labios separados, ha estado comiendo grumos de tierra? . . . Se pone una mano con gusto a tierra sobre los labios con gusto a tierra. Se entierra, se calla. (261–62)

> A mouthful of dirt. A mouthful of dirt, as if the world were coming down on him—burying him? . . . the taste of a mouthful of dirt. Has he been dragging himself around with his mouth open, panting with

8: *Tierra en la boca:* Decadence, Death, and a Decent Burial

his mouth hanging open? has he been eating dirt clods? . . . He puts one dirt-flavored hand up to his dirt-flavored lips. He buries himself, he shuts up.

It is interesting, given the climate of events the year *Tierra* was written, that this crucial scene should end with the equation of silence to death, as if to imply that to be silenced—or censored?— were to be buried alive. Ramos decides that his only remaining course of action, the last measure of choice left to him, is to choose the policeman to whom he will surrender. He chooses his uncle, a man who may be able to obtain some mercy for him, since, in the novel's last words, "Total, ¿a mí que van a hacerme estos milicos?" ("After all, what can these cops do to me anyway?") (293). He has encountered the void. Nothing could be worse than that.

In *Tierra en la boca*, Martínez Moreno certainly does "dramatize the void," as Holquist says of the postmodern crime story. *Tierra* is a leap down into the void of the lumpen proletariat from the "drama of the elites" seen in Martínez Moreno's previous novels. In this, his last fictional novel, he ends his career in fiction by presenting the reader with a narrative that is radically simplified in form when compared to his previous works. It is also one in which he presents a much harsher view of the human condition. In *Luces*, Eugenio lives and dies by choice in a world of objects, seeking to escape *la deca* in the memories they evoke. In the end he dies by that choice, recognizing himself to be as empty as the milk bottle on the doorstep next to him. The novel ends as he awaits the milkman who will find them both, no more than objects, "con las primeras luces" ("by dawn's early light").

The "post-*deca*" world of *Tierra en al boca* is one that begins with an even worse situation than that with which *Luces* ends. In the scale of values of *Tierra en la boca*, objects seem to have more vitality than do human beings themselves. As a result, as Rosell has pointed out, is that all that remains for them to do is to join with the objects, to be buried. They are presented to us, figuratively speaking, with dirt already in their mouths. *Tierra en la boca* is definitely a novel bound to leave a taste of bitter realism in the reader's mouth.

Thus, to return to Salisbury-Ginsburg's question: why write such a novel? I believe Giardinelli offers an answer. In his opinion, writers in Marínez Moreno's circumstances of the early 1970s

> *tienen que ser* negros, duros. Ya no pueden hacer una ficción clásica. Y por eso mismo, la literatura ha tenido algo de revolucionaria para

las letras lationamericanas de estos tiempos que llamaríamos de *posboom* (emphasis in original). (Giardinelli 1984, 64)

they must be dark and hard. They can no longer create classic fiction. And for that very reason, literature has had some revolutionary quality for the Latin-American letter of these times we call the *postboom*.

At the end of this study's first chapter, I cited the views of Italian philosopher Gianni Vattimo on the issue of modernism and postmodernism. Speaking of the end of modernism, he said:

La forma moderna de vivir la historia era progresista y progresiva. Imaginaba un desarrollo indefinido del tiempo. Este progreso era un valor, como si la historia mejorara. El concepto moderno se acaba cuando ya no sentimos que es necessario ese avance. No hace falta más ser vanguardista. (Vattimo 1987, 8)

The modern way of living history was progressivist and progressive. It imagined an indefinite development of time. This progress stemmed from a value which held that history bettered itself. The concept of modernity comes to an end when we no longer feel the need for such advancement. We no longer need to be avant-garde.

Perhaps it is appropriate from the point of view of a Western European philosopher to speak in such a leisurely manner of historical advancement and avant-gardeism as options. I would venture that in the case of the Uruguayan novelist in question, a year after the fall from democracy to militarism of Latin America's longest-standing, the issue brought with it a greater sense of urgency, one that went to the heart of the relevancy and possibility of historical advancement and avant-gardeism. Nonetheless, what results is a novel that embodies the positive qualities Vattimo ascribes to postmodern art. It is an art that is

menos fetichista. Está más inserto en la comunidad social . . . y se vuelve más comunicativo, más comprensible. . . . Veo una nueva humanización del arte, un retorno al mundo de los sentidos, una menor intelectualización. (Vattimo 1987, 8)

less fetishistic. It is more involved in the social community . . . and it becomes more communicative, more comprehensible. . . . I see a new humanization of art, a return to the world of the senses, less intellectualizing.

In his last novel, Martínez Moreno writes in a milieu marked

8: *Tierra en la boca:* Decadence, Death, and a Decent Burial

by the passing of *la deca* in his social reality, and leaves it and the form to which it gave rise in his novels of the "boom." His response is to bury the modernism of his past works with *Tierra en la boca*, planting the seeds of a new, postboom and postmodern novel in the overturned soil. Given this new and difficult beginning for such a mature novelist, it is all the more unfortunate that the circumstances that brought about such a brave departure for his writing career smothered any further fruits these seeds might have borne, sending him into an exile in real life much like that of the Primitivo of his own first novella.

9

El color que el infierno me escondiera: After the Fall

After a steady stream of literary production until 1974, Martínez Moreno's literary career was interrupted for almost seven years by events in his native Uruguay. In addition to being a novelist, Martínez Moreno was the nation's foremost criminal defense attorney. After the Uruguayan military coup of 1973, it befell him to defend his colleagues—including Juan Carlos Onetti—against the savage attacks of the country's military dictatorship upon the literary community.

Martínez Moreno never lacked in admiration from critics and novelists among his Latin-American peers. In his prologue to the 1979 Spanish edition of Juan Carlos Onetti's collected works, Emir Rodríguez Monegal establishes the importance of Onetti's canon—a body of work much better known to an international readership than Martínez Moreno's—by comparing it to the works of the leading novelists of his time, a list that included Carlos Fuentes, Mario Vargas Llosa, and Carlos Martínez Moreno.[1] Yet Chilean novelist José Donoso, in his book *The Boom in Spanish American Literature: A Personal History* (1977), complains that, in spite of their obvious qualities, Martínez Moreno's works have "stayed locked within their national boundaries" (Donoso 1977, 24). He adds that "the lists of the hardships and sacrifices" of novelists such as Martínez Moreno

> could be continued *ad infinitum* in order to disprove the fascinating legend . . . circulating in certain parts of Latin America about the fabulous success of the boom novelists in the United States and in Europe—the idea that "they are fashionable." That is nothing more than a relative truth. . . . Martínez Moreno works obscurely in his law office in Montevideo. (63–64)

9: *El color que el infierno me escondiera:* After the Fall

It is Donoso's view that

> the public . . . sees a large number of writers—all with solid reputations, and whose names reach, in some areas more than in others, the entire Spanish-speaking world—grouped a little below the main body of the boom. (112)

Ironically, Martínez Moreno's literary fortunes began to change in exile with the publication of his only nonfiction novel. *El color que el infierno me escondiera* (The color hell would hide, translated into English in 1988 as *El Infierno*) (1981) is the product of the author's experiences during this bitter hiatus from 1974 to 1980.[2] Written in Mexico after a bomb blast at his Montevidean home forced him into exile in 1978, *El color* is part documentary narrative and part personal memoir cast in a narrative collage bound together by a structure borrowed from Dante's *Inferno*. The war between the Uruguayan government and the Movimiento de Liberación Nacional–Tupamaros had reached its most savage peak between 1970 and 1972. The ranks of the security forces were purged in favor of hard-liners who would eventually take power and create a dictatorship. Drastic measures were introduced in order to defeat any opposition to military rule after the coup in 1973. The most widespread of these measures was the use of professional, systematic, and institutionalized torture allegedly introduced to the Uruguayan security forces by a U.S. government official referred to by Martínez Moreno only as "the Adviser."[3] *El color que el infierno me escondiera* concerns itself with events stemming from the discovery of this character's alleged activities by elements of the Uruguayan Left. The audacity of kidnapping and executing such a figure can afford a revolutionary movement the international limelight and much leverage. However, it can also represent an escalation of a different type. This second type of escalation is one of despair in the face of backlash. It is an escalation that, morally, leads to the *deca* of the MLN–T itself as it finds itself forced to lower its standards for the application of violence in the face of looming defeat. The agonizing ethical twilight of the Tupamaro movement is soberly depicted in the sad description of the execution of an innocent peon by the MLN–T in "Operación Tatú" ("Operation Armadillo"). With the publication of his accounts drawn from this crucible of Uruguayan history, Martínez Moreno not only achieves some much-deserved and much-delayed critical acclaim, but also draws attention to a much-neglected subject area. As James Polk points out in his review of *El color* for the *New York Times*,

> Thus far, the Uruguayan experience during the "dirty wars" in the southern cone of Latin America has been pretty much slighted. The journalist Eduardo Galeano, the novelist Marta Traba and the film maker Costa-Gavras are among the few who have set works there, but most practitioners of what could be called "the literature of the disappeared" have stuck to Chile and Argentina, with occasional excursions into Brazil. So "El Infierno" reminds us forcefully of a neglected corner of terror and reminds us in stark, matter-of-fact terms not easily forgotten. (Polk 1988, 22:4)

Why Martínez Moreno's writing and Uruguay's experience during the "dirty war" did not receive greater attention prior to the publication of *El color* is anyone's guess. In dealing with this horrid chapter of Uruguayan—and human—history, the author definitively bridges the gap between the personal and the social seen previously in his treatment of *la deca*. In so doing, *El color* simultaneously combines the intimism of novels such as those of Onetti, with the social commentary of writings such as those of Benedetti, while never sacrificing the depth of the former nor the breadth of the latter. Given the keen insights of *El color* regarding the relationship between those two aspects of reality, one can argue that this last novel would have become the centerpiece of his work regardless of the country Martínez Moreno had chosen for his subject matter. Though the novel is firmly grounded in Uruguay's cultural, sociopolitical, and historical milieu, its meaning far transcends any national or temporal boundaries.

El color moved David William Foster to include Martínez Moreno in a chapter of his revisionist postboom study, *Alternate Voices in the Contemporary Latin American Narrative*, and rightfully so. Upon publication in 1981, it was awarded first prize in the Concurso Internacional Proceso–Nueva Imagen for its treatment of militarism in Latin America. The jury that selected it for this distinction consisted of such illustrious literary figures as Julio Cortázar and Gabriel García Márquez, among others.

As far as his own canon is concerned, *El color* is the culmination of the theme that holds Martínez Moreno's body of work together, the process he observed in Uruguayan society both on the individual and social levels and that he called *la deca*. Martínez Moreno's spiraling stylistic experiments in expressing his moral vision of *la deca* are what distinguish him as a novelist of the boom. When the 1960s *deca* yields to the 1970s "inferno" of Uruguay's military dictatorship, however, the change in Martínez Moreno's novels is abrupt. In *El color* it is no longer possible to speak of him as a boom author. This watershed in Martínez Moreno's canon pinpoints a drastic shift in a boom author's aesthetic values in response to a sociopolitical cataclysm. As such, it has significant implications for the historical definition of the revisionist tendencies of the postboom.

El color is Martínez Moreno's only documentary novel. From its first pages, it is evident, however, that Martínez Moreno intends to depart from the conventional narrative strategies employed by his contemporary documentary novelists. In it he deals directly with the military repression that served as an agonizing coda to the Uruguayan *deca* chronicled throughout his writings. But, what is more, to quote John King again, in *El color,*

> Martínez Moreno bravely confronts a theme which urgently requires historical revision: the nature of guerrilla movements in Latin America. . . . In the recent past, the *guerrilla* was a subject either of hagiography, for example Julio Cortázar's *A Manual for Manuel* (and to this I would add Benedetti's novel on the Uruguayan Tupamaros, *El cumpleaños de Juan Angel* and Galeano's *La canción de nosotros*) . . . or demonology. . . . Now a more balanced historical account is emerging, but to my knowledge this is the first . . . [novel] . . . reflecting this process. (Martínez Moreno, iii)

By including the Tupamaros in his critical revision of Uruguay's fateful experience in the 1970s, however, *El color* became Martínez Moreno's *El paredón* for his own country—a novel touching a most sensitive nerve in the national psyche and thereby provoking loud controversy. For the Tupamaros, it is a vindictive last straw in a heated, two-decade-old argument over violence versus nonviolence as the means for bringing about the changes needed to confront Uruguay's crisis in the late 1960s and early 1970s. As one might expect, Martínez Moreno's brave confrontation with this controversy was not without its consequences. The novel's reception immediately embroiled the author in a bitter debate that still clouds critical judgment of his works in Uruguay today, over a decade later. The sharpest criticism comes, as one might expect, from Uruguay's MLN–T, now a significant sector of the Frente Amplio, a leftist coalition Martínez Moreno himself helped found in 1970. At the time of its founding, the MLN–T supported the Frente Amplio in principle, but considered such nonviolent attempts at electoral change naive, claiming armed rebellion was the only realistic means of bringing about change. The fraudulent outcome of Uruguay's 1972 elections, the ensuing 1973 overthrow of even that government, and the right-wing military overthrow of Allende's Frente Popular coalitional government in Chile seemed to vindicate the MLN–T's position. The armed victory of another Frente, the Nicarguan FSLN, in 1979 seemed to make any arguments against violent change irrelevant. For Martínez Moreno to insist yet again on his nonviolent views from exile in 1981 appeared to some, particularly MLN–T supporters, to be unseemly stubbornness flying in the face of history.

Today the MLN–T would object to Martínez Moreno's moral indictment of choosing the path of violent change for very differnt reasons. In an unprecedented wave of toppled dictatorships surpassed only by the fall of communism in Eastern Europe, elections became to 1980s Latin America what guerrilla warfare was to Latin America in the 1970s. Elections and revolutions exchanged places as far as which was quixotically romantic and which was the realistic path to change, even for the continental models of victorious revolution, Nicaragua's FSLN. With the re-emergence of its leadership from a decade of bitter solitary confinement and torture at dictatorship's end in 1985, the MLN–T command was quick to adapt to the times and abandon arms, seeking political legitimacy in the Frente Amplio coalition. The nonviolent left, mindful of and still stinging from the rhetoric of the 1970s MLN–T's calls to arms, was slow to accede. Some, fairly or unfairly, even blamed the MLN–T for the severity of the dictatorial regime, claiming the MLN–T's actions had provoked a backlash. It was a delicate time, as the pieces of the past were put back together and open stock was taken for the first time in twelve years. The appearance of Martínez Moreno's somber refutation of the MLN–T's former argument was not helpful to the promotion of the MLN–T's new nonviolent image. Though in no way so intended, it almost seemed like an "I told you so" from the grave.

With all this complex controversy surrounding the novel, it is important to recall that Martínez Moreno had defended many Tupamaros himself as an attorney and that his own son had reportedly joined the movement. Yet the novel's reception by the movement is typified by the fact that, upon its publication in Mexico, an exiled Tupamaro found his way to Martínez Moreno's home, rang the bell, identified himself, and spat in the author's face.[4] In spite of having been acclaimed internationally and duly awarded Uruguay's own highest literary prize in 1987 after the author's death and the country's return to democracy, *El color que el infierno me escondiera* remains, for Uruguay, a subject of heated polemic as it challenges the country to digest the most bitter chapters of its horrible recent history.

The polemic has in no way been mitigated by the novel's critical success in both Spanish and in English translation, by the author's death, or by Uruguay's return to democracy and the subsequent amnestying of all Tupamaros. A recent interview with Eleuterio Fernández Huidobro, the current, widely respected leader of the Tupamaro movement and an author himself, confirms that *El color* has made Martínez Moreno a pariah to many leftists he once defended.[5] It is his contention that Martínez Moreno carried a grudge against the Tupamaros that dated back to their earliest days. As he sees it, the Tupamaros deserved their renown as the world's most efficient and elusive urban guerrilla movement. They eventually inspired the Sandinistas on to victory, as seen in Commander Omar Cabezas' admiring reference to them in his gripping testimonial account of the Sandinista revolution, *La montaña es algo más que una inmensa estepa verde* (*The Hills are Something More than an Immense Green Steppe*).[6] The MLN–T's reputation was for efficiency and daring creativity in combat, not for brutality. In its day, its efficiency garnered the MLN–T an image that prompted popular comparisons of their real-life activities to the fictional ones of the contemporary television series *Mission Impossible*. Nonetheless, it was not always so, particularly at the movement's beginnings, and there, too, was Martínez Moreno. As early as 1966 a combination of carelessness and bad luck nearly caused the MLN–T to expose its clandestine organization and self-destruct before the movement even had a chance to engage in any effective actions against the government. Faced with the prospect of falling into the hands of the authorities, one of the Tupamaros contacted Martínez Moreno to represent them in seeking safe conduct to political asylum out of the country. Fernández Huidobro's account of the incident in his *Historia de los Tupamaros* summarizes the general attitude of the Tupamaros toward Martínez Moreno and his novel on them:

> Esa noche contó (el compañero Tupamaro) que hacía días había comenzado las gestiones para pedir asilo y que cierto abogado de nota, que luego escribiría novelas muy ácidas sobre los tupamaros, cerró una puerta en la cara, diciéndole: *"Jódanse."* Comenzaban a deslindarse campos. (Emphasis in original.) (Huidobro 1989, 3:75)

> That very night (our Tupamaro comrade) told us that several days before he had begun to make the necessary arrangements for asking for political asylum and that a certain attorney of note, who would

later go on to write very acidic novels about the Tupamaros, slammed the door in his face saying to him: *"Go fuck yourselves."* Battle lines were beginning to be drawn.

Before considering his somewhat strongly worded views on Martínez Moreno and his attitudes toward the MLN–T, it is important to establish that Eleuterio Fernández Huidobro is no casual observer when it comes to Tupamaro history. Neither is he just another Tupamaro. Next to the MLN–T's late founder, Raúl Sendic, he is one of the most respected of the original Tupamaros—or the most notorious, depending on one's point of view. Denied the option of political asylum and exile when Martínez Moreno refused the Tupamaros legal representation when their underground network was compromised in 1966, Huidobro went on to become second only to founder Sendic himself in the reconstruction of the MLN–T. He was captured in the MLN–T's most notorious operation, which involved taking the city of Pando, in October 1969. He escaped from prison and returned to action as commander of one of the MLN–T's two military "columns," masterminding some of its boldest actions in its heyday. He was apprehended again in a spectacular shoot-out at a safe house in Montevideo in April 1972, just one month before the MLN–T's definitive military defeat. During his years as an active guerrilla, he was seriously wounded by gunfire four times. He is the most distinguished living Tupamaro veteran.

Tupamaro founder Raúl Sendic died in early 1989 from lingering complications related to torture while one of the "Hostage Nine" along with Huidobro. Huidobro then became the MLN–T's top surviving strategist. As such, he has directed its amazingly successful conversion to peacetime as participant in electoral politics. The eventual inclusion of the MLN–T in the reborn Frente Amplio coalition meant that, backed by the MLN–T—participating as a political party in elections for the first time in elections in 1989—the new Frente won the mayorship of Montevideo. In Uruguay, that office is the second most powerful post in the country. Attaining the mayorship at the ballot box was the greatest victory the left had ever won in any election in Uruguay's history. In addition the Tupamaros have established the country's most successful new book publishing house, a widely distributed weekly newspaper, and one of the country's most powerful radio stations.

In freedom, Huidobro has become one of Uruguay's most outstanding authors in helping Uruguayan society digest the country's double nightmare during the Tupamaro War and the ensuing brutal dictatorship. Along with his series of official Tupamaro histories, Huidobro has written the three-part *Memorias del calabozo* (The dungeon memoirs) (Huidobro and Rosencoff 1989). A gripping memoir of his unspeakably cruel ordeal, *Memorias del calabozo* was written in conjunction with fellow Tupamaro and critically renowned playwright Mauricio Rosencof. A simply narrated, riveting tale of suffering and the triumph of the human spirit, *Memorias del calabozo* deserves to be considered alongside *The Diary of Anne Frank* as a classic first-person narrative in the literature of survival. Similarly, Martínez Moreno's *El color* brings to mind literary comparisons with such a work as Solzhenitsyn's *Gulag Archipelago*.

Since each has so much to offer in shedding crucial light on this dark chapter in Uruguayan history, it is particularly painful, though perhaps inevitable, that there should be a lingering rivalry—whatever the source—between the two writers, for the correct version of the truth. In their sincere, relentless, self-sacrificing pursuit of their ideals, both men deserve respect for their accomplishments, whether one agrees with them or not. With absolutely every possible ounce of respect for Eleuterio Fernández Huidobro, as well as with genuine gratitude for his willingness to discuss the matter candidly in a private, lengthy interview with me, I can only differ with his description of Martínez Moreno's treatment of the Tupamaros as "acidic" in *El color* or any other book, as well as in any conversation that can be independently verified. It is understandable that the Tupamaros should be somewhat sensitive to the discussion of the ethics of their inner workings by an outsider. However, the exact source of the very high level of resentment on the part of the MLN–T for Martínez Moreno is—and perhaps will always remain—a mystery known and understood only by them, hidden from public view once by lawyer-client privilege and now, forever, by the grave.

Despite its controversial significance as a Uruguayan document, the more detached reader will find in *El color* a novel of universal significance. As Polk says,

> Martínez Moreno is clearly a moralist, and as such is much more interested in exploring how individuals function in a moral vacuum. . . . That such people emerge from the Inferno with some semblance of themselves intact is the most the author allows. Otherwise, he leads us through a society of extremes, a nation without any habitable middle ground. (Polk 1988, 22: 4)

The essence of the *El color* is not politics, but ethics—the ethical questions raised by man's inhumanity to man in Uruguay's holocaust. Martínez Moreno deftly steers a course between manichean visions of his country's tragedy by leading the reader through the personal trials of a vast sampling of characters who played a part in Uruguay's holocaust. Yet these characters are not presented merely as soldiers and guerrillas. Instead, high government officials held hostage, torture victims, Tupamaros, military officers, and political prisoners are presented—through personal testimonials, letters, and reports—as the children, parents, husbands, mothers, wives, lovers, and grandparents they also were.

Martínez Moreno organizes their personal stories by dividing the novel's twenty-two chapters into an internal structure of four alternating portions. The first and third portions juxtapose the opposing poles of Uruguay's inferno, depicting the inner workings of the security forces and the Tupamaros at key moments that defined their fates. Martínez Moreno offers the reader what one could call, to turn a phrase from Echeverría's "Radiografía de la Pampa," a "radiological" view of an Uruguay's Inferno.

The first portion begins with a chapter on the U.S. aid torture instructor titled "The Adviser and his Beggar's Opera" beginning with the words, "As the Cuban tells it." The Cuban in question, Manuel Hevia Cosculluela, alleges himself to have been a double agent who had allegedly infiltrated the CIA after "escaping" Cuba for "asylum" in the U.S. Sent to Uruguay by the CIA, as alleged in his book *Pasaporte 11333: Ocho años con la CIA* (Passport 11333: Eight years with the CIA), Cosculluela claims to have witnessed the actual classes in which Montevideo's police and military were taught the use of cattle prods on live subjects (Cosculluela 1988). However, Cosculluela's credibility, though high in certain sectors of Uruguayan society, obviously has not been established in other sectors of society due to the ongoing U.S. blockade of Cuba and the Cuban regime's own censorship. Therefore, Martínez Moreno is careful never to use any name in reference to the character of the Adviser, preferring only the generic, functional title. Though obviously originating in a legal necessity to avoid libelous or slanderous characterizations of any actual person who may have passed through those tumultuous times, it plays an important part in the author's literary plan of attack on this most difficult subject. It serves to ward off the temptation to concentrate only on the acts of particular individuals, important though they may be, so as to focus on the larger tableau of human morality. In this way, *El color* is markedly different from the Costa Gavras film treatment of the period in Uruguay. Costa Gavras's film concentrates on the political intrigue of the times. Martínez Moreno asks us to mourn, not only for his tortured Uruguay, but for how its suffering adds yet another chapter to what remains, as of yet, an unending record of modern sadism and fratricide, a record running from Auschwitz to Argentina, from Cambodia to Chile. *El color* manages to achieve this universality by being, above all, not an historical treatise, nor a legal brief, but, timelessly, a novel.

As the novel opens, the Adviser has established a secret torture academy in his own neighborhood in Montevideo as part of the government's program to neutralize the Tupamaros. In setting the scene, Martínez creates an almost theatrical sense bordering on the tragically inevitable in presenting this crucial character playing his central role in this fatal national drama. Shocking acts unfold before the reader, almost entirely without comment. The Adviser speaks for himself in a monologue worthy of a Dr. Mengele, but presented dispassionately: evil eerily devoid of malice. Martínz Moreno's commentary on the phenomenon that the Adviser represents is provided by the backdrop of the character's life, a backdrop that includes the contradicting roles of devout Catholic, opera lover, and father of a large family. The reader is thus relentlessly challenged by a portrait of villainy that prompts inevitable questions as to the relevance of religious, cultural, and family values to the root of evil. The Adviser is depicted as having set up a torture house only blocks away from his own quiet suburban home in Montevideo. In so doing, Martínez Moreno says symbolically, quoting Dante, "he made his own house his scaffold. . . . Then he climbed it. We all did" (Martínez Moreno 1988, 78).

Thus, the Adviser is not introduced in the novel as some sort of hooded sadist in a secret dungeon's torture chamber. Quite to the contrary, the narrator describes him in the first person as a man of refinement and taste he remembers having seen at the opera in Montevideo. The description sketches the narrator's impressions of the Adviser in lines that might serve to make some sort of human connection with what was, under the circumstances of Uruguay at the time, the Wholly Other.

> One night I got a glimpse of him, close up, without knowing who he was. Though it was only that once, his face, his discreet charm and well-concealed portliness made such an impression on me that the day his photograph appeared in *El Día* I recognised him immedi-

ately. . . . *The Kibbutz* had not held his attention on stage. I've often wondered since, whether despite his name, he was unable to understand Italian. He had allowed his half-moon spectacles to slip down his nose, so that the tortoiseshell arms stood out clearly above his ears, where they opened two slender furrows in his well-groomed silvery hair. . . . Barely a few days later, on August 1st, I saw his photograph in the newspaper. (3–4)

The elegance and charm in the initial description of the Adviser are disconcerting in a portrait of a character so heinous as a torture instructor. Martínez Moreno juxtaposes his mild, bureaucratic demeanor at the opera with the coldness of his first session in the torture school he has established.

"Gentlemen: everything we are going to do here is absolutely necessary." (His pale, expressionless eyes are fixed somewhere above his audience's head—the army men in uniform, the police officers in smart suits as though they were attending an official function). "If you don't agree, there's no room for you here. . . . This is a lecture: you are here to learn. It is part of a complete course. . . . I didn't come to this country to waste my time. . . . The art of interrogation is a complex one. . . . What we are aiming for here is that a person should feel alone and defenseless, completely cut off from reality, face-to-face with infinite fear. To achieve results at this stage there should be no interrogation as such . . . [n]o questions: nothing but blows and insults. . . . However, harsh they may be, words are bound to produce familiarity between the people involved. Whenever two people talk, they cease to be completely alien to each other . . . the aim is to provoke panic, a solitude that is so desperate we can later offer to alleviate it in return for whatever we are interested in obtaining. The deepest despair . . . a process of self-destruction . . . terror that has no limits is the worst kind, an infinite terror . . ." he muses, clearly engrossed in his words . . . "not a single word that might help him relate to another human being. . . . Have you all understood clearly what I've been saying?"

Nobody has ever spoken to them like this before. It is all very clear, but at the same time they are stunned. Torture, in the hands of the police officers, had always been a confused affair . . . a brawl in which . . . [t]hey lost control. . . . The Adviser offers them a different perspective . . . [n]o hatred, no display of emotion. No fear, no arrogance. Method and more method. . . .[T]he look in the Adviser's eyes: "They were like plastic, showing no spark of life." . . . [T]hey have [never] come across the devil, but they dimly realise that were they to do so, he would appear to them in similar disguise. (13–17)

The Adviser's recognition of words, of language itself, as the basis of all human community, reveals much about Martínez Moreno's own view of language in a plainly didactic manner that distinguishes this novel from those of his boom period in the 1960s. Martínez Moreno appears to have completed the transition noted in the 1974 novel *Tierra en la boca* from the style of his boom novels to a postboom aesthetic. *El color* is a far cry from the clumsy, after-the-fact didacticism tacked on to the end of the 1970 novel *Coca*. In that case, Martínez Moreno's ill-considered didacticism marred an otherwise fine novel by destroying the verisimilitude of an otherwise masterfully drawn *deca* character with an uncharacteristically idealistic speech. Marie-Louise's unlikely soliloquy on Che Guevara is an unconvincing epilogue for a novel whose characters' most salient trait has been their childish self-absorption in their own problems. They, like the protagonists of the author's previous novels, are characters of Martínez Moreno's boom aesthetic. Hence, they inhabit his *deca* world, a private hell to which they cling although they recognize it to be infernal. These are characters so fearful of change that they are willing to endure hell even in the most turbulent of public circumstances, much like Fuentes' Artemio Cruz.

In *El color,* such resistance to change turns from a willingness to endure hell to a willingness to inflict it as private stoicism turns to public sadism. Martínez Moreno still employs the baroque narrative strategies that earned him the nickname of "Justiciero barroco" ("baroque lawman"). However, in the brutally intrusive police state of *El color*'s Inferno, the separation between personal and public hell no longer holds. Consequently, the author steps out from behind his role as master puppeteer to editorialize, commenting personally upon the fates of his characters and how he has chosen to portray them. Both directly and indirectly, Martínez Moreno reveals to the reader the extent of the despair Uruguay's suffering has visited upon him. As a result, he also divulges his reason for writing a novel in a manner he had never allowed himself in the past, to reveal his desperate faith in the healing power of words. In his first chapter on the Adviser, he makes his didactic intent clear. With typical irony, he conveys his message through the unlikeliest of characters. As Martínez Moreno's Adviser says, *"However harsh they may be, words are bound to produce familiarity"* (emphasis mine) (13). Thus, the very description of Uruguay's Inferno, however difficult both for the author and for the reader, is an act of restoration. As the book's epigraph from Dante states,

> . . . And at his touch the colour they had worn
> Ere Hell had overcast it, they regained.
>
> Dante, *Purgatory*, Canto I (Martínez Moreno 1988, v)

The meaning of the novel's title and the author's purpose in "touching" upon the horrible subject of Uruguay's recent history is clear. In Martínez Moreno's postboom view as revealed in *El color*, the writer can ill afford the luxury of Art for Art's sake alone. Instead, the writer's role in society is to rescue society from the hell it creates for itself. While not claiming the power to transform society, literature can heal by bringing humanity into painful contact with even the most atrocious but true aspects of human nature.

This is an interesting case of an author's coming about full circle in his attitude toward the relationship between literature and society in narrative. Martínez Moreno's first writings were inspired by his youthful passion for the republican cause during the Spanish civil war. However, in *El color* he renounces what Lennard Davis, writing in Edward Said's *Literature and Society*, has called the novelist's "authorial disavowal" that he worked so hard to maintain in his novels in the years of the 1960s boom (Davis 1980, 120).

"Authorial disavowal," says Davis, is, in the "social history of fact and fiction," traditionally one of the very means by which the novel is conventionally defined. Yet, as he points out, the now familiar dichotomy between fact and fiction, journalism and the novel, did not assist the birth of the modern novel as a genre. Artistic concerns were not to blame so much as fear of government censorship and of vague, embryonic libel and slander laws in the seventeenth century. Only then did the distinction become desirable as a source of protection for writers. In fact, says Davis, until the late sixteenth and early seventeenth century, according to the *Oxford English Dictionary* "the word *novel* seems to have been used interchangeably with the world *news*" (Davis 1980, 126). One of the examples Davis gives of such a book is, interestingly enough, a novel published in 1606 with the title *News from Hell*.

El color is Martínez Moreno's "News from Hell." Ironically, in *El color* he abandons "authorial disavowal" and the distinction between fact and fiction, news and novel, for the same reason it was adopted in the first place by the earliest modern novelists: as a reaction to government intrusion. Having already paid the price of exile for his views, he no longer cares to observe such a

9: *El color que el infierno me escondiera:* After the Fall

distinction since he no longer has anything to lose. Consequently, he breaks with this central convention of the modernist definition of the novel blurring the line between fact and fiction in postmodern (some would argue, premodern) fashion. In *El color* the definition of the postboom and postmodern novel cannot be seen to involve yet another new avant-garde form. Rather, it is a return to a more straightforward social realism, though one informed by the experiments of the boom all the same.

Thus, if *El color*'s didactic purpose is to demonstrate that the word can heal by connecting the reader with even the most atrocious human experiences, then Martínez Moreno is generously therapeutic in his descriptions of the Adviser's lessons. In his typical Flaubertian fashion, while never sensational, he spares the reader no detail. The Adviser has the police round up some *bichicomes*, people now known in the U.S. as "the homeless," as subjects for a cruel session of show-and-tell. Martínez Moreno's humanist view that *no* human being is dispensable was earlier the source of his controversial commentary on the Sosa Blanco trial in *El paredón*. Here the same stubborn sense of values is evident in the dignifying pathos of the description of the *bichicomes'* suffering. One, whom he calls "The Prophet" for lack of a name and because his beard and wild eyes make him resemble an Old Testament character, is

> [s]tripped of his clothes.... He doesn't say a word, blinking.... The assistants have brought in a stretcher.... They lay the bearded tramp down on it ... [and] secure him.... [T]hen a man in shirtsleeves begins to probe at him with a cattle prod.... He presses it to his penis, his scrotum, very precisely, almost delicately, as surgically as the adviser has been recommending. Despite the straps, the tramp begins to writhe on the board; he screams. It's a brief, hoarse yelp that lacks either power or intensity, the scream of someone unaccustomed to it, who is suddenly horrified to find he cannot avoid doing so....
>
> "Look at the way his balls are shaking, dammit!" the colonel sputters....
>
> "Colonel," [the Adviser] says, "it would be better if you used the correct terms for the different parts of the body. I would also ask you to remember your military discipline. And please, could you not speak unless spoken to." (Martínez Moreno 1988, 20–21)

Martínez Moreno gives voice to the voiceless Prophet in this scene as he juxtaposes him with the Adviser's desire for absolute control of the word even when uttered in alarm at the outer limits of human (inhuman?) experience. In such juxtaposition lies the novel's modus operandi for conveying the author's message and the aspect of the novel that most typifies its postboom, didactic sensibility. In contrast to the Adviser, for whom a large funeral will eventually be held, these, the Holy Innocents of the story, are not memorialized. "El color" will not be restored completely until they are, so Martínez Moreno builds them a literary memorial:

> A city is a honeycomb. Each layer is unaware of what is going on underneath. In this system of tunnels, the *bichicomes* live at the lowest level. They are oblivious to what is going on above their heads. There is never anything to ask them. Though their lives are at stake, they don't know what to reply. If one or four of them die, it's all the same. A *bichicome* is not an adviser. There are no flags at half-mast for a *bichicome*'s death, no expressions of remorse, no threat of national disgrace, no burial mounds, no pleas for them to be spared, nothing. A *bichicome* dies when he cannot withstand any more torture, not because someone refuses to bargain for his life. If one or four of them die from the prod or drowning in their own vomit, it is not because their executioner wants any secrets from them. Nobody wants to ask the *bichicomes* anything, nobody is anxious for their answers. It's simply a question of testing the limits of their resistance, how long their ribs, testicles, arms, or lungs can hold out. This is torture at its most gratuitous, a pure form of torture as experiment. (26)

From these introductory scenes to the Adviser's Uruguayan underworld, Martínez Moreno goes on to portray the 1969 abduction by the MLN–T of financier Dr. Gaetano Pellegrini Giampietro in the second chapter, "Il Dottore Gaetano." Presented as a monologue recorded on tape as a statement for posterity, in Gaetano's observations Martínez Moreno provides an uncommon view of the Tupamaraos close up:

> [T]hey questioned me about some of the bank's transactions. They tended to think of all bank or stock negotiations which they did not understand as illicit, crooked, and fraudulent. I tried to explain the mechanisms of each operation, like someone explaining the big bad wolf to frightened children. One of the young guys had previously worked in a bank, I could tell. . . . There was a certain left-wing Manicheism in (his) judgments. (35)

This is undoubtedly a passage that did not serve to endear Martínez Moreno to Tupamaro leader and Eleuterio Fernández Huidobro. Though not mentioned by name, the former bank teller turned guerrilla leader mentioned here is most certainly Huidobro. Of course, if this were a conventional novel employing "authorial disavowal," one could argue that the accusation of "Manicheism" is Gaetano's and not Martínez Moreno's. Yet such is not the case here. In any case, it is the author who is always ultimately responsible for the deliberate selection of material to be narrated, whatever the generic considerations. Perhaps it is to Martínez Moreno's credit that, in selecting his material for *El color*, he allows each of the players in the drama to say his piece no matter how "harsh" his words might be. In no way can it be said that Martínez Moreno prefers Gaetano's voice to that of the Tupamaros; he also "allows" the Dottore to damn himself in his own words with an admission of his fascist past:

> "Mussolini was never great," replied the young man. "Fascists can't be great."
> I replied, " . . . I'm no longer a fascist, but I would never dare deny his potential greatness as you do."

To remind us of the reason why fear of fascism was so relevant to Uruguayan reality, between "Il Dottore Gaetano" and another kidnapping we witness the secret burial of the *bichicomes* in "The Beggar's Opera (II)." Only then are we treated to the testimonial of cabinet minister and presidential confidant Ulysses Pereira Reverbel, the only man who can claim the distinction of having been kidnapped and released by the MLN–T twice (in 1968 and 1971) in "Ulysses' Monologue." Again the story takes the form of a first person narrative after the victim's release. However, this time it is a monologue spoken to a certain "Marenales"—one of Pereira Reverbel's Tupamaro abductors—and not merely into a tape recorder. As the chapter unfolds, the scene is revealed to be a private moment police allow Pereira Reverbel to have with one of his kidnappers, Julio Marenales Saenz, an actual Tupamaro arrested in the case on 8 October 1968. Marenales Saenz was tortured with electric shock by police for five days. He escaped detention and was not recaptured until the MLN–T's final defeat. The interconnectedness of all participants in this human drama, so well illustrated in Martínez Moreno's memorial to the *bichicomes*, is only reinforced by Reverbel's stubborn, vain, and ultimately pathetic attempts to deny it. He is grateful for the treatment he received from Marenales in captivity. Notwithstanding, he disclaims any responsibility for the consequences—certain torture—of his picking Marenales Saenz out of a police lineup, which he is about to do. "*I fulfill my duty and you can't accuse me of wanting revenge*" (54). It is such a revealing journey into a petty, self-absorbed mind that one almost chuckles upon reading of his second abduction by the MLN–T years later.

Having set the narrative into motion by juxtaposing the MLN–T's kidnappings and the state's torture, the first portion of the novel ends with two more chapters on the subject of the Adviser, "The Adviser (I)" and "(II)." In these final chapters on the North American, the author plumbs the psyche of this family man of such contradictory moral fiber. As his descriptions insistently make obvious, Martínez Moreno's Adviser is more frightening than any stereotypical Marquis de Sade. It is his banal realism that makes him so: he is a twentieth-century Everyman whose job happens to be in the middle management of a bureaucracy of pain. The Adviser goes to work each day to demonstrate the use of a cattle prod on live, innocent victims as if they were medical school cadavers and he were teaching anatomy to future pediatricians and gynecologists.

In depicting the Adviser's kidnapping, interrogation, and execution by the Tupamaros, Martínez Moreno subtly takes the view that the MLN–T's violence only served to further the Adviser's goals. By their own admission, resorting to violent methods against representatives of foreign governments only created martyrs in the international community and evaporated whatever sympathy for their cause that may have existed in the Western bloc. Thus, in yet another of Uruguay's many tragic ironies, the Tupamaros assisted their own adversaries in seizing the moral high ground, at least imagewise, in this crucial conflict over the future of Uruguayan society. In making the fatal decision to resort to kidnapping, the MLN–T put itself in the no-win situation of winning a battle to lose the war. From that point on, the government's torture tactics alone could no longer be blamed for creating the moral vacuum in the country. The government could now point to someone else as having committed atrocities in the conduct of the war. However lopsided the government's comparison of its own atrocities to those committed by the MLN–T might be (and they were bound to be extremely distorted comparisons), the Tupamaros had lost that precious, absolute moral high ground it had previously occupied in resisting the holocaust the state sought to visit upon the Uruguayan people. The execution of kidnap victims now provided a pretext for state terror in the guise of counterterrorism.

The consequences for a variety of Uruguayans from various

9: *El color que el infierno me escondiera:* After the Fall

walks of life are the subject of six chapters pointedly sandwiched between the first and third portions of the novel. "Candelabra" is the gentle portrait of a Tupamaro woman in prison who is driven insane by torture. In a masterfully moving and ironic episode typical of Martínez Moreno's style, she inadvertently leads her captors to wonder whether the hallucinatory candlelight dinners in her cell aren't real; the reader is left to wonder who might be the more sane after all. "Release Papers," a chapter in which a husband is forced to watch the rape of his beloved by his interrogators, answers the question by illustrating the mad, brutal depths to which the security forces fell.

"Red Indians," which appears as a short story in Martínez Moreno's posthumous short story volume *Animal de palabras* (Animal of words), is the heart-wrenching story of a child of war. A wounded little girl is left by her Tupamaro parents in the garden of her grandfather, who she calls "the Chief." Her nickname for her grandfather attracts the attention of an army captain, who submits the four-year-old child to an interrogation. In the little granddaughter's ordeal, the reader witnesses how a war such as Uruguay's can tear a family apart at the seams, simultaneously devouring past, present, and future generations in the process. "The Soldier with the Arm in Plaster" tells how those families' grief is cynically exploited for gain by the corrupt military. In an absurdly humorous scheme, a prison guard makes a business of carrying letters between prisoners and their families in the hollow of a fake cast he wears on his arm, delivering them for pay to families too desperate to refuse the letters and too frightened to report the extortion.

With this interlude illustrating the ripple effect the war's escalation has had upon the general populace, Martínez Moreno returns to its combatants in the second half of the novel with a devastating probe into the collapse of the Tupamaro revolutionaries' highest ideals. In a series of chapters entitled "Caragua," he analyzes the ethical implications of the execution of an innocent *peón* on the orders of the Tupamaros' high command. The MLN–T's reason for the execution—"security"—ominously echoes the national security doctrine followed by the state to justify its actions. The MLN–T has begun to resemble that which it most opposes.

Though the MLN–T was known as an exemplary guerrilla movement for its restraint and organization, Martínez Moreno deliberately and mercilessly explores this, the Tupamaros' least proud episode, not as an exercise in political propaganda, but so as to reveal the moral consequences of resorting to violence in the name of ideals. This is a theme visited before in Martínez Moreno's controversial novel on the executions of the Cuban revolution, *El paredón*. It also appears often in the works of his closest Latin-American counterpart, Mario Vargas Llosa, most notably in the Peruvian's epic treatise on fanaticism, *The War of the End of the World*.

In the "Caragua" chapters of *El color*, however, Martínez Moreno makes his point nakedly; as the first line of "Caragua (III)" puts it, "A man's death should always be central to any drama" (171). Unfortunately for the MLN–T, in this case the drama to which a man's death becomes central here is a drama whose denouement is the Tupamaros' loss of the moral high road—and with it, the war. The murder of the Adviser has unleashed a ferocious counteroffensive against the Tupamaro rebellion. The military, resorting to ever more barbarous acts as means to its end, has eliminated all middle ground in the conflict and stands poised to engulf all of Uruguayan society. The Tupamaros, beaten back, desperately go underground to carry on their struggle—not just clandestine, but literally underground. As a defensive measure, they launch "Operation Armadillo," a plan to build a system of tunnels in the countryside similar to those of the Viet Cong in the Vietnam War. In the course of building the first of these tunnels, a *peón*, a member of the underlcass they are sworn to defend, is captured by the guerrillas when he unwittingly stumbles upon the mouth of the Tupamaros' tunnel system while chasing a stray horse.

Immediately, the Tupamaros sense their dilemma. In the interest of security, they should execute their prisoner so as to guarantee he will not reveal, wittingly or unwittingly, the existence and location of their tunnel network—the last hope for their movement's survival and the fulfillment of its promise of liberation. On the other hand, to be consistent with their proletarian ideals, the Tupamaros should release the *peón*—at the risk of jeopardizing the lives of hundreds of comrades and, with them, the last chance of resistance to a Uruguayan military dictatorship.

The pages describing the agony of the Tupamaro leadership at a war council to discuss this dilemma reveal the soul of Martínez Moreno's *Inferno*. As is the case repeatedly in the history of Western civilization from the Crusades to Stalin and Hitler, the road to hell is paved with good intentions gone bad. The crux of the issue, as seen in Martínez Moreno's depiction of the debate, is in the irony of the individual's dehumanization as s/he is made

9: *El color que el infierno me escondiera:* After the Fall

subservient to a greater "good." The arguments are the usual familiar ones; however, now they will be played out in concrete, not abstract, terms: a person will live or die by the outcome of the debate. To one youthfully militant member of the council deciding his fate, the *Peón* is "two eyes and a tongue" and nothing more (135). The eldest member of the council, an anarchist known as the Priest who is as close as any character to being Martínez Moreno's alter ego in the novel, the fate of the *peón* represents much more. It is a watershed, a fateful decision that will decide the course of their movement and how it will be judged by posterity. As he says, the very fact that the *peón*'s fate presents them with a dilemma proves that

> We have made a revolution greater than ourselves. Yes, and what do we do with it now? It is no use. . . . The revolution should be on the level of those who make it. If it is not, it will not work. It should express everybody's highest achievements, of course, but nothing else, no more than that. The highest level, but no higher. Everything for the revolution, but also for the man who makes it. Because the ideal and purpose of revolution is to diminish the power of one man over other men. (140)

As is too often the case, pragmatism triumphs over such idealism, and the *peón* is executed with the comment, "Of necessity, men are never equals" (145). Marínez Moreno's entire canon's message could be summarized as a protest against the existence of such "necessities" in a world claiming to be civilized. The moment the MLN–T embraces such "necessity" the soul of the Tupamaro rebellion is executed with him: the *L* in the acronym—"liberation"—loses a great deal of its human dimension of meaning. As the Anarchist puts it:

> At the beginning, when we robbed the Monty Finance Company and the San Rafael Casino, we were Robin Hoods, we wanted justice, we were crusaders against injustice, defenders of the poor. But after that, after we had been forced to kill, we became, in the minds of the majority, murderers, wild animals cornered in their dens, teeth and claws at the ready. And now, for logistic reasons, that transformation was complete. We were digging the grave of a man whom we would never ever have reason to believe was anything but innocent.
> "*Compañeros*, it is done. And I now realize who it is we are burying."
> "Who?" they asked, allowing him to exercise his fantasy for a moment (was he going mad?).
> "We are burying Robin Hood," he said. (181)

The guerrillas have guaranteed the survival of the movement for a time, but they also have taken an ethical short-cut which no longer allows them to hold clear claim to moral superiority over their adversaries. It is a testament to the literary powers of Martínez Moreno that such an easily overlooked, singular incident could take on such significance in his writings.

In no way, however, do the "Caragua" chapters imply that Martínez Moreno dismissed the suffering of the Tupamaros in their mortal struggle. In the book's second half, two chapters in particular deal with what it is like to make the supreme sacrifice for one's ideal—only to be defeated. Once again, he does not couch this drama in heroic terms, but humanizes it on an individual scale by discussing the MLN–T's defeat not in terms of political or military goals, but in terms of the thwarted desires of lovers and families. He reminds the reader once again that Uruguay's fall into the Inferno meant that countless private dreams were fed to the flames of a public hell. " . . . Paradise on Earth," the only chapter inserted between the Caragua chapters, is a vignette illustrating what that meant in terms of concrete human suffering. It is 13 June 1972, the last few weeks of the Tupamaro struggle. Sendic will be wounded and captured on 1 September. Rightist death squads now roam Montevideo's strees with impunity. Since the 15 April formal declaration of "internal war" by the government, one of the MLN–T's two column commanders, Eleuterio Fernández Huidobro, has been wounded and captured in a horrific gun battle. Leaderless, several hundred Tupamaros have fallen into government hands. Huidobro's column, now disintegrating, is based in the dunes east of Montevideo in which the summer home community of "Paradise on Earth" is nestled, camouflaged as weekenders at the beach. Here Martínez Moreno directs the reader to witness the meaning of the death of a Tupamaro.

He is never named, but he is described as one of the higher ranking members of the MLN–T and a veteran. The Tupamaros dug the tunnel from his cell for their spectacular prison break on 6 September 1971 in which 106 Tupamaros, Sendic included, escaped right from under their guard's noses. "Now as he is being hunted down, he knows they will not take him prisoner this time; they will shoot him" (152).

Yet what concerns this veteran Tupamaro in the hour of his defeat and death is not so much a sense of remorse for the loss of a better future for his country. He has done all he could for the popular struggle. It is the private loss, the loss of a future

9: *El color que el infierno me escondiera:* After the Fall

with his beloved, which grieves him most. But now, waiting for the security forces to attack, there is no time for doubting:

> it would be no use either, to talk to each other, to toss questions back and forth between the two of them. They were tired and this was another barren vigil. Months ago now they had decided not to have the child which she had given up asking him for and which he had not wanted to give her. War was not the time for it, and a hideout not the place. . . . Nobody can believe, nobody can admit that they may have to pass their last hours in a trap. "I'm staying right here, they can come and get me," Jay (his *compañera*) had said. Her right leg was fractured, the bone exposed; she had fainted after falling into a deep ditch, in her small, truncated, curtailed attempt at flight. . . .[H]e kissed her once, one last time, distraught, as he laid her down again on the pine needles at the edge of the ditch. And then—just as she could not suppress a cry, as shafts of pain stabbed her again—only then did he begin to run, to put distance between them and disperse the pursuer's fire. . . . His fall was a void. . . . The blow, so long expected/unexpected, impels him forward like an axe blow, a searing, it burns more that it hurts, it flames, it envelops, it darkens, it blinds, it asphyxiates.
> He opens his arms.
> Opens his mouth.
> Falls. (259)

It would be difficult for even the most hardened cynic to avoid being moved by this man's fall over the edge of the Inferno as he sacrifices his own life to save his wife's in this ironically named "Paradise on Earth."

For other Tupamaros, defeat brings concern for other loved ones—if not a lover, then for parents. "Karonicki" is a chapter named for a Tupamaro who was one of Martínez Moreno's clients during the months of the government's final offensive and victory. As his name would indicate, this Tupamaro is Polish. However, in another of this book's many bitter ironies, he is not only Polish, but Jewish, his parents having come to Uruguay as refugees from Europe and the Warsaw ghetto massacre of Jews by Hitler's forces during World War II. Now the demon of murderous antisemitism they fled has pursued their family across the ocean. In prison, the son is singled out by army officers for torture since, as the officer puts it, "Bolshies, Zionism, and Cosa Nostra" are the "three forces that will destroy the world" unless destroyed first. Karonicki's parents implore Martínez Moreno to find a way to get him out of prison so they can leave Uruguay and immigrate to— of all places for an anti-Yankee revolutionary—the U.S., where they have relatives. "We're Jews and we've already been in one concentration camp. We didn't die because we were young and strong, like he is now. but who knows whether this time . . ." (196). Try as he might, the author fails to obtain their son's release, with the expected consequences. A couple who survived torture under Hitler in Europe for their Jewishness and put it behind them to start a new life so as to face it "never again" live to see their tormentor's ideas rise from the grave to slaughter their own son as they helplessly sit by.

The plight of this Jewish couple and their son points to what Martínez Moreno the political scientist thinks of those who dismiss comparisons of Uruguay's "dirty war" to Nazi Germany and Fascist Italy. So does Dr. Gaetano's reappearance in the novel's very next chapter, as he compares his own years in Uruguay to memories of his father's tenure as one of Mussolini's ministers. Martínez Moreno's juxtaposition of the two renders hypocritical and absurd the endless hair-splitting of certain intellectuals—particularly certain North American intellectuals—who chose to focus with riveted attention upon a fabricated, petty debate over the "difference" between terms like *authoritarian* and *totalitarian* while ignoring their own governments' backing of regimes spreading dictatorship all over the hemisphere. Such conveniently self-serving, abstracted arguments delayed and blunted an effective response by the international community, prolonging the suffering of numerous Karonickis. The novel's treatment of the historical record on the point bears witness to the price paid in blood by thousands for whom help was delayed while others argued abstractions that, if humanity had been part of the equation, should have been moot points.

Martínez Moreno, while a leftist, amply proved himself over the years to be an independent thinker. He and his colleagues in exile argued for the importance of the historical comparison between the dictatorships of the Southern Cone and those of the Axis powers. By contrast, certain North American academics who disallowed any link between the two on ideological grounds seem to have taken their cues from a conservative establishment in power both in the U.S. and in Great Britain. For them to oppose regimes installed with the help of a previous conservative U.S. president's administration—that of Richard Nixon—was politically inconvenient. That political expediency, not intellectual integrity, drove certain conservative intellectuals' attitudes toward the Southern Cone was amply made evident, in this writer's view, at the outset of the Falklands War in 1982. It was truly sad how quickly these same intellectuals, intellectuals who previously had accused others of hyperbole at the mention of Nazism and fascism in connection with Southern Cone dictatorships, abandoned those once vehement arguments once the British, not South Americans civilians, became the target of a general's military madness.

The comparison of the Southern Cone dictatorships to World War II's Axis alliance of Nazism and fascism was—and still is—not only of intellectual importance; it is important to the current process to which *El color,* like all of contemporary Uruguayan society itself, is dedicated: the process of digesting and learning from the horror of the past so it will never be repeated. To deny the drawing of obvious and necessary comparisons between the South American holocaust and the European holocaust is to deny the Southern Cone's "dirty war" its necessary historical context. Such a context is required for Uruguayans and others to learn from the extensive research conducted by the Jewish community into how a society recovers from such devastatingly prejudicial self-destruction. It is no coincidence—any more than the fact that Martínez Moreno included "Karonicki" and "Nino" in *El color*—that Uruguay's human rights commission named its inquiry into the "dirty war" after the motto of the Jewish Holocaust survivors: *Uruguay: nunca más,* or *Uruguay: Never Again.* Uruguayan historian Federico Fasano Martens has called Uruguay's experience during the 1970s and 1980s that of a dictatorship of a "lumpen fascismo anémico que quiere ser y no puede" ("an anemic lumpen fascism that wants to be but can't) (Martens, 1980, 126). "Karonicki" is a chilling illustration of that notion.

Of course, the gravest injustice of Uruguay's "dirty war" was that it did not end with the defeat of the combatants in the MLN–T. It turned an entire nation into innocent bystanders caught in the crossfire. According to Lawrence Weschler's 1989 *New Yorker* piece, after the defeat of the MLN–T and the military coup a year later, "The whole country was run like a prison. The actual prisons were merely the punishment cells." U.S. aid was used to conduct a census and create a state-run computer system that issued identity cards to all citizens classifying them as belonging to one of three categories:

> "A" citizens were politically trustworthy, and hence could be employed by the state (Uruguay's principal employer), could travel freely, and were extended certain minimal freedoms. "B" citizens were deemed ideologically suspect, and hence could be employed privately

but not by the state (tens of thousands were fired); their external travel privileges were severely limited; and they faced continual petty (and sometimes not so petty) harassment by the security services. "C" citizens weren't citizens: they were pariahs, stripped of all their rights, and even of the possibility of employment. (Any private company that endeavored to employ a "C" citizen invited a crippling series of government audits.) And anyone at any time could suddenly find himself reclassified "C"—because, after all, the state knew everything. (Weschler 1989, 75)

Thus, for Uruguay, military dictatorship did not merely mean that a few thousand militants, students, unionists, and journalists were rounded up, though rounded up they were. The country was subjected to a comprehensive, fanatical purge:

between 1973 and 1982 twenty-eight newspapers and magazines— including *Marcha* . . . —were shut down. . . . Censorship was ironclad. Unions were gutted, schools purged and revamped. (Weschler 1989, 75)

In comparison to Chile and Argentina, however, Uruguay is a relatively tiny country, and the above effects of the dictatorship— repeated everywhere in the Southern Cone—had a more profound effect:

everyone knew someone—knew several people, in fact—in prison or under torture. The military wanted it that way—relied on the fear that such knowledge engendered. (Weschler 1989, 74)

Thus was created a sizable population of "sandwich" people; people caught between the government and the guilt by association of some family tie to a relative who, whether truthfully or not, had been branded a "subversive." To be one of the "sandwich" people was tantamount to wearing Hawthorne's scarlet letter. As the title of James Polk's review of *El color* bears witness, there was "no middle ground" in dictatorial Uruguay. No past favor owed or relationship shared could make up for one's being a "sandwich" person.

The wife in the chapter titled "Julio and the General" is just such a person. Rather than being the story of a fallen Tupamaro, hers is the more common stock of a relative of one of the "disappeared." As Martínez Moreno states in the chapter's introduction:

the "disappeared" do not gradually slip away from us like a drowning man in his last futile, fruitless effort to save himself. There are no

9: *El color que el infierno me escondiera:* After the Fall

eddies, no submerging heads, no whirlpools in which an arm waves desperately then disappears. . . . The "disappeared" of our times, however, falls already dead from the torture factory, naked, broken, and often mutilated, tied to a block of cement, or bound with wire at feet, wrists, and knees. . . . this is the story of the "disappeared." (Martínez Moreno 1988, 206–7)

A woman's husband, Julio, leaves his house on 1 August 1977—five years after the end of the Tupamaro war—to run some errands, and simply never returns. Eventually, embassies, U.S. civil rights leaders, and even UNESCO intercede on his wife's behalf to locate him, all with no results.

Finally, she writes the general who is commander-in-chief of the armed forces, since it so happens that her husband Julio had been the General's elementary school teacher years before. The General has known for two months that Julio was abducted from Uruguay by security forces and killed, as were many others, in neighboring Argentina in a joint "antisubversive" operation of the two countries' secret police. The General realizes it was a case of mistaken identity. However, he launches a sham, cover-up investigation and tells Julio's wife that her husband has been seen abroad, that he has run off on her, because

> For him the conventions of the system were much stronger and truer than a simple childhood memory. . . . The General wasn't about to burn his fingers by asking questions within his own order, a world where he was somebody, and have others accuse him of sentimentality and weakness. . . . Only failures, or incurable sentimentals, only cowards, receive orders from their own memories. . . . Case closed. (215)

Such is the lot of a "sandwich" person in a society driven mad by fear, a society in which being human is seen as a sign of cowardice—even in a general.

"Mar Mediterráneo" shows how such standards were applied within the military as well, confirming the fear the General expresses about being seen as weak by his peers. Though different in nature, the episode is as significant to Uruguay's history as was the attempted assassination of Hitler by Field Marshal Rommell and his coconspirators for German history. As the Tupamaros were defeated, the military's "hard liners" used the humanitarian inclinations of the "soft liners" within the armed forces in order to ferret them out and purge them before the coup d'etat. Those purged ended up "disappearing" themselves, just like the colonel and naval captain of Martínez Moreno's chapter, who wind up being tortured in one of the "safe" torture houses the Adviser left behind.[7]

The clever ruse behind the purge involved calling a truce and negotiating a conditional surrender with the MLN–T in mid-1972, ostensibly in order to prevent further unnecessary bloodshed. As the recent historical account *La tregua armada* makes clear, Martínez Moreno is accurate in declaring that it was a trap from the start (Martínez Moreno 1988, 220).[8] The Tupamaros were so weak they could only negotiate not whether, but to whom Sendic would surrender on their behalf. However, whatever military unit was credited with Sendic's capture was sure to be in the best position in the competition for the spoils of the war—power—later on.

The unit that approached the MLN–T proposing a truce and negotiations, in turn, had been told, as Martínez Moreno's colonel in "Mar Mediterráneo" attests, that the negotiations were part of a mid-1972 special operation called "Operation Counter-Coup." Supposedly, they had to obtain Sendic's surrender even if on conditions, since another military faction was allegedly plotting to take over the government. Time was of the essence: if their unit could capture Sendic first, they would save Uruguay from fascism. They were to tell the MLN–T that they were the "peruanista" or "Peruvianist" faction of the military. As such, they were the faction that, if forced to do so, would only stage a coup d'etat like that of Peru in 1968—to institute leftist reforms and forestall fascism.

In reality, as Martínez Moreno reports, there was no Operation Counter-Coup and there were no real "peruanistas." That the astute Tupamaros should have made the grave error of trusting in such an unlikely scheme was almost incredible; their apparent gullibility may have been due to their hopes for another General Seregni. As the MLN–T leader and historian Eleuterio Fernández Huidobro himself put it, "Los tupamaros se equivocaron feo" ("the Tupamaros made an ugly mistake") (Huidobro 1989, 158). The whole affair was a double-cross by the fascistic military officers themselves that went by the name "Operation Takeover." Not only were the officers who participated double-crossed, however; so were the Tupamaros. They soon discovered that Amodio Pérez, one of their own MLN–T leaders, had cut a deal with the hard-liners running Operation Takeover. Pérez had been betraying them during the entire course of the negotiations in return for certain guarantees of liberty and, in a bid for fame and fortune, even a book deal. His betrayal was discovered too late: Sendic was wounded and captured by a hard-line unit within a few weeks. He and many other Tupamaros were to serve time in prison camps along with some of the very same soft-line officers with whom they had attempted to negotiate. The worst of the ironies is that the purge of the military revealed that "quienes menos efectivos habían sido en la lucha contra el MLN, más fascistas eran" ("those who had been the least effective in the struggle against the MLN were the most fascistic") (Huidobro 1989, 144). By the same token, some of the soft-liners were the most seasoned veterans of the war and had wanted most to end it. Their reward was to share the same cells with some of their foes in arms.

No story such as that told in *El color* would be complete without its collaborators, the passive Pontius Pilates who, unlike the active Judas Iscariots, wash their hands as they look the other way. Again, in *El color*, an unlikely character fills this role: the president, Juan María Bordaberry, the protagonist of the chapter "The Pine Grove." Bordaberry, Martínez Moreno's "Devout Man," was a protegé of rightist President Jorge Pacheco Areco, "the Boxer," in the 1971 elections. Elected amidst allegations of fraud, Bordaberry cut a deal with the military to keep him on as a puppet civilian president after their coup d'etat. He earned the nickname of "Devout Man" because, in a country with the highest ratio of declared atheists in the Western world (34%), he made a point of appeasing his conscience with a "personal confessor" (Martens 1980, 77; Martínez Moreno 1988, 233). He prefers to deal with the fact that, as "The Pine Grove" demonstrates, his country is being run by death squads simply by refusing to deal with it: "His concept of innocence and guilt seems to bear a strange relationship to details known or not known. He prefers not to know" (Martínez Moreno 1988, 239). Meanwhile, the bodies of executed victims mysteriously continue to appear in places, as the chapter's title indicates, like pine groves.

As Martínez Moreno observes the rapid rise and fall of a generation born to the slaughter of the Southern Cone in the 1970s, he provides keen insights into the forces that drive what we now call the generation of the postboom and distinguishes it from its predecessor:

> I do not think that either promising poets especially, or intellectuals especially, died when the guerrilla organization was wiped out in those years. *Young people* were destroyed; that is, men and women, examples of the human condition, people with something new to say,

many of them with no place to say it. *Fer la cittá sovra quell'ossa morte;* that is what is left for us in the years to come. Build the city over their dead bones. Not on the cast-off skins of poets who fell silent and changed, but on the bones of men and women who had a passion for life and were sacrificed to the Order of the Barracks. (244)

The titles of subsequent postboom novels—Skármeta's *Ardiente paciencia* (Burning patience), Peri Rossi's *La nave de los locos* (Ship of fools), and Giardinelli's *Qué solos se quedan los muertos* (How lonely are the dead), just to name three—suffice to show that Martínez Moreno's assessment at the conclusion of *El color* amounts to a literary manifesto for the postboom. This novel, like Martínez Moreno's entire literary canon's treatment of *la deca* and what lay beyond it, marks a revisionist transition in Latin-American literature. It is a revision both in style and theme the significance of which we are only now becoming aware, and which we are—perhaps provisionally—labeling the "postboom." Martínez Moreno's works are consistently a process in which art anticipates life, for any of the ideas just entering into the critical domain today can be found embodied in his canon beginning a generation ago. As observers of contemporary literature ask themselves what could possibly lie beyond the avant-garde canon of the boom, perhaps they should look to the novels of Martínez Moreno to find an answer already there, waiting for their discovery.

Chronology

1917 Born 1 September, Colonia, Uruguay.
1920 Family bankrupted, moves to Melo, Uruguay.
1925 Family moves, for last time, to Montevideo.
1933 Colorado Party leader Gabriel Terra stages coup.
1936 Writes short stories inspired by republicans in Spanish civil war.
1938 First short story, "En niño que prepara su muerte" (The child who prepares his death), published in *AIAPE* 22 December. Joins prestigious newspaper *El País* as reporter.
1939 Franco defeats republicans in Spain.
1942 Leaves *El País;* contributes to *Mundo Uruguayo* under pseudonym Alejandro Tour.
1943 Joins *El Diario* news staff, begins contributing to *Marcha*.
1944 Wins first literary contest sponsored by *Mundo Uruguayo* and *AIAPE* with short story "La otra mitad," later title of second novel.
1948 Valedictorian at law school graduation; becomes public defender for criminal courts of Montevideo.
1952 International correspondent covering Bolivian revolution from La Paz; begins friendship with Bolivian revolutionary leaders Paz Estenssoro and Siles Suazo.
1956 Novella *Cordelia* wins first prize in literary contest sponsored by *Número*.
1957 Wins literary contest sponsored by Scandinavian Air Systems; first prize is four month stay in Europe. Contributes to *Marcha* during travels.
1959 Observer at trial of Sosa Blanco at invitation of Castro regime.
1960 First short story collection, *Los días por vivir,* published. Novella *Los aborígenes* wins second prize in contest sponsored by *Life en Español*.
1961 Both novellas published. First full-length novel, *El paredón,* awarded second prize by Seix Barral after tying for first place four times. Movimiento Nacional de Solidaridad con Cuba (MNSC), urban nucleus of the Tupamaros, formed.
1962 Unión de Trabajadores Azucareros de Artigas (UTAA) marches on Montevideo led by founder and later Tupamaro leader Raúl Sendic.
1963 *El paredón* published by Seix Barral to storm of controversy. First armed action by MLN-T (Movimiento de Liberación Nacional–Tupamaros) as rifle club robbed of firearms.

1964 *La otra mitad* accepted for publication by Seix Barral; censored by Spanish government for immortality. Writes *Con las primeras luces*. MLN–T carries out first bombing.
1966 First national convention of MLN–T; first Tupamaro killed in action. *La otra mitad* and *Con las primeras luces* published, the former in Mexico to circumvent censors. Travels to PEN Club International in New York City.
1967 Short story collections published in second editions. Attends Latin American Congress of Writers in Mexico city; joins with Benedetti to denounce "pro-imperialist" writers. MLN–T safehouse discovered. President Gestido dies after only months in office. New president Pacheco Areco closes two newspapers and bans six leftist parties in first week in office.
1968 Second national MLN–T convention; Tupamaros kidnap and release presidential crony and cabinet minister Ulysses Pereira Reverbel; waves of robberies and bombings. Police kill student leader Líber Arce at head of demonstration. General Líber Seregni resigns rather than obey president's orders to send troops against unarmed civilians; later to be presidential candidate for leftist coalition. Short story volume *Los prados de la conciencia* published.
1969 MLN–T acts at will: three banks robbed in twenty minutes 2 May. First defeat in Operation Pando 8 October; financier Dr. Gaetano Pellegrini Giampietro kidnapped and released; newspaper *Extra* closed; words related to MLN–T forbidden.
Three short story volumes published: *La sirena y otros cuentos, Las bebidas azules,* and *Cuentos de la ciudad.*
1970 Thirteen Tupamaro women escape prison; robberies, bombings continue. Republican Guard troops mutiny over mistreatment of captured Tupamaros in Operation Pando and lack of support from government; disbanded.
31 July: foreign government official kidnapped; 12,000 troops search Montevideo house by house for him.
7 August: Sendic captured.
9 August: foreign government official executed.
Fourth novel, *Coca,* published.
1971 MLN–T supports Broad Front leftist coalition in national elections. Martínez Moreno considered for vice presidential spot on ticket with Seregni but not selected; Montevideo rally draws 140,000. MLN–T kidnaps and releases British ambassador and, for second time, Pereira Reverbel. MLN–T cell in army discovered; right-wing death squads appear. 106 Tupamaros, Sendic included, escape prison 6 September. In November Pacheco protegé Juan María Bordaberry wins elections; serious fraud suspected. New book of short stories, *De vida o muerte,* published, along with book on law, *Jurisdicción civil y jurisdicción militar,* summary

Chronology 197

of Martínez Moreno's milestone fourteen-month case before Supreme Court against military's judicial abuses.

1972 MLN–T leader Amodio Pérez captured with plans to President's house 24 February; escapes prison with fourteen other Tupamaros 12 April. MLN–T executes four death squad leaders 14 April. Police raid captures MLN–T second commander Eleuterio Fernández Huidobro; eight killed, several hundred Tupamaros captured.
15 April: government declares "state of internal war."
19 May: playwright and Tupamaro leader Mauricio Rosencoff captured.
25 July: Colonal Artigas Alvarez, brother of commander of Joint Chiefs, assassinated, ending truce and negotiations.
1 September: Sendic wounded and recaptured; MLN–T effectively defeated.

1973 Martínez Moreno publishes *Los días que vivimos,* book exposing illegal steps government adopted to defeat Tupamaros.
8 February: army and air force stage abortive coup; navy resists, backing President Bordaberry.
7 May: former Tupamaro leader Amodio Pérez betrays MLN–T, turning government witness.
14 May: General William Rosson, commander of U.S. Southern Command in Panama, arrives in Montevideo.
18 June: Ernest Siracusa becomes new U.S. Ambassador to Uruguay.
27 June: President Bordaberry backs an all-out coup d'etat; massive arrests and police repression, congress occupied by troops.

1974 Juan Carlos Onetti and others on jury of *Marcha* literary contest arrested after awarding prize to story offensive to dictatorship; Martínez Moreno retained as attorney. Jurors exiled; story's author, Nelson Marra, to serve five years in prison. Martínez Moreno removed from twenty-five year post as public defender. "Disappearances" become routine.

1976 Bordaberry removed by military; replaced with elderly country lawyer. Former senate opposition leader and Martínez Moreno associate Zelmar Michelini, congressman Gutiérrez Ruiz, and several others "disappeared" in broad daylight and murdered in joint secret police operation in Buenos Aires, Argentina. 1971's opposing presidential candidate, former senator Wilson Ferreira Aldunate, receives political asylum at Austrian embassy and testifies before U.S. Congress; U.S. aid cut off for human rights violations.

1977 Amnesty International denounces Uruguay as Latin-American country with highest rate of political prisoners. Andrei Sakharov and forty other Soviet dissidents protest Uruguayan repression.

1978 Martínez Moreno's home bombed by right-wing death squad.

Phone tip from officer warns of plan to "disappear" him; flees to Spain, then Mexico. Made full professor of political science at Mexico's national university; becomes columnist for newspaper *La Jornada*.

1979 Addresses French parliament on human rights violations.

1980 Uruguayan dictatorship puts plan to legitimize military rule to "yes" or "no" plebiscite; loses to landslide "no" vote.

1981 General Gregorio Alvarez made last president of Uruguayan dictatorship. Martínez Moreno's last novel *El color que el infierno me escondiera* wins international award in Mexico.

1984 Massive protests since "no" vote force dictatorship to negotiate for elections. Political prisoners, MLN–T included, released; Seregni hailed as hero after nine years' imprisonment. Revealed each of top nine Tupamaro leaders kept in solitary in separate cells around country for over a decade. Existence of concentration camps acknowledged, opened to public shock.

1985 Colorado candidate Julio Sanguinetti wins presidential election tainted by major opposing candidates Seregni and Aldunate's "disqualification" from running; Aldunate jailed. Martínez Moreno's longtime friend and next-door neighbor in exile, *Marcha* founder and editor Carlos Quijano, dies in Mexico.

1986 Carlos Martínez Moreno dies of a heart attack in Mexico City 6 February 1986; profusely eulogized in Uruguayan press. In August Sanguinetti announces amnesty for military human rights violators.

1988 Posthumous short story collection *Animal de palabras* published; *El color que el infierno me escondiera* published in English translation as *El Infierno* to favorable *New York Times* reviews.

Notes

Chapter One. Life and Times

1. See the chapter "*Batllismo* and its Opponents: Ideology in Twentieth-century Uruguay," in Martin Weinstein, *Uruguay: The Politics of Failure* (London: Greenwood Press, 1975), 20–50.
2. For an English-language discussion of the socioeconomic background to the Tupamaro War from the Tupamaro point of view see Carlos Wilson, *The Tupamaros: The Unmentionables* (Boston: Branden Press, 1974), 35–41.
3. Any claims, for obvious reasons, remain unverifiable at this time. For a broad range of viewpoints, the interested reader should consult Manuel Hevia Coscullela, *Pasaporte 11333: ocho años con la CIA* (Montevideo: Editorial TAE, 1988), U.S. government witnesses before the U.S. Congress, House Subcommittee on International Organizations of the House Committee on International Relations, *Human Rights in Uruguay and Paraguay*, 94th Cong., 2nd sess., 1976, and *Uruguay, Nunca Más*, Servicio Paz y Justicia (Montevideo: Altamira, S.R.L., 1989).
4. Mentioned in the "Mar Mediterráneo" chapter of Martínez Moreno's *El color que el infierno me escondiera* and the subject of an entire book by Tupamaro leader and historian Eleuterio Fernández Huidobro, *La tregua armada* (Montevideo: Editorial TAE, 1989).
5. For a detail account of the events leading up to and immediately following the forced closing of parliament that came to be known as Uruguay's "soft" military coup ("golpe blando" or "autogolpe") of 27 June 1973, see Weinstein, *Uruguay*, 131–34 and Edy Kaufman, *Uruguay in Transition: From Civilian to Military Rule* (New Brunswick, N.J.: Transaction Books, 1979), 111–15.
6. New York's Edward Koch, quoted in Federico Fasano Martens, *Después de la derrota: un eslabón débil llamado Uruguay* (México, D.F.: Editorial Nueva Imagen, 1980), 77.
7. See Philip Agee, *CIA Diary* (Harmondsworth, England: Penguin, 1975).
8. See Thomas Hauser, *Missing* (New York: Avon Books, 1978), 18, 24, and 27. *Missing* was originally published under the title *The Execution of Charles Horman: An American Sacrifice*.

Chapter Two. *Los aborígenes*

1. Interview with Carlos Martínez Moreno, July 1985, tapes available in my private library.
2. For an extensive discussion of the crucial role the Tupamaro rebellion played in recent Uruguayan history, see the introduction to chapter 9 "After the Fall: *El color que el infierno me escondiera*. For a thumbnail sketch of Tupamaro history, see James Kohl and John Litt, *Urban Guerrilla Warfare in Latin America*

(Cambridge: MIT Press, 1974) 173–309. The Tupamaro guerrilla war touched Martínez Moreno both personally and professionally when he served as defense attorney for several MLN–T members.

3. This is common knowledge to anyone who knows of Martínez Moreno's life outside of literature, since he was affiliated with the leftist journal *Marcha* from its founding in 1939, was a founding member of the Broad Front, a leftist political coalition, and was, at the time of his death, writing for a leftist Mexican daily, *La Jornada*. He also was directing dissertations on political science at the Universidad Nacional Autónoma de México. For the record, however, he was never a Marxist, and laughed at the common misconception of many that he was, a misconception he attributed to his defense of those persecuted for their involvement in Marxist movements in Uruguay in the 1960s and 1970s. His human rights stance was consistent and nonideological, as his position in the Padilla case in the early 1970s bears out—he refused to sign the public letters circulating among writers either defending or condemning Castro. At the same time, he held and acted upon strong political beliefs of his own. My source for this information is the author himself in a taped interview held at his home in July of 1985, which I now have in my private library.

4. For a complete explanation of the meaning of this term, which Brushwood uses to describe nineteenth-century Latin America's themes in literature, see John S. Brushwood, *Genteel Barbarism: New Readings of Nineteenth-Century Spanish-American Novels* (Lincoln: University of Nebraska Press, 1981).

Chapter Three. *Cordelia*

1. Such a thing occurs in John S. Brushwood, *La novela hispano-americana del siglo XX: Una vista panorámica*, trans. Raymond L. Williams (México, D.F.: Fondo de Cultura Económica, 1984). At the end of this extremely useful book, Professor Brushwood offers a nearly year by year listing of the most significant novels of the century, through 1980. It is commendable that he lists Martínez Moreno among Latin America's most significant writers of narrative as early as 1960. However, the fact that Martínez Moreno's publications listed for both 1960 and 1961—*Los días por vivir* and *Cordelia*, respectively—are listed under the heading of "novels" could create some confusion regarding the novelist's work. His first actual novel does not appear until *El paredón*, in 1963. Both books listed in 1960 and 1961 are actually novellas included in short story anthologies.

2. For a full explanation of these terms and the theoretical concepts behind them, please see the introduction and first chapter of Gerard Genette, "Order" in *Narrative Discourse: An Essay in Method* (Ithaca: Cornell University Press, 1980) 28–85. The complexity with which Martínez Moreno uses shifting focalization, analepses, and diegetic discourse can be seen at its peak in *La otra mitad* (1966). A detailed analysis of some of its complex features can be found in Joan Rea Green, "The Structure of the Narrator in Contemporary Spanish American Fiction," diss., University of Texas-Austin, 1976.

3. These aspects of Martínez Moreno's works are dealt with sympathetically in Angel Rama, *La generación crítica 1939–1969* (Montevideo: Editorial Arca, 1972), 95. All subsequent quotes are from this edition and will appear with page numbers in parentheses.

In an interview with Uruguayan writer Ricardo Prieto in Montevideo in August of 1986, only months after Martínez Moreno's death, I discovered that some critics a generation younger put these same qualities of Martínez Moreno's work in a less favorable light. Prieto bemoaned his "lack of warmth" and his "over-intellectualizing" as a legacy that burdens his own writing and that of his generation. According to Prieto, his generation wishes to depict reality from a less critical point of view. Personally, I evaluate the difference of opinion between the two generations of writers in a Bloomian sense, taking it as a healthy and, perhaps, inevitable sign of the "anxiety of influence."

Chapter Four. *El paredón*

1. See Josefina Delgado, *Nueva novela latinoamericana*, ed. Jorge Lafforgue (Buenos Aires: Paidós, 1969), 114–30.
2. See Hayden White, *Metahistory: The Historical Imagination in Nineteenth-Century Europe* (Baltimore: Johns Hopkins University Press, 1973), 29. The table (Bonnycastle's Paradigm) is reproduced on page 202. See also Stephen Bonnycastle, *"The Tropics of Discourse:* A Paradigm Worth Using," *The Journal of Literary Theory* 3 (July 1982): 32–33.

Chapter Five. *La otra mitad*

1. See Fernando Ainsa, *"La otra mitad:* Cuando el amor se refleja en la muerte," *Temas* (Montevideo), 12 (1966): 49–54.
2. See Joan Rea Green, "The Structure of the Narrator in the Contemporary Spanish-American Novel," diss., University of Texas-Austin, 1970.
3. See Roland Barthes as cited in Barbara Johnson, *The Critical Difference: Essays in the Contemporary Rhetoric of Reading* (Baltimore: Johns Hopkins University Press, 1980), 6.
4. See also Roland Barthes, "Textual Analysis of a Tale by Edgar Poe," *Poe Studies* 10, 1 (June 1977): 1–12. For Holquist's comments on Poe's place in the canon of the detective genre, see Holquist 1971, 140.

Chapter Six. *Con las primeras luces*

1. Information taken from an interview held with the author at his home in Mexico City, July 1985. Available in my personal library.
2. For a clear-eyed and corrective view of this relationship of Faulkner to the Latin-American novel, see John S. Brushwood, "La importancia de Faulkner en la novela hispanoamericana," *Letras Nacionales: Literatura Comparada* (Columbia—EEUU) Núm. 31, 1976, 7–14. In this article, Brushwood particularly emphasizes the experience of time in Faulkner's novels and how that has been important to Latin American writers. The fragmentation of the narrative produced a reduction in causal logic, substituting an inner logic based upon both the characters' experiences within the work and the readers' experience before the text. Brushwood also comments on how the frequent shift in narrator, verb tense, and setting changes the reader's appreciation of history: a setting becomes all settings, a point in time becomes all times. Gail L. Mortimer's study, which is also cited in this chapter, deals particularly with time in literature through Faulkner. Her study's subtitle, "A Study in Perception and Meaning," bears out how the

Bonnycastle's Paradigm

	Stage 1: Metaphor	Stage 2: Metonymy	Stage 3: Synecdoche	Stage 4: Irony
Dominant mental process	Naming things, or learning the accepted names of things.	Connecting things with neighbours in time and space.	Forming wholes by relating parts to each other. Idealising and integrating.	Recognizing the inadequacies of the integration achieved in stage 3.
Characteristic Psychological state	Numinous experience. Individual lost in an enormous new world. Implicit faith in immediate experience. Hysteria, fetishism.	Desire to analyze things, to reduce things, to a more basic level of organization; tendency toward positivism; ego very involved?	A complex reticulated structure present in the mind. Possessing a grand and panoptic vision (Blake, Coleridge). Obsessional?	Awareness of different viewpoints; uncertainty about things-in-themselves. Paralysis; mimicking as a way of taking action. Ego dissolved.
Appropriate stage in the development of a student of literature	Discovering literature as field of interest. Great admiration for individual authors. Utter lack of understanding for other "major" authors. Little or no interest in criticism.	Establishing connections between authors usually by locating them in their historical context. Accumulation of detailed knowledge without a strong sense of over-all pattern.	Development of a comprehensive pattern for literature-as-a-whole, in the manner of Frye, or a hierarchy based on merit, or a historical synthesis. Investigating the basis for this pattern can lead to structuralism.	The discovery that the order in stage 3 is based on your own idiosyncratic conditions of development (class, education, place in the family constellation, your body, etc). Everything depends on "what lang. you speak", objectivity disappears. Deconstruction flourishes; attention focuses on criticism, because the "approach" determines what you see in a work of literature.
Related Ideology	Anarchist	Radical	Conservative	Liberal
Stage in the development of a civilization, according to Vico	Age of the gods. Gods ae projected on nature by man. Little social organization.	Age of heroes. Strong men dominate the institutions of a more complex society. Class divisions are established.	Age of common humanity transcending class divisions. Development of written law; equal rights for all men.	Age of dissolution and the *ricorso* or recycling. The human origin of institutions and standards is revealed; men no longer revere them, and seek their own private pleasures instead of the public good.

Notes

relative experiences of time possible in literature can make one aware of the contingent nature of being and time—contingent on one's experience of it more than of one's definitions of it.

3. See Linda Hutcheon, "Theorizing the Postmodern: Towards Defining a Poetic," panel on Postmodernist Straregies, Conference On Postmodernism: Text, Politics, Instruction, Lawrence, Kansas, 2 May, 1987.

4. Mortimer deals extensively with the literary treatment of time through Faulkner and makes many observations that go far beyond a mere analysis of the author's work.

Chapter Seven. *Coca*

1. See Carlos Martínez Moreno, *Con las primeras luces* (Barcelona: Editorial Seix Barral, 1966), 174.

Chapter Eight. *Tierra en la boca*

1. See note on 7 to "Chapter One. Life and Times."
2. The story referred to here, "El guardaespaldas," (The bodyguard) by Nelson Marra, was published in *Marcha*, No. 1671, 8 February 1974, 28–31. The editorial "Tres meses y medio después" (Three and a half months later), *Marcha*, 24 May 1974, 4–5, describes the ordeal Onetti, Quijano, Marra, Ruffinelli, Rein, and *Marcha* itself suffered that year.
3. Interview with Carlos Martínez Moreno in Mexico City, July 1985, on tape in my personal library; interview with Juan Carlos Legido in Motevideo, June 1989. See Carlos Fagúndez, "Cronología y bibliografía," ed. Rómulo Cosse, *Onetti: papeles críticos* (Montevideo: Linardi y Risso, 1989), 282.
4. See Avenir Rosell, "El habla popular montevideana: A propósito de *Tierra en la boca*," *Texto crítico*, No. 6 (1977).

Chapter Nine. *El color que el infierno me escondiera*

1. See Emir Rodríguez Monegal in *Juan Carlos Onetti: Obras completas* (Madrid: Aguilar, S.A. de Ediciones, 1979), 11.
2. See Carlos Martínez Moreno, *El color que el infierno me escondiera* (México, D.F.: Editorial Nueva Imagen, 1981), 3–4. In contrast with all previous quotations from Martínez Moreno's novels in this study, the translated quotations used here are from Ann Wright's translation of Carlos Martínez Moreno, *The Inferno* (London: Readers International, 1988) and not the author's.
3. The role of U.S. advisers in the teaching of torture in Brazil and Uruguay during this period has been amply documented by former *New York Times* investigative reporter A. J. Langguth in his book *Hidden Terrors* (New York: Pantheon Books, 1978).
4. Anecdote from an interview with Juan Carlos Lelgido, Uruguayan novelist and close Martínez Moreno associate, August 1986, in Montevideo.
5. Interview with Eleuterio Fernández Huidobro at the headquarters of the Movimiento de Liberación Nacional–Tupamaros (MLN-T), July 1989, Montevideo, on tape in my private library.

6. See Omar Cabezas, *La montaña es algo más que una inmensa estepa verde* (Managua: Editorial Nueve Nicaragua, 1987), 189.

7. The house in question, "that fabulous torture mansion bang in the middle of the residential suburb of Punta Gorda," was probably much like the house at Rambla República de México Ave. 5515, the house pictured in *Uruguay: nunca más*, 113, photograph 13.

8. See also Eleuterio Fernández Huidobro, *La tregua armada* (Montevideo: Editorial TAE, 1989), 114 and 158.

Bibliography

Works Cited

Editions of Novels Analyzed

Martínez Moreno, Carlos. 1970. *Coca.* Caracas: Monte Avila.
———. 1966. *Con las primeras luces.* Barcelona: Editorial Seix Barral.
———. 1961. *Cordelia.* Montevideo: Editorial Alfa.
———. 1981. *El color que el infierno me escondiera.* México, D.F.: Editorial Nueva Imagen.
———. 1988. *El Infierno.* Translated by Ann Wright. London: Readers International.
———. 1963. *El paredón.* Barcelona: Editorial Seix Barral.
———. 1966. *La otra mitad.* México, D.F.: Editorial Joaquín Mortiz.
———. 1967. *Los aborígenes.* Montevideo: Editorial Alfa.
———. 1974. *Tierra en la boca.* Buenos Aires: Losada.

History and Criticism

Benedetti, Mario. 1969. *Literatura uruguaya siglo XX.* Montevideo: Alfa.
Bonnycastle, Stephen. 1982. "*The Tropics of Discourse:* A Paradigm Worth Using," *Journal of Literary Theory* 3 (July): 32–33.
Brushwood, John S. 1984. *La novela hispanoamericana siglo XX: una vista panorámica.* México, D.F.: Fondo de Cultura Económica.
Campos, Jorge. 1966. "Sociedad y decadencia: *Con las primeras luces* de Martínez Moreno." *Insula* (Madrid), No. 241 (December): 11.
Cosculluela, Manuel Hevia. 1988. *Pasaporte 11333: ocho años con la CIA.* Montevideo: Editorial TAE.
Donoso, José. 1977. *The Boom in Spanish American Liturature: A Personal History.* New York: Columbia University Press.
Fasano Martens, Federico. 1980. *Después de la derrota: un eslabón débil llamado Uruguay.* México, D. F.: Editorial Nueva Imagen.
Faulkner, William. 1987. *As I Lay Dying: The Corrected Text.* New York: Vintage Books.
Foster, David William. 1985. *Alternate Voices in the Contemporary Latin American Narrative.* Columbia: The University of Missouri Press.
Giardinelli, Mempo. 1984. *El género negro.* México, D.F.: Universidad Autónoma Metropolitana.

Huidobro, Eleuterio Fernández. 1989. *Historia de los Tupamaros III: el MLN.* Montevideo: Editorial TAE.

———, and Mauricio Rosencoff. 1989. *Memorias del calabozo.* Montevideo: Editorial TAE.

Leenhardt, Jacques. 1981. "La enstructura ensayística de la novela latinamericana." In Angel Rama, *Más allá del boom: literatura y mercado.* México: Marcha Editores, S.A.

Lewald, Ernest H. 1967. "Carlos Martínez Moreno: *Con las primeras luces.*" *Books Abroad* 41 (Summer): 324–25.

Luchting, Wolfgang A. 1971. "Carlos Martínez Moreno's *Coca.*" *Books Abroad* 45 (Summer): 488–89.

Martínez Moreno, Carlos. 1985. Personal interview, 5 July.

Martens, Federico Fasano. 1980. *Después de la derrota: un eslabón débil llamado Uruguay.* México, D.F.: Editorial Nueva Imagen.

Mortimer, Gail L. 1983. *Faulkner's Rhetoric of Loss: A Study in Perception and Meaning.* Austin: University of Texas Press.

Polk, James. 1988. "No Middle Ground." *The New York Times Book Review,* 30 October, Sec. 7, 22:4.

Orthmann, Nora. 1976. "Life and Works of Carlos Martínez Moreno." Ph.D. diss., University of Toronto.

Rama, Angel. 1972. *La generación crítica 1939–1969.* Montevideo: Editorial Arca.

———. 1981. *Más allá del boom: literatura y mercado.* México, D.F.: Marcha.

Ravazzani, Ana-María. 1981. "La narrativa de Carlos Martínez Moreno." Ph.D. diss., University of California–Irvine.

Rodríguez Monegal, Emir. 1967. "Cara y cruz de Carlos Martínez Moreno." *Mundo Nuevo* (Paris) 10 (April): 79–85.

———. 1979. Prologue. *Juan Carlos Onetti: Obras completas.* Madrid: Aguilar.

Rosell, Avenir. 1977. "El habla popular montevideana: a propósito de *Tierra en la boca.*" *Texto crítico* 6: 25.

Salisbury-Ginsburg, Liz. 1982. "Downfall of a Democracy: Carlos Martínez Moreno and the Uruguayan Experience." Ph.D. diss., University of California–Davis.

Shakespeare, William. 1972. *King Lear.* In *The Complete Signet Classic Shakespeare.* New York: Harcourt Brace Jovanovich, Inc.

Velázquez, Pablo Cejudo. 1985. *Uruguay, el ciclo de la violencia.* San José: Editorial Universitaria Centroamericana.

Weschler, Lawrence. 1989. "A Reporter at Large: The Great Exception." *The New Yorker* (3 April).

Theory

Barthes, Roland. 1974. *S/Z: An Essay.* New York: Hill & Wang.

———. 1977. "Textural Analysis of a Tale by Edgar Poe." *Poe Studies* 10 (June): 1–12.

Davis, Lennard J. 1980. "A Social History of Fact and Fiction: Authorial Disavowal in the Early English Novel." In Edward Said, ed., *Literature and Society.* Baltimore: The Johns Hopkins University Press.

Derrida, Jacques. 1982. *Margins of Philosophy.* Chicago: University of Chicago Press.
Hassan, Ihab. 1982. *The Dismemberment of Orpheus: Toward a Postmodern Literature.* New York: Oxford University Press.
Holquist, Michael J. 1971. "Whodunits and Other Questions: Metaphysical Detective Stories in Post-War Fiction." *New Literary History* 3 (Autumn): 135–56.
Johnson, Barbara. 1980. *The Critical Difference.* Baltimore: The Johns Hopkins University Press.
Merrell, Floyd. 1982. *Semiotic Foundations: Steps Toward an Epistomology of Written Texts.* Bloomington: Indiana University Press.
Todorov, Tzvetan. 1977. *The Poetics of Prose.* Ithaca: Cornell University Press.
Vattimo, Gianni. 1987. Interview. *El posmodernismo o la transformación de la utopias.* With Fermín Févre. *Clarín: cultura y Nación* (15 October): 8.
White, Hayden. 1973. *Metahistory: The Historical Imagination in Nineteenth-Century Europe.* Baltimore: The Johns Hopkins University Press.

Works Consulted

Berman, Marshall. 1982. *All That is Solid Melts into Air.* New York: Simon & Schuster.
Deleuze, Gilles, and Félix Guattari. 1977. *Anti-Oedipus: Capitalism and Schizophrenia.* New York: Viking Press.
DeMan, Paul. 1979. *Allegories of Reading.* New Haven: Yale University Press.
Derrida, Jacques. 1976. *Of Grammatology.* Baltimore: Johns Hopkins University Press.
Fish, Stanley. 1980. *Is There a Text in this Class?* Cambridge: Harvard University Press.
Handelman, Susan A. 1982. *The Slayers of Moses.* Albany: SUNY Press.
Hardison, O. B. 1981. *Entering the Maze: Identity and Change in Modern Culture.* New York: Oxford University Press.
Hartman, Geoffrey. 1980. *Criticism in the Wilderness.* New Haven: Yale University Press.
———. 1981. *Saving the Text.* Baltimore: The Johns Hopkins University Press, 1981.
Lyotard, Jean Francois. 1984. *The Postmodern Condition: A Report on Knowledge.* Manchester: Manchester University Press.
Rimmon-Kenan, Shlomith. 1983. *Narrative Fiction: Contemporary Poetics.* London: Methuen.
Robbe-Grillet, Alain. 1959. *Jealousy.* New York: Grove Press.
Said, Edward, ed. 1980. *Literature and Society.* Baltimore: The Johns Hopkins University Press.
Sinai, I. Robert. 1978. *The Decadence of the Modern World.* Cambridge: Schoenbaum Publishing Co.
Weschler, Lawrence. 1990. *A Miracle, A Universe: Settling Accounts with Torturers.* New York: Pantheon Books.

Index

Aborígenes, Los (Martínez Moreno), 10, 29, 30, 35–49; alienation in, 35, 36, 38–39; bohemians in, 43; Bolivia as setting for, 37, 151; Cándido Lafuentes (character), 42, 44; cultural identity issues in, 40, 140; *la deca* in, 42–45, 48–49, 147; ethnic autobiography in, 40; "genteel barbarism" in, 37–39, 125; Ilse (character), 43; irrelevance in, 37–38; Latin American cultural identity and, 37, 39–40, 140; modernism and, 151; as predecessor to *El Paredón*, 35–36; Primitivo (character), 36, 37–45, 127–28, 130, 140, 165; *quietismo* of elites in, 44–45, 127–28; Ventura (character), 43
Adultery: in *La otra mitad*, 30–31, 50, 88, 89, 101–3, 105
Agee, Philip, 32
Agrarian reform, 17
Agustini, Delmira, 105
AIAPE, 28, 29
Ainsa, Fernando, 90
Albañiles, Los (Leñero), 91
Aldunate, Senator Wilson Ferreira, 26, 197, 198
Alguien tiene que enterrarnos, 33
Alienation: in *Los aborígenes*, 35, 36, 38–39; in *Cordelia*, 55; in *La otra mitad*, 90, 92, 102, 103; in *El paredón*, 78, 82, 86–87; in *Tierra en la boca*, 158
Allende, Salvador, 32, 170
Alternate Voices in the Contemporary Latin American Narrative, 168
Alvarez, Colonel Artigas, 24, 197
Alvarez, General Gregorio ("Goyo"), 24–25, 198
Amnesty: for human rights crimes, 26, 27
Amnesty International, 25, 197

Anarchistic attitude: in *El paredón*, 78–80
Animal de palabras (Martínez Moreno), 183, 198
Antipsychological aesthetic: in *Tierra en la boca*, 152–54
Areco, Pacheco, 22–24, 193
Argentina, 11, 26, 190, 191
"Arquitectura mental": in *Cordelia*, 59–61, 98, 100
Artigas, Jose, 19
As I Lay Dying (Faulkner), 110, 117–18, 122
Association/alienation subcode: in *La otra mitad*, 95, 98, 100, 102, 103
Astiller, El (Onetti), 38
"Autojustificación": in *Con las primeras luces*, 123
Avant-gardism, 164

Barthes, Roland, 10, 92
Batista, Fulgenico, 29, 64, 67
Batlle y Ordóñez, José, 16, 17, 79
Batllismo, 16, 18
Bebidas azules, Las (Martínez Moreno), 31, 196
Benedetti, Mario, 11, 17, 18–19, 45, 49, 58, 90, 168; criticism of *El paredón* by, 65–67
Bichicome (homeless), 179–80, 181
Blanco (National) party, 15, 26; economic issues and, 17–18; election of, 17; in *El paredón*, 86
Bohemians: in *Los aborígenes*, 43
Bolivia, 31; revolution, 29; as setting for *Coca*, 128, 129, 142–44; as setting for *Los Aborígenes*, 37, 151
Books Abroad (Lewald), 110
Boom literature, 166–69
Boom in Spanish American Literature, The (Donoso), 166–67

Bordaberry, Juan María, 24, 25, 26, 193, 197
Bourgeois democracy, 19
Brazil, 17
Broad Front (Frente Amplio), 22, 26, 172; Martínez Moreno's involvement in, 31, 196; mayorship of Montevideo won by, 26, 27, 172; MLN-T in, 27
Brum, Baltazar, 79
Brushwood, John, 37, 58, 92, 109, 150

Cabezas, Omar, 171
Campos, Jorge, 111
"Candelabra" (Martínez Moreno), 183
Castro, Fidel: in *El paredón*, 67–68, 81, 84, 88; firing squads, 64; Operación Verdad, 64–65; reactions to, 21–22
Censorship: of *La otra mitad*, 30–31, 109
Central Intelligence Agency (C.I.A.), in Uruguay, 32, 174
Chile, 32, 170, 190
C.I.A. Diary (Agee), 32
Civilización/barbarie, 11
Coca (Martínez Moreno), 10, 29, 31, 37, 127–44, 196; Bolivia as setting for, 128, 129, 142–44; the Captain (character), 127–43, 158; characters, 128–29; crime novel style, 47; cultural chauvinism in, 136–40; decadence in, 46; *la deca* in, 128, 129, 138, 141, 144, 177; disenchanted elites in, 139–40; epilogue, 142–44, 177; flaws in, 128, 142–44, 177; fragmented narrative in, 132, 141–42; Che Guevara in, 142–44, 177; irony in, 130–31, 136–37; Marcel (character), 129, 134, 135, 140; Marie-Louise (character), 129, 131, 133–36, 138–42, 177; Martínez Moreno's expectations for, 128; passivity in, 129–30, 135–36, 140; personal identity in, 138–40; point of view in, 128; *quietismo* in, 127; self-destructiveness in, 133–34, 138; sociohistorical analysis of, 131–33, 136
Codes: association/alienation subcode, 95, 98, 100, 102, 103; cultural, 93–103; power subcode, 94, 97, 98, 99, 101, 102, 103; reflective subcode, 93, 94, 96–97, 98, 100, 101, 102; social, 94–95; in text, 92–93

"Coloradismo": denunciation of, 66
Colorado party, 15, 17, 18, 22, 26, 78
Color que el infierno escondiera, El (El Infierno) (Martínez Moreno), 10–11, 34, 146, 160, 167–94, 198; Advisor (character), 174–77, 179–80, 182; *bichicome* in, 179–80, 181; Cosculluela, Manuel Hevia (character), 174; *la deca* and, 168–69; dehumanization in, 184–86; didactic purpose of, 177–79; ethics in, 174, 183–86; evil portrayed in, 175, 182; fear of fascism in, 181; language in, 176–77; Marenalez Saenz, Julio (character), 181; MLN-T and, 21, 169–72, 180–87; narrative structure in, 174; Pellegrini Giampietro, Gaetano (character), 180–81; Pereira Reverbel, Ulysses (character), 181; political philosophy revealed in, 177–78; as postboom literature, 177–78, 194; as social realism, 179; title of, 178; torture portrayed in, 175–77; value of, 173–74, 189
Communist Party, 19
"Como el Uruguay no hay," 27, 36
Con las primers luces (Martínez Moreno), 10, 31, 109–26, 127, 196; allegory in, 113; "autojustificación" in, 123; Bob (character), 113, 114, 115–16, 120, 137–38; death in, 110–15, 117–20, 123–26, 153, 163; *la deca* in, 109–16, 118, 120–26, 138, 152; denial in, 114, 118, 120; downward spiral in, 121, 123, 124, 125–26, 141; Eugenio (character), 109, 112, 113–25, 129, 138, 141, 148, 163; "fence-sitting"/inertia in, 113, 115; flux in, 116; *Guerre Grande* and, 11–12; intimism in, 109; irresponsibility in, 46; language in, 118; modernism and, 151; motion-in-stasis in, 120–21, 123; paradoxes in, 114; *tercerismo* in, 109; texture of, 110; "tympanizing" in, 124–26; writing of, 109–10
Conservatism: in *El paredón*, 82–84
Conversación en la Catedral (Vargas Llosa), 132
Cordelia (Martínez Moreno), 10, 29, 30, 35, 50–61, 127, 195; Aldo (character), 60; alienation in, 55; death in,

55, 114; *la deca* in, 48–49, 52, 56, 60, 147; immortality in, 56; irony in, 58–59; irresponsibility in, 50, 54, 57; judgment in, 54; *King Lear* and, 55, 56–57; lack of faith in progress in, 60–61; *la deca* in, 45–46, 50; loss and grief in, 55; mental architecture in, 59–61, 98, 100; narrative structure, 53, 60–61; point of view in, 53, 59; political commentary in, 60; as precursor to *La otra mitad*, 50; publication of, 50; Robledo (character), 50, 54–60, 98, 100, 114, 138; Susana (character), 28, 51, 54–60, 100; title of, 54–55

Cosculluela, Manuel Hevia, 174
Crime novels. *See* Detective novels
Critical Difference, The (Johnson), 108
Criticism in the Wilderness (Hartman), 72
Cuba: firing squads, 64, 67–68; National Movement of Solidarity with Cuba (MNSC), 21, 195; Operación Verdad (Operation Truth), 64–65, 80, 81; as setting for *El paredón*, 37, 62–68, 73–76. *See also* Castro, Fidel
Cuban revolution, 18–19, 29, 30; Latin American cultural solidarity and, 36; as model for Uruguay, 20, 68–69, 74–76; as theme of *El paredón*, 62–69, 80–87, 88; trials following, 29, 31; Uruguayan reactions to, 21–22
Cuentos de la ciudad (Martínez Moreno), 31, 196
Cultural chauvinism: in *Coca*, 136–40
Cultural codes: in *La otra mitad*, 93–103
Cultural identity, 36; in *Los aborígenes*, 37, 39–40, 140. *See also* Identity
Currency: devaluation of, 17

Dante, 175, 177–78
Davis, Lennard, 11, 178
Death: in *Los aborígenes*, 44; in *Con las primeras luces*, 110–15, 117–20, 123–26, 153, 163; in *Cordelia*, 55, 114; in *La otra mitad*, 90–91; in *El paredón*, 85; in *Tierra en la boca*, 153–56, 160, 163
Death of Artemio Cruz, The (Fuentes), 111–12
Deca, la, 10; in *Los aborígenes*, 42–45, 48–49, 147; in *Coca*, 46, 128, 129, 138, 144, 177; in *El color que el infierno escondiera*, 168–69; in *Con las primeras luces*, 109–16, 118, 120–26, 138, 152; in *Cordelia*, 45–46, 48–49, 50, 52, 56, 60, 147; crime, moral casuality and, 47; as defined by Martínez Moreno, 35–36; denial and, 138; as downward spiral, 121, 123, 124, 125–26, 141; in early novellas, 35–36; of elites, 147; loss of faith in progress and, 48; of lower classes, 46, 147–50; *Marcha*, 18; military takeover of Uruguay and, 147–50; of MLN-T, 167; in *La otra mitad*, 46, 88, 89, 90–91, 92, 94, 101, 103–8; in *El paredón*, 46, 64, 65, 76, 78–79; postmodernism and, 47–49; in *Tierra en la boca*, 46, 147–50; urban guerrilla movement and, 20
Deconstructionism, 72, 108, 125
Dehumanization, 184–86
Delgado, Josefina, 69, 90
Denial: in *Coca*, 138; in *Con las primeras luces*, 114, 118, 120; of death, 114; *la deca* and, 138; of loss, 118
Derrida, Jacques, 10, 124–25
Detective novels: flouting of, in *La otra mitad*, 93–94; *La otra mitad* as, 47, 89–90, 97; postmodernism and, 152–53; *Tierra en la boca* as, 151, 155–56, 158–59; traditional, 93–94, 155–56
Detective novels, metaphysical, 90–102, 107
Diario, El, 29
Días por vivir, Los, 29, 30, 195
Días que vivimos, Los, 33, 197
Dictatorships: Terra regime, 17–18
"Dirty war," 167, 168, 189. *See also* Movimiento de Liberacion Nacional-Tupamaros (MLN-T); Uruguay
"Disappeared" people, 33–34, 190–92, 197, 198
Disequilibrium: in literary theory, 72
Documentary novels: *El color que el infierno escondiera* as, 169
Donoso, José, 166–67
Downfall of a Democracy: Carlos Martínez Moreno and the Uruguayan Experience (Salisbury-Ginsburg), 9, 68

Economic issues, 17–18
Ejercicio del criterio, El (Benedetti), 45

Elites: *la deca* and, 147; disenchanted in *Coca*, 139–40; *quietismo* of, in *Los aborígenes*, 44–45, 127–28
Emergency Security Measures (Medida Prontas de Seguridad), 23
"Equilibrium-disequilibrium-equilibrium," 72
Escritor latinoamericano y revolución posible, El (Benedetti), 45
Essayistic novels: *El paredón* as, 71–72, 73, 77
Estenssoro, Paz, 29, 37
Ethical movements, 77–78
Ethics: in *El color que el infierno escondiera*, 174, 183–86; in *El paredón*, 64, 74
Ethnic autobiography: in *Los aborígenes*, 40
Evil: portrayed in *El color que el infierno escondiera*, 175, 182
Executioner's wall *(paredón)*, 64–65, 68, 82–83, 86, 87
Exports: textiles, 17
Extra, 32–33

Falklands War, 188–89
Fasano Martens, Federico, 189
Fascism, 181, 188, 189
Fatiga social, 78–79
Faulkner, William, 110, 111, 113–14, 117–18, 122
Federalists (Argentina), 11
"Fence-sitting": in *Con las primeras luces*, 113
Fin de la modernidad, El (Vattimo), 47
Firing squads, Cuban, 64, 67–68
Flaubert, 53
Foster, David William, 168
Frente Amplio coalition, 169–70, 172. *See also* Broad Front
Fuentes, Carlos, 111–12

Generación crítica (Generation of 1945), 10, 18, 36; cultural identity and, 36, 37; intimism and, 58; Latin American elite and, 45
Genette, Gerard, 51
"Genteel barbarism," 37–39, 125
Gestido, Oscar, 22–23, 196
Giardinelli, Mempo, 155–56, 163–64
Golpismo, 19

Goyo (Alvarez, General Gregorio), 24–25
"Grammar of narrative," 72
Great War. See *Guerra Grande*
Green, Joan Rea, 90
Grief: in *Cordelia*, 55
Guardaespaldas, El (Marra), 146
Guerra Grande (Great War), 11–12, 15, 16
Guevara, Che, 31, 142–44, 177

Hartman, Geoffrey, 72
Hassan, Ihab, 125
Historiography, 76
Holquist, Michael, 10, 47, 91, 93, 96, 151, 152, 153, 159–60, 163
Homelessness, 179–80, 181
Huidobro, Eleuterio Fernández, 23, 171–73, 180, 186, 192, 197
Hutcheon, Linda, 113

Identity: cultural, 36, 39–40, 140; national, 70, 74, 88; personal, 88, 90, 91, 92, 97–98, 106–8, 138–40
Ideology: preconceived understanding of novels and, 73; of totality, 90
Immortality: in *Cordelia*, 56
Indeterminacy: in literary theory, 72
Inertia: in *Con las primeras luces*, 113, 115. *See also* Passivity; *Quietismo*
Infierno, El. See *Color que el infierno me escondiera, El (El Infierno)*
Inflation, 17
Intellectuals, 45
Intimism, 58, 109
Ironic tropology, 84
Irony: in *Coca*, 130–31, 136–37; in *Cordelia*, 58–59
Irresponsibility: in *Con las primeras luces*, 46; in *Cordelia*, 50, 54, 57

Jews: torture of, 187–88
Johnson, Barbara, 108
Judgment: in *Cordelia*, 54
Juntacadáveres (Onetti), 38
Jurisdicción civil y jurisdicción militar (Martínez Moreno), 31, 196–97
Justice: revolution and, in *El paredón*, 66–68, 74

Kant, Emmanuel, 98
King, John, 169

Index

King Lear (Shakespeare), 55, 56–57
Kissinger, Henry, 32

Land ownership, 17, 19–20
Language: in *El color que el infierno escondiera*, 176–77; in *Con las primeras luces*, 118; in *La otra mitad*, 97–99; in *Tierra en la boca*, 148
Latin America: boom literature, 166–69; cultural identity, 36; postboom literature, 147, 164–65, 168, 193–94
Leenhardt, Jacques, 70–71, 73, 77
Leftists: Areco regime and, 23; criticism of *El paredón* by, 63–69, 73, 86, 87; criticisms of *El color que el infierno escondiera* by, 169–72; division into hard and soft camps, 19; land ownership and, 19–20; Martínez Moreno as leading voice, 19; nonviolent vs. violent, 21, 22, 169–70, 182. *See also* Broad Front; Movimiento de Liberacion Nacional-Tupamaros (MLN-T)
Leiris, Michel, 124
Leñero, Vicente, 91
Lewald, H. Ernest, 11, 110
Liberalism: in *El paredón*, 84–87
Life and Works of Martínez Moreno (Orthmann), 9
Literary style: content and, 76–77
Literature modes: anarchistic, 78–80; as blend of narrative and moral essay, 77; conservatism, 82–84; liberalism, 84–87; in *El paredón*, 77–87; radical, 80–82
Literature and Society (Said), 11, 178
Loss: in *Cordelia*, 55
Luchting, Wolfgang, 128, 143

Madame Bovary (Flaubert), 53
Marcha, 18, 19, 28–30, 33, 35, 145–46, 147, 195, 197
Marenalez Saenz, Julio, 181
Margins of Philosophy (Derrida), 124
Marra, Nelson, 146, 197
Martial law, 17–18
Martínez, Afredo, 27
Martínez Moreno, Carlos: as attorney, 29, 31, 146, 166; birth, 27; as a boom author, 168–69; characterization, 51, 53–54, 131–33; childhood, 27–28; chronology, 195–98; crime novel style, 46–47; death of, 28, 29, 34, 198; defense of *Marcha* literary prize decision, 146; as drama critic, 28–29; early published works, 28–29; exile in Mexico, 28, 29, 34, 147, 167, 198; as existential (intellectual) writer, 51; family, 15–16, 27–28; *la Generación crítica* and, 36, 37; as international correspondent, 29; intimism, 58; life, 27–34; MLN-T and, 169–73; narrative structuring, 50–54, 58, 60–61; Operación Verdad participation, 64–65; perfectionism, 29–30; political involvement, 31–34; political philosophy, 19, 21, 28, 177–78; as a postboom author, 169; short stories published by, 29–31; social and personal aspects of work, 131; sociohistorical analysis of works of, 131–33; writing style, 46–47, 49, 50–52, 58
Martínez Moreno, Carlos (father), 27
Más allá del boom: literatura y mercado (Rama), 150
Medidas Prontas de Seguridad (Emergency Security Measures), 23
Memorias del calabozo (Huidobro), 173
Méndez, Aparicio, 25
Mental architecture: in *Cordelia*, 59–61, 98, 100
Merrell, Floyd, 72–73
Metahistory (White), 76
Metaphysical detective novel: *La otra mitad* as, 90–102, 107
Metonymy: in *El paredón*, 81–82
Military dictatorship: amnesty for, 26, 27; budget of, 27; peaceful overthrow of, 25–26; powers granted to, 24; repression by, 25, 188–91; takeover by (1973), 24, 25, 145–46, 149–50. *See also* Uruguay
MLN-T. *See* Movimiento de Liberacion Nacional-Tupamaros (MLN-T)
MNSC, 21, 195
Modernism, 151–52, 164
Monegal, Emir Rodríguez, 62, 69. 90, 166
Montevideo, 26, 27, 172; C.I.A. in, 32
Moral decay, 47. *See also Deca, la*
Moreno, Eduardo, 27
Mortimer, Gail L., 113–14, 117–18, 122

Motion-in-statis: in *Con las primeras luces*, 120–21, 123
Movimiento de Liberacion Nacional-Tupamaros (MLN-T), 18, 19, 31, 195–98; in *El color que el infierno me escondiera (El Infierno)*, 21, 180–87; *la deca* of, 167; defeat of, 24, 186–93; as efficient and creative, 171; ethics and, 183–86; formation of, 19–20; illegal control of, 33; kidnappings by, 23, 180–82; Martínez Moreno and, 31, 169–73; official party status, 26–27; Pacheco government and, 22–24; peak of fighting with government, 167; stages of, 20–21; violence by, 170, 182, 183–86
Movimiento Nacional de Solidaridad con Cuba (MNSC), 19, 21, 195
Muerte de Artemio Cruz, La (Fuentes), 111–12
Mundo Uruguayo, 28–29, 195

Name change: in *El paredón*, 81
Narration de Carlos Martínez Moreno, La (Ravazzani), 9
Narrative: grammar of, 72
Narrative structure, 58; in *Coca*, 132, 141–42, 150; in *Con las primeras luces*, 152; in *Cordelia*, 51–54, 60–61, 150; in *El color que el infierno escondiera*, 174; fragmented, 132, 141–42, 150; juxtaposition of past and present, 58; in *La otra mitad*, 53; retrospective, 152; in *Tierra en la boca*, 152, 163
National (Blanco) party, 15
National identity, 36; as theme in *El paredón*, 70, 74, 88. See also Identity
National Movement of Solidarity with Cuba (MNSC), 21. See also Cuba
Nazism, 187–88, 189
New Critical approach, 90
Nicaragua, 170, 171
"Niño que prepara su muerte, El" (Martínez Moreno), 28, 195
Nixon, Richard, 32, 188
Nonviolence: return to democracy and, 25–26; vs. violence debate, 169–70, 182
Novels: documentary, 169; "equilibrium-disequilibrium-equilibrium" in, 72; essayistic, 71–72, 73, 77; ideological reading of, 73; metaphysical, 90–102, 107; postboom, 147, 164; simplicity in, 151. See also Detective novels
Nueva Novela Latinoamericana (Delgado), 69
Número magazine, 50

Onetti, Juan Carlos, 11, 29, 33, 38, 49, 58, 112, 146, 166, 168, 197
Operación Verdad (Operation Truth), Cuba, 64–65, 80, 81
Operation Counter-Coup, 192
Operation Pando, 196
Operation Takeover, 192–93
Orga, la. See Movimiento de Liberacion Nacional-Tupamaros (MLN-T)
Orthmann, Nora, 9, 48, 52
"Otra mitad, La" (Martínez Moreno), 29, 195
Otra mitad, La (Martínez Moreno), 10, 30, 88–108, 128, 195, 196; adultery portrayed in, 88, 89, 101–3, 105; alienation in, 90, 92, 102; association/alienation subcode in, 95, 98, 100, 102; Carlos (character), 89, 91, 99, 106, 108; censorship of, 30–31, 109; Cora (character), 89, 91–92, 96, 98–108; *Cordelia* as precursor to, 50; as a crime novel, 47, 89–90, 97; cultural codes in, 93–103; death theme in, 90–91; *la deca* in, 46, 88, 89, 90–91, 92, 94, 101, 103–8; flouting of detective genre in, 93–94; language in, 97–99; limited point of view in, 89, 91, 92, 97–98, 105; Mario Possenti (character), 46, 50, 53, 58, 89, 91–108, 128; as a metaphysical detective story, 90–91, 93–102, 107; narrative structure, 53; the "other half" in, 89, 92, 96, 97, 100, 101, 102, 106–8; personal identity in, 90, 91, 92, 97–98, 106–8; as *policial metafísica*, 90–92; power subcode in, 94, 97, 98, 99, 101, 102, 103; reflective subcode in, 93, 94, 96–97, 98, 100, 101, 102; social codes in, 94–95; "tabúes" in, 100–103; uniqueness of, 88–89

Pacheco Areco, Jorge, 18
País, El (Martínez Moreno), 28–29

Index

País de la cola de paja, El (Benedetti), 19
Paradoxes: in *Con las primeras luces*, 114; in *La otra mitad*, 90
Paredón, 64–65, 68, 82–83, 86, 878
Paredón, El (Martínez Moreno), 10, 29, 62–87, 143, 195; *Los aborígenes* and, 35–36; alienation in, 78, 82, 86–87; anarchistic attitude in, 78–80; "antiquietista" reading of, 67; author's father as basis for character, 28; Benedetti's criticism of, 65–67; conservatist attitude in, 82–84; crisis of faith in government and, 18, 19; critical backlash against, 63; Cuban revolution treated in, 21, 62–69, 73–76, 80–87, 88; death motif in, 85; *la deca* in, 46, 78–79, 147; as denunciation of "coloradoismo," 66; as essayistic novel, 71–72, 73; ethical theme of, 64, 184; executioner's wall in, 64–65, 68; Julio Calodoro (character), 45, 68, 69, 70, 74–87, 88, 115, 127, 132, 147; leftist criticism of, 63–69, 73, 86, 87; liberalism in, 84–87; Matilde (character), 86–87; metaphors for Uruguay in, 79–80; misreading of, 64; national identity as theme in, 70, 74; as Oedipal struggle, 69; publication of, 35; *quietismo* as theme of, 65, 68, 73–76, 87; radical attitude in, 80–82; Raquel (character), 82, 85; Ravazzani's criticism of, 67–68; rightist criticism of, 69; sexual motif in, 85; as symbolic of revolutionary justice, 66–68; *tercer mundismo* (thirdism in), 87; title of, 64–68, 73, 82–83, 86, 87
Passivity: in *Coca*, 129–30, 135–36, 140. See also *Quietismo*
Pellegrini Giampietro, Gaetano, 180–81, 188, 196
Pereira Reverbel, Ulysses, 181, 196
Pérez, Amodio, 192, 197
Personal identity, 36; in *Coca*, 138–40; in *La otra mitad*, 88, 90, 91, 92, 97–98, 106–8; in *El paredón*, 88. See also Identity
Peruanistas, 192
Point of view: in *Cordelia*, 53, 59; limited, in *La otra mitad*, 89, 91, 92, 97–98, 105; shifting, in *Coca*, 128

Political metafísica: La otra mitad as, 90–102, 106
Political commentary: in *Cordelia*, 60
Polk, James, 168, 173–74, 190
Postboom Latin American literature, 147, 164–65, 168, 193–94; *El color que el infierno escondiera* as, 177–78
Post-deca, 10; *Tierra en la boca* as, 145, 150, 151, 156, 163–65
Postmodernism: detective story as, 152–53; moral decay and, 47–49; *Tierra en la boca* and, 147, 149–53, 156, 158–59, 164
Power subcode: in *La otra mitad*, 94, 97, 98, 99, 101, 102, 103
Prados de la conciencia (Martínez Moreno), 31, 196
"Problematizing": in *Cordelia*, 54
Progress: loss of faith in, 48, 60–61
Prolegomena to any Future Metaphysic (Kant), 98

Quietismo, 45; in *Coca*, 127; in *La paredón*, 65, 68, 73–76, 87. See also Inertia; Passivity
Quijano, Carlos, 18, 29, 34, 146, 147, 198

Radical attitude: in *El paredón*, 80–82
Rama, Angel, 18, 51–52, 58, 150
Ravazzani, Ana-María, 9, 62–63, 64; critique of *Coca*, 129, 130, 136–37, 142–43; critique of *Con las primeras luces*, 114, 117, 120, 121–22; critique of *El paredón*, 67–68
Realism, social, 179
Reality: transitional view of, 49
"Red Indians" (Martínez Moreno), 183
Reflective subcode: in *La otra mitad*, 93, 94, 96–97, 98, 100, 101, 102
Rein, Mercedes, 146
"Release Papers" (Martínez Moreno), 183
Repression, 25, 32
Revolution: justice and, in *El paredón*, 66–68; motives for, 85; national identity and, in *El paredón*, 72–73
Reyles, Carlos, 39
Rightists: critical backlash against *El paredón*, 63, 69–70
Romantic emplotment: in *El paredón*, 79–80

Rome: in *Los aborígenes*, 38–39
Rosell, Avenir, 149, 160, 163
Rosencof, Maurico, 173, 197
Rosson, General William, 197
Ruffinelli, Jorge, 29, 146

Sábato, Ernesto, 70
Said, Edward, 11, 178
Sakharov, Andrei, 25, 197
Salisbury-Ginsburg, Liz, 9, 68, 148–49, 150, 153–54, 163
Sandinistas, 171
"Sandwich" people, 190–91
Sanguinetti, Julio, 26, 198
Saving the Text (Hartman), 72
Self-destructiveness: in *Coca*, 133–34, 138
Semiotic Foundations (Merrell), 72
Sendic Antonaccio, Raúl, 21, 23, 172, 186, 192, 193
Seregni, General Líber, 26, 31, 32–33, 196, 198
Sexual motif: in *El paredón*, 85
Shakespeare, William, 55
Sherlock Holmes, 93–94, 96, 99
Siracusa, Ernest, 197
Siren y otros cuentos (Martínez Moreno), 31, 196
Sobre héroes y tumbas (Sábato), 70
Sobremurientes (survivors who are as good as dead), 38, 44, 46, 49, 110, 145
Sobrevivientes (survivors), 38, 40, 44
Social change: ethics in, in *El paredón*, 64, 68, 73
Social codes: in *La otra mitad*, 94–95
Social fatigue, 78–79
Social realism: *El color que el infierno escondiera* as, 179
Sociohistorical analysis: of works of Martínez Moreno, 131–33, 136
"Soldier with the Arm in Plaster, The" (Martínez Moreno), 183
Soviet Union, 25
Spain: censorship of *La otra mitad* in, 30–31, 109
Suazo, Siles, 29
Sugar workers, 22
Suicide: in *Tierra en la boca*, 160–61
Synecdochical tropology: in *El paredón*, 83

"Tabúes": in *La otra mitad*, 100–103
Tercerismo (thirdism), 18, 87, 109
Tercer mundismo (third world-ism), 87
Terra, Gabriel, 28
Terra regime, 17–18
Text: encoded texture of, 92–93
Textiles, 17
Tierra en la boca (Martínez Moreno), 10, 33, 145–65; alienation in, 158; antipsychological view of, 152–54; as crime novel, 151, 155–56; dark skepticism ("noir genre") in, 155–57, 162; death in, 153–56, 160–61, 163; decadence in lower classes in, 46, 147–48; Font (character), 147–48, 153, 157, 158, 160–61; Isabel (character), 147–48, 157; language in, 148; Luján (character), 147–48, 161–62; military takeover and, 145–46; narrative structure, 150, 163; as postboom Latin American novel, 147; as *postdeca*, 145, 149–50, 151, 156, 163–65; postmodernism and, 147, 149–53, 156; Ramos (character), 147–48, 157, 159–60, 162–63; senseless crime in, 154–57; suicide in, 160–61; void in, 160, 163
Todorov, Tzvetan, 72
Torture, 25; by Uruguayan security forces, 167, 174, 181–83; of Jews, 187–88; portrayed in *El color que el infierno escondiera*, 175–77, 181–82. *See also* Violence
Tragic emplotment: in *El paredón*, 80, 81
Tupamaros. *See* Movimiento de Liberacion Nacional-Tupamaros (MLN-T)
"Tympanizing," 124–26

Union of Sugar Workers of Artigas (UTAA), 22, 195
Unitarios (Argentina), 11
United States: anticommunist containment policy, 32; C.I.A. involvement in Uruguay, 32, 174
Uruguay: as amusement park, 80; as *Avestruz* (ostrich), 79, 87; bureaucracy, 17; C.I.A. involvement in, 32, 174; classification of citizens, 189–90; Cuban revolution as model for, 68–69, 74–76; democratic govern-

ment in, 25–26; "dirty war," 167, 168, 189; "Europeaness" of, 36; *Guerre Grande*, 15–16; human rights commission, 189; Latin American identity of, 36–37; loss of innocence of, 79; metaphors for, in *El paredón*, 79–80; military takeover, 24, 25, 145–46, 149–50; national identity, 36, 70, 74, 88; as neutral/pacifist, 16, 18; portrayed in *Tierra en la boca*, 145–46, 149–50; purge in, 190–93; repression, 25, 188–91; textile exports, 17; torture, 167, 174, 181–83. *See also* Military dictatorship
Uruguay: Never Again, 189
UTAA (Union of Sugar Workers of Artigas), 22, 195
Utopia: future, desire for, 80, 87; past, desire for, 78, 86; as present, 82, 86

Valázquez, Cejudo, 21
Vargas Llosa, Mario, 132, 184
Vattimo, Gianni, 47–48, 164
Vida o muerte, De (Martínez Moreno), 31, 196
Violence: ethics of, 183–86; vs. nonviolence, 21, 22, 169–70, 182. *See also* Torture

War of the End of the World, The (Vargos Llosa), 184
Warren, Robert Penn, 90
Weschler, Lawrence, 189
White, Hayden, 10, 76–78, 81, 86
Wool exports, 17

Yo, El Supremo (Martínez Moreno), 71–72